Stefan Zweig, r  essay ...g. apner, d
in Vienna in 18. .to a wealthy Austrian-Je
30s Zweig enjoyed great literary fame and w
authors in the world. With the rise of Nazism, Zweig moved to England
where, in 1940, he became a British subject. Following a lecture tour of
South America and a period in New York, he moved to Brazil where in
1942, in despair at the future of Europe, he and his wife committed suicide.

Lotte Zweig (née Altmann) was born in 1908 into a middle-class family of
merchants in the Prussian city of Kattowitz. Soon after Hitler gained power
in Germany, she moved to London. In 1934 Lotte was employed by Stefan
Zweig as a multilingual secretary and research assistant. They married in
1939 and the following year left their home in Bath for the Americas.

Darién J. Davis is an associate professor of history at Middlebury College,
Vermont, USA. He has written on race, migration and twentieth century
intellectual and cultural history.

Oliver Marshall is an independent historian based in Sussex, England,
who has published on South American and international migration history.
He has been a research associate at the University of Oxford's Centre for
Brazilian Studies and its Latin American Centre.

04419416

STEFAN AND LOTTE ZWEIG'S SOUTH AMERICAN LETTERS

New York, Argentina and Brazil
1940–42

Edited by
Darién J. Davis and Oliver Marshall

continuum

2010

The Continuum International Publishing Group
80 Maiden Lane, New York, NY 10038
The Tower Building, 11 York Road, London SE1 7NX

www.continuumbooks.com

Copyright © 2010 Darién J. Davis and Oliver Marshall

Library of Congress Cataloging-in-Publication Data
A catalog record for this book is available from the Library of Congress.

ISBN: 978-1-4411-0987-3 (hardback)
978-1-4411-0712-1 (paperback)

Typeset by Pindar NZ, Auckland, New Zealand
Printed in the United States of America by Thomson-Shore, Inc

Contents

Acknowledgements

Many people have helped us bring this work to fruition. First and foremost we would like to thank Eva Alberman, Lotte Zweig's niece and Hannah and Manfred Altmann's daughter. In addition to giving us unrestricted access to Lotte and Stefan Zweig's correspondence and for permission to reprint Lotte Zweig's letters, Eva was always generous with her time and she patiently answered our many questions and queries as well as commenting on the entire manuscript. We would also like to thank Sonja Dobbins and Williams Verlag for permission to reprint the Stefan Zweig letters. We also appreciate the help of Michael Simonson of the Leo Baeck Institute Archives in New York for providing information on the Ernst Feder estate.

Countless librarians and archivists have assisted us in tracking down information to enable us to put the letters in context. We would like to thank the staffs of the Österreichische Exilbibliothek (Vienna), the British Library (London), the National Archives (London), the University of London's Senate House Library, the Biblioteca Nacional (Rio de Janeiro), the Fundação Getúlio Vargas (Rio de Janeiro), the Biblioteca Central Municipal Gabriela Mistral (Petrópolis), the New York Public Library, the University of Miami Library and the Daniel A. Reed Library, SUNY Fredonia.

We are also grateful to the many individuals who have provided suggestions and encouragement and who have responded to our queries. Together, their interest and advice convinced us of the importance of pursuing this project. In particular, thanks are owed to Jeffrey B. Berlin, Leslie Bethell, Alberto Dines, Michael Hall, Zuleika Henry, Majorie Lamberti, Peter and Liselotte Marshall, Oliver Matuschek, Klemens Renoldner, Carol Rifel and Ursula Trafford, and to the two anonymous readers of the manuscript. John McCarthy and Mario Higa provided us with valuable suggestions for the translation of the Luis Camões poem used in the epigraph. Ashley Kerr very ably helped to type and organize many of the letters. Jo Marcus and Dr Virgínio Cordeiro de Mello were delightful guides to Petrópolis, offering their vivid memories of the city in the 1940s, with the latter also providing insights into the problem of asthma there.

Darién Davis would also like to thank Middlebury College for its financial support for trips to London, Vienna and Rio de Janeiro. It has been a pleasure to have worked with Haaris Naqvi, our editor at Continuum Books. Throughout the publishing process Haaris has been a great source of encouragement and has always shown great enthusiasm towards our book. Thanks are also owed to Sara-May Mallet for efficiently guiding the book through production.

Finally, we are indebted to the support of Karin Hanta and Margaret Doyle. Since the outset of the project Karin has commented on the manuscript and provided translations from German to English, including explanations regarding Viennese German usage. Margaret provided many helpful suggestions, in particular through her careful reading of the Introduction. Without the support of Karin and Margaret this book would have been more difficult to complete.

Abbreviations

HA   Hannah Altmann
LA   Lotte Altmann
MA   Manfred Altmann
HA&MA   Hannah Altmann and Manfred Altmann
FZ   Friderike Zweig
LZ   Lotte Zweig
SZ   Stefan Zweig

[–?] Unable to decipher writing.
[. . .] Replaces sections specifically concerning Eva Altmann.

No mar, tanta tormenta e tanto damno;
Tantas Vezes a morte aperecibida!
Na terra, tanta guerra, tanta engano,
Tanta necessidade aborrecida!
Onde pode acolher-se um fraco humano?!
Onde terá degura a curta vida,
Que não se arme e se indigne o céu sereno
Contra um bicho da terra tão pequeno?!
—Luís de Camões

On the sea, such storms and damning misfortune;
Death, many times, attendant!
On the land, such battle, so many miscalculations
Such dire hardship!
Where can a frail human soul find shelter?!
Where can a short life find tranquillity,
A place where a small earthy creature
Is safe from Heaven's wrath?!
—Translated by the editors

For New Year 1941, Stefan Zweig sent friends and family a printed postcard featuring Canto 1, Stanza 106 of Luís de Camões epic poem *Os Lusíadas* (*The Lusiads*, 1572) in Portuguese, along with his German translation.

Introduction

The suicide of the internationally acclaimed author Stefan Zweig in the Brazilian mountain resort of Petrópolis on 22 February 1942 shocked and bewildered his friends, family and admirers around the world. 'He, who loved life so much . . .', lamented Klaus Mann, son of the German writer Thomas Mann. 'He seemed so strong and so secure . . .', echoed the French dramatist Romain Rolland. The poet Jules Romains received the news with profound remorse and sadness in exile in Mexico. Other writers such as Emil Ludwig, Paul Stefan, Heinrich Mann, Berthold Viertel and Thomas Mann erupted in anger and disappointment.[1] In trying to make sense of the suicide, the Belgian painter Frans Masereel remarked that despite his death, Stefan Zweig's work would endure, and in it we would find 'reasons to love life'.[2]

The news and commentary focused almost exclusively on the 61-year-old writer. At most, only in passing was it mentioned that the great literary figure did not die alone: at his side, with her left arm wrapped around him was his 34-year-old wife, Charlotte Elisabeth Altmann — or 'Lotte', as she was usually known.[3] Though Lotte had lived and travelled with Stefan in Europe, North and South America, remarkably little has been revealed about her or about the couple's relationship and their life in exile together. Scholars, biographers and journalists have tended to dismiss Lotte as a shy young wife in awe of her great husband, too weak to have any real impact on his attitude, actions or work. Some biographers, including Stefan Zweig's ex-wife Friderike Zweig, have even suggested that her so-called silence may have contributed to his death. The German writer Thomas Mann expressed anger towards Stefan Zweig and was critical of Lotte Zweig:

> . . . as for Stefan Zweig? He can't have killed himself out of grief, let alone desperation. His suicide note is quite inadequate. What on earth does he mean with the reconstruction of life that he found so difficult? The fair sex must have something to do with it, a scandal in the offing? . . .[4]

Understandably, yet notably, the historiography has been uneven.[5] Almost all of Stefan Zweig's biographers have mistakenly characterized Lotte Zweig as a 'silent woman', largely due to the dearth of written material available on her.[6] Oliver Matuschek has published information, albeit brief, that has been useful in understanding Lotte's family background in general and Lotte in particular. Lotte Zweig's life has fallen victim to a traditional interpretation of women: in the absence of traditional sources, biographers have relegated her solely to the role of obedient secretary and observer, rather than seeing her as an active participant in her marriage, and have ignored or minimized her professional inputs. As Lotte's letters in this collection show, she was far from silent and did not shy away from stating her opinions. While her outlook on life was often similar to that of her husband's, her views should not be dismissed as being merely his. Although much younger than Stefan Zweig, and from a less wealthy family, Lotte came from a prosperous background with similar cultural values. Like her husband she was multilingual, able to write and converse in English, French and German, understand Yiddish, and, while in South America, she learned Portuguese and Spanish. We also know that Lotte had learned Esperanto, probably before she met Stefan Zweig, suggesting that she independently held internationalist ideals.[7] But fundamentally, her letters reveal a voice that is strong and distinct, enabling a fuller understanding of her own mental and physical health and placing both Zweigs in a new light.

In order to more fully understand both Zweigs, it is helpful to look at Lotte and Stefan as fellow exiles and travellers, stripped of homeland and national loyalty. They occupied an ambiguous physical and mental state making them a 'liminal couple' of the kind described by anthropologist Victor Turner as being 'neither here nor there; they are betwixt and between the positions assigned and arrayed by law, custom, convention, and ceremony.'[8] This space, constructed in a time of war and chaos, was nonetheless a comparatively privileged one: it allowed the Zweigs to choose their place of exile and to continue travelling, due to the security offered by Stefan's income from his substantial royalties and from lecture fees, and thanks to the relative freedom of holding an Austrian passport and, later, a British one.

Zweig and his literary reputation

Stefan Zweig was born in Vienna on 28 November 1881 to a wealthy, cosmopolitan and secular Austrian-Jewish family. In addition to his native German, Zweig was brought up learning Italian, French and English and he received a privileged education in Vienna against a background of anti-Semitic sentiment that was never far below the surface in the Austro-Hungarian capital. He decided not to enter his family's textile manufacturing business, instead choosing to concentrate on writing. He adopted a pacifist stance during World War I, moving to Switzerland and urging fellow European intellectuals to oppose the conflict. At the same time he generally eschewed organized groups because he believed that true freedom was a spiritual impulse that required informality. Certainly in his writing, rather than addressing politics, Zweig was more interested in exploring the psychological propensities and sensitivities of the human condition, a goal that was influenced in no small part by his friend and fellow Viennese, Sigmund Freud. Zweig's vision also explains why his writings garnered such universal appeal.

During the 1920s and 1930s, Stefan Zweig became firmly established as the German language's most translated of authors and one of the twentieth century's most respected literary figures, receiving praise from his contemporaries in Europe and in the Americas. Zweig's elegant and supremely readable works of newly psychoanalytical-inspired fiction, biography and other writings had been translated into English, French, Portuguese, Spanish, Chinese and numerous other languages. Among his most famous novellas is *Letter from an Unknown Woman* (first published in 1922), a haunting tale of a woman destroyed by love. Zweig's many other fine and enduring novellas that were published between the wars include *Amok* (1922), a tale of obsession and, eventually, suicide, and *Twenty-four Hours in a Life of a Woman* (1927), described by Sigmund Freud as 'a little masterpiece', while the novel *Beware of Pity* (1938) explores guilt and emotional blackmail. Zweig's reputation abroad, however, rested mostly on his biographies of historical and literary figures, with *The New York Evening Post* claiming that Zweig's 'style, pellucid and vivid, all muscle and nerve',[9] would change the American perception that German writers were difficult to read. In a review published in 1935 of Zweig's new biography *Mary, Queen of Scots*, the literary magazine *Books* wrote that his impartiality was 'so unusual as to be practically unique', while the *Atlantic Bookshelf* remarked that Zweig's writing had a 'poetic quality', with a 'vital, surging and inspiring tone'.[10] Such praise could equally have been applied to his books on subjects as varied as Balzac, Dickens and Dostoevsky

(1920), Nietzsche (1925), Casanova, Stendhal and Tolstoy (1928), Freud (1932), Marie Antoinette (1932) and Magellan (1938), among others.[11]

Political ambivalence

Foreseeing Nazi-Germany's domination of Europe, Stefan Zweig left Austria in October 1933, five years before the *Anschluss*, the annexation of Austria into Greater Germany by Hitler's regime. Zweig chose England as his place of self-imposed exile precisely because it afforded him a measure of anonymity that he would not have managed elsewhere in Europe, where he was a celebrated figure. In London, wrote the biographer Donald Prater, he would actually enjoy 'indifference and isolation'.[12]

Zweig's general refusal, in Austria or elsewhere, to join political organizations hostile to the Nazis, or even sign petitions, met with intense criticism both during his exile and after his death. Two common accusations levelled against Zweig were that his pacifist stance was naïve and that he failed to use his celebrity status to achieve publicity for anti-Nazi causes. Some critics went further. In her 1943 review of *The World of Yesterday*, Zweig's memoirs, the German-Jewish political theorist Hannah Arendt offered a withering dissection of Zweig's character when she accused him of being out of touch with the lives of ordinary Jews, referring to him as a 'bourgeois Jewish man of letters, who had never concerned himself with the affairs of his own people'. To Arendt, Zweig was to be disdained for being deliberately aloof from the struggles going on around him.[13] Zweig's belief in what he called 'the intellectual unification of Europe',[14] may have been premature, but the ideal, expressed during such a dark period, was a precursor to the movement that eventually created the European Union. As far as political involvement is concerned, he was not without certain attachments. He had long been a member of PEN, the international writers' organization, the character of which was increasingly politicized during the course of the 1930s, and in 1938 in London he became a founding member of the Free German League of Culture (*Freier Deutscher Kulturbund*), made up of individuals of various political persuasions. Although Zweig hated to appear at political gatherings, in exile he sometimes agreed to participate in causes in support of fellow writers.

In a note sent in 1939 to his friend H. G. Wells discussing his hope that his application for British naturalization — and therefore a British passport — would soon be granted, Zweig explained that he felt that he had a duty to speak publicly against fascism:

I hope not to appear presumptuous in stating the purely statistic fact that from all writers in the German language not one has to-day a larger public in all languages than myself and that only very few could have such an influence in neutral countries on both sides of the ocean. Just in these critical weeks I received very important invitations for lectures and broadcasts in the United States and different European countries [that] could serve the cause of Democracy. But I am paralysed as long as I am branded an "Enemy Alien" and nothing is more painful than to be idle in a time where everybody's service is a moral duty.[15]

Two lives cross in London

It was in London in 1934 where Stefan Zweig and Lotte Altmann first met. Despite their differences in age and professional standing, the family backgrounds of Stefan and Lotte Zweig did not contrast as significantly as biographers have sometimes assumed. And while Stefan Zweig introduced Lotte to many famous writers and artists, for her part, Lotte introduced Stefan to the lively circle of professionals and intellectuals associated with her own family.

Lotte Altmann was born on 5 May 1908 into a middle-class family of merchants in the industrial city of Kattowitz in the Prussian province of Silesia. Even though her grandfather had been a rabbi in Frankfurt and her mother was religiously observant, Lotte, with her three older brothers, was not.

After the conclusion of World War I and the independence of Poland in 1918, the inhabitants of what is now called Katowice were permitted either to remain in their hometown with Polish citizenship or to retain their German nationality and move to what remained of Germany. As a consequence, the Altmanns, like many other families, were separated: Lotte's brothers Hans and Richard remained in Katowice to look after the family's well-established business selling electrical and industrial goods; Lotte, her brother Manfred and their parents chose to move to Frankfurt. Manfred Altmann went on to study medicine in Frankfurt and Berlin. Lotte completed high school, but it appears that she did not attend university.

In January 1933 the Nazis gained power in Germany, signalling the beginning of official restrictions of Jews. In April the new government passed the Law for the Restoration of the Professional Civil Service, which excluded Jews from state employment including in the civil service, schools, universities and hospitals.[16] A month later, Manfred Altmann left Germany because of the restrictions on Jewish doctors working in state medicine and after anonymous threats for treating a patient who had been beaten up by members of the Gestapo, the German secret police. England was a natural destination for Manfred, who, like his sister and brothers, spoke English and had previously visited London, where they had close relatives who were well established there. Later that year, Manfred's wife, Hannah, and their young daughter Eva, joined him in London where he had opened a medical practice. In 1934 Lotte Altmann also travelled to England, spending a short period improving her English at Whittingham College in Sussex before moving in with her brother and his family in London. Although she would later leave and enter Britain on a number of occasions, she used her brother's home as her London address until 1935.[17] Other members of the Altmann family, including Manfred's and Lotte's mother Therese, an aunt and their brother Hans, would later join them.[18]

Lotte's employment history is more difficult to determine, and detailed information about her life in Kattowitz is not known. In Britain her immigration status initially prohibited her from legally working. When she arrived at Dover from Calais on 14 May 1934, the presiding immigration officer determined that she was 'very undecided as to the probable length of her stay', but nevertheless allowed her to enter the country for up to three months on the condition that she would not accept 'any employment, paid or unpaid'.[19] While in London, Lotte requested and received several extensions to remain in Britain.[20] In 1934, Stefan Zweig contracted her to work as his secretary and research assistant although, officially at least, she was initially only employed while they travelled abroad together. On 20 February 1936, after taking up permanent residence in London, Zweig was granted permission from the Ministry of Labour to hire Altmann to work for him while in Britain.[21]

Most biographers accept the claim by Friderike Zweig (Stefan Zweig's first wife) that she was responsible for recruiting Lotte Altmann to serve as Stefan Zweig's secretary and assistant.[22] According to Friderike Zweig, she recruited Lotte in 1933 through Woburn House, the Bloomsbury home of several Anglo-Jewish organizations assisting Jewish refugees. This, however, seems implausible as Friderike Zweig returned to Austria in March 1934, while Lotte did not move to England until May of that year.[23] Instead, evidence suggests that the Viennese journalist Peter Smollett, and his wife Lotte, mutual friends of Stefan Zweig and the Altmann family, may have been the ones who introduced the two.[24] Another possibility is that they met through Otto M. Schiff, a London banker and founder of the Jewish Refugees Committee, a body based at Woburn House that supported the admission, hospitality, accommodation, financial help, training and re-emigration of German-Jewish refugees in Britain.[25] According to a letter from Schiff to the Ministry of Labour, Stefan Zweig asked him to recommend 'a secretary who was absolutely perfect in German, and who also knew English well, at the same time possessing some knowledge of literary work'. Schiff reported that he had suggested Lotte Altmann.[26]

Lotte played a key role in bringing Zweig's biography of Mary Stuart to fruition, not only as typist and research assistant, but also as a travelling companion who had filled his life with new energy, as he confided to his friend Joseph Roth.[27] Alberto Dines has gone as far as suggesting that many of the descriptions that Zweig wrote of Mary Stuart could have easily applied to Lotte.[28] Stefan Zweig was enthralled with the subject of his biography, who was young, inexperienced and immature, yet cultivated and gracious. While Stefan Zweig was working on *Mary Stuart* in London with Lotte, his wife Friderike Zweig stayed behind in Austria. Friderike, an Austrian writer and journalist, had married Stefan in 1920, bringing two daughters, Alix Elizabeth and Susanne Benediktine, to the marriage. Like many Austrian Jews, she, her daughters and her sons-in-law remained in Austria until the *Anschluss* in 1938, when they fled to France, Portugal and finally the United States.

In January 1935, Stefan Zweig embarked on his first voyage to the Americas since leaving Austria. Having lost the security that Austria provided him, the 'Flying Salzburger' (as Hermann Hesse dubbed Zweig) would continue to traverse the world.[29] Though Zweig may have understood that he would never be able to return to Austria, he was not a typical emigrant and he certainly did not regard himself as a refugee. Already in 1935 he claimed that he had no talent for emigration, upon which his friend the Viennese novelist and playwright Franz Theodor Csokor admonished him not to leave 'the land that has nourished you'.[30]

Zweig was not seduced by New York, the city of immigrants. On the contrary, he found the place unbearable, although financially profitable and ebullient with optimism. In New York, he signed autographs, gave interviews, attended conferences and visited the major tourist attractions. He enjoyed what he called 'the mix of peoples and cultures' but complained of the lack of cafés and of the horrible interviews he felt forced to endure.[31] When Zweig returned to Europe in early 1935, he had no desire to go back to New York, despite the faith in life and in progress that he felt Americans exhibited.[32]

Meanwhile, in 1934, Zweig returned briefly to Austria to finalize the sale of his house in Salzburg and to visit his mother in Vienna. He returned to England and later that year he moved into a flat at 49 Hallam Street, in central London, effectively making his move to Britain permanent. He seemed pleased with his new arrangement and with life in England. In a letter to Friderike, who had remained in Austria, Zweig reported that many of his friends and associates (including the Austrian writers Paul Frischauer and Fritz Kortner) were nearby and that the atmosphere in London was 'pleasant and quiet'.[33] In less than a year, however, he would be travelling again, this time to South America.

The South American tour of 1936

In August 1936 Stefan Zweig travelled to South America as a guest of the Argentine branch of PEN and of the Brazilian government. Zweig's books were becoming increasingly available in both Spanish and Portuguese and he had excellent relationships with translators and publishers in both Brazil and Argentina, South America's largest literary markets. On 21 August he arrived in Rio de Janeiro, where Marcelo Soares, the Brazilian minister of foreign affairs, was waiting at the docks to receive him. This was only the beginning of the Brazilian hospitality. Driven about the city in a limousine and escorted by his own personal host and guide, the charming aristocratic Jaime (Jimmy) Charmont, Zweig felt immediately at home, seemingly enjoying being pampered as an honoured guest. On 26 August he wrote to Friderike that Brazil '. . . is wonderful from morning till night. The beauty, the colourfulness, the magnificence of this city is unimaginable . . .' He also commented on race relations in Brazil, claiming that "there are no racial questions, Black and White and Indian, one quarter, one eighth, the wonderful Mulattoes and Creoles, Jewish and Christian live together in peace . . .'[34] These thoughts would remain with him until his death, and he would publish similar views in his impressionistic 1936 essay 'Kleine Reise nach Brasilien' and in his 1941 book-length travelogue *Brazil: Land of the Future*.[35]

Zweig's days were filled with interviews, conferences, book signings and a host of social and literary events including ones hosted by the Ministry of Foreign Relations, the Brazilian Academy of Letters, the National Institute of Music and the Jockey Club. In the midst of all this activity, Zweig still found time to pen his observations of Brazil and to correspond with his friends in Europe. He was impressed by his own success and how admired he was in Brazil, even by the country's president, Getúlio Vargas, and his daughter and confidant Alzira.[36] In a contrast to the ethnic and religious hatred that was sweeping Europe, Brazil, he wrote, was a 'country made for him', a place where he believed Jewish refugees were 'extremely happy'.[37]

Without a doubt Zweig's most important literary contact in Brazil was the young Abrahão Koogan, his Brazilian publisher. Koogan had arrived in Brazil from Ukraine with his parents in 1920 and by the early 1930s, he and his brother-in-law had purchased the Editora Guanabara. The publishing house would eventually produce translations of many German-speaking writers including Sigmund Freud and Stefan Zweig. Koogan and Zweig corresponded in French and German, first with the formality of a writer and his publisher and then, despite the thirty-year age gap, as two friends. Koogan played a significant role in securing Zweig an official invitation from the Brazilian government, and while in Brazil he also often served as host and interpreter, and, at least initially, was Zweig's main entrée into Brazilian intellectual circles.[38]

In late August 1936, Stefan Zweig made his first visit to Petrópolis, a small town in the mountains near Rio de Janeiro, which was reminiscent of the European resorts that he enjoyed so much. The landscape and atmosphere of Petrópolis reminded him of Semmering, a mountainous region to the southwest of Vienna, and he found the cooler climate there to his liking. In the mid-nineteenth century, Petrópolis became the unofficial summer capital of Brazil, with the Brazilian emperor and the royal family maintaining residences there. Petrópolis also experienced a wave of German immigration, its legacy being architectural touches, bakeries and family links that remained well into the twentieth century. With power residing in Petrópolis during the summer months, Brazilian aristocrats, government officials, foreign diplomats and businessmen gravitated to the mountain town and its mansions, villas, bungalows, hotels and boarding houses — the range of accommodation types reflecting the wealth and status of the summer residents. With the end of the Brazilian monarchy and the establishment of the republic in 1889, Petrópolis maintained its importance as Brazil's summer centre for social and political influence well into the twentieth century, only fading with the inauguration in 1960 of Brasília as the country's new federal capital and the transfer of power and influence away from Rio de Janeiro.

By all accounts, Zweig was impressed with Brazil, although his main reason for going to South America was to attend the PEN convention in Buenos Aires. In the beginning of September 1936, he left Santos, in the state of São Paulo, on board the British ship, the *Highland Brigade*, arriving in Buenos Aires a few days later. After Brazil, Zweig was disappointed by Argentina, despite the warm reception that he received there. He wrote to Friderike that 'the air here is not so good as in Rio' and he explained to her that the conference was 'boring'.[39] In spite of that, at the convention he met many of his old friends and fellow writers, including Jules Romain, who was elected president of the international secretariat of PEN, French novelist and poet Georges Duhamel, German biographer Emil Ludwig, and German novelist and poet Paul Zech, who had emigrated to Argentina in 1933. While in Buenos Aires, Zweig took advantage of the opportunity to meet with his Argentine literary agent, translator and friend Alfredo Cahn, who had organized meetings and readings for him. After the end of the convention, Zweig chose not to remain in Argentina but instead returned to Europe.

Back in London Zweig continued to see Lotte Altmann, and they began appearing together in public. In early February 1937, Lotte accompanied Zweig to Naples and Milan, where she worked on his book on Ferdinand Magellan, the Portuguese explorer. By the end of the year, Friderike and Stefan Zweig's relationship was over: he returned to Salzburg to sell his house, and Friderike and her daughters moved to Vienna. Stefan then left Austria for what would be the last time — although the divorce would not be official until the following year. Then, in late January, Zweig and Lotte travelled to the Portuguese coastal resort town of Estoril, near Lisbon, relaxing and discreetly developing contacts that would be useful later to help, among others, Friderike. When they returned to London, a series of events would change their lives completely and sever Stefan Zweig's relationship with Austria forever.

In March 1938, Germany annexed Austria, rendering Zweig's Austrian passport void. Following the *Anschluss*, the German government began a series of civil reforms that would strip away the rights of people of Jewish descent. Stefan's mother died that same year and his brother, who had moved in 1919 to Czechoslovakia to be close to the family's business, emigrated to the United States, settling in New York. Stefan Zweig's European world was being decimated and the property of his major Viennese publisher, Herbert Reichner, was confiscated, and with it went one of his major sources of royalties in Europe. Stefan Zweig was now stateless while Lotte Altmann, although still holding a valid German passport, could not return to Germany. By the end of 1938 they separately submitted British naturalization applications, each providing evidence that they fulfilled the residency requirements.[40]

In the midst of all the turbulence and uncertainty, Zweig decided to visit North America to promote his work, having been granted a Certificate of Identity by the British Home Office, enabling him to travel without a passport.[41] On 17 December 1938 he boarded the SS *Normandie* for New York. Once there, he set about on a frenetic tour that included thirty cities across the United States and Canada, giving lectures and conducting book signings. He returned to London on 3 March 1939, just twelve days before Germany invaded Czechoslovakia.

The refuge of Bath

Seeking refuge from the frenzy of London, Altmann and Zweig spent the summer of 1939 in Bath, a town in Somerset that had long been a haven for English writers. The hilly, graceful resort reminded Zweig of his residence on Kapuzinerberg, in the city of Salzburg. There Zweig returned to his writing, with Lotte to assist him.

Bath would come to occupy a special place in the lives of both Stefan Zweig and Lotte Altmann, and they would refer longingly to their home there in many of their letters from the Americas. By the summer of 1939, Zweig's divorce from Friderike had been finalized, and on 6 September 1939, just a few days after Britain declared war on Germany, Stefan Zweig and Lotte Altmann married in a civil ceremony at Bath Registry Office. Joining them for the celebration was Stefan's friend and solicitor Arthur Ingram, Lotte's brother Manfred Altmann and her sister-in-law, Hannah Altmann.[42]

In Bath, Stefan Zweig later purchased Rosemount, an imposing early Victorian house, decorating it with furniture and pictures that he had sent from his former home in Salzburg. Creating a new home in England reflected the couple's desire to construct a refuge following their marriage. In a letter to the banker Siegmund Warburg that Stefan Zweig wrote on his wedding day, a sense of urgency and desire for personal peace was palpable:

> I wish to tell you immediately that I have married today here in Bath Lotte Altmann. It was my intention to do so after my naturalisation, but I do not know [if] this will be possible now . . . I have the intention of settling here and have nearly bought already an old modest house with a marvellous! garden of more than a[n] acre . . . and what is more — quietness and a healthy distance from this mad world . . . So my dear friend, let us do the best to keep fit for all ordeals, which are expecting us . . .[43]

For a few months, Stefan and Lotte Zweig settled into a routine based around his writing, mainly on his Balzac book. But the house was also a refuge for friends from London and, in particular, members of the extended Altmann family. Manfred and Hannah's daughter Eva and Hannah's sister, Martha, and niece, Ursula, came to live with them, the children attending a local school. Hannah and Manfred, who had been naturalized in 1938, were permitted to travel freely between London and Bath and were regular visitors to Rosemount, deepening the friendship with Stefan Zweig that began in London and forging a special bond that is apparent in the letters that he would later write to them.

The return to America

On 23 August 1939 Germany and the Soviet Union signed the Treaty of Non-Aggression, agreeing to remain neutral if either country were attacked. Two days later, Poland and Britain signed the Common Defence Pact that provided for mutual military assistance if either country came under attack. Germany launched an attack on Poland less than a week later and on 3 September Britain responded by declaring war on the invading power. In April 1940 Germany invaded Denmark and Norway and in the following month attacks were launched against France, Belgium, Luxembourg and the Netherlands. At the end of May British troops were evacuated from Dunkirk, leaving Britain isolated in Europe against Germany.

Against this background, the Zweigs turned their attention to leaving Europe. Stefan wrote to his friend Max Herrmann-Neiße, a fellow writer in exile in England, that he had planned a long trip to South America and that they would 'not see each other for a long time.'[44] In March 1940, shortly after his naturalization had been approved, Stefan Zweig received a British passport. As Lotte was now married to a British subject, she was able to acquire his new nationality by simply signing a declaration affirming that she wanted to be British. Passports in hand, the Zweigs were now free to travel. Thus, Stefan Zweig readily accepted another invitation to travel with Lotte to South America via New York.[45] At the same time he remained engaged in his own writing projects in addition to speaking out about the plight of European writers and artists, and helping his friends financially.[46] Throughout their travels, he lobbied his many contacts to secure visas and to arrange travel for a host of friends and colleagues from Austria and Germany. Although he was rarely publicly vociferous in his anti-Nazi protests, he joined the Free German League of Culture, aided the National Council for Civil Liberties and maintained his support for PEN, the international writers' organization.[47]

Lotte and Stefan Zweig arrived in New York City on 30 June 1940. Once there, they made plans for the arrival of Eva Altmann, whose parents, Hannah and Manfred, had made the difficult decision to send her to the safety of the United States. While in New York, Stefan Zweig was also making preparations for his trip to South America and setting out his research and travel agenda for the book he planned to write on Brazil; he was also looking forward to meeting Abrahão Koogan again, as well as other friends and acquaintances.[48]

After a month in New York, the Zweigs embarked for South America on the SS *Argentina*, arriving in Rio de Janeiro on 21 August 1940. The letters reproduced here begin on 14 August 1940, the first letter having been written while onboard the passenger liner. In his first letter to Hannah and Manfred Altmann in London, Zweig wrote with relief, 'we were glad to leave New York because we could not stand longer this "jolly news" in such a time.' Lotte's letter from the ship also documents the hectic life in New York due to work that she was doing there with the film director Berthold Viertel. The Zweigs were absorbed with working on a screenplay of *Das Gestohlene Jahr* (*The Stolen Year*) for Viertel,[49] who had made a name for himself in the theatre, had previous experience in Hollywood, and would later work on almost all of Greta Garbo's films. But Lotte continued to write about the security and wellbeing of her family and in particular her niece Eva.

Lotte and Stefan made two trips together to South America, the first lasting from August 1940 to March 1941, and the second from August 1941 to February 1942. The Zweigs returned to the United States between these trips, staying in or near New York City. Brazil was both a sanctuary from the pressures of war and a place that Stefan Zweig truly admired. But Brazil was also a burden to the Zweigs, precisely because it was so removed from all that was familiar to them, as well as being physically so distant from their widely scattered friends and family. In their descriptions of the country and its people, both Lotte and Stefan Zweig wavered between high praise and gratitude for individuals they encountered there and grumblings about the difficulties of relocating in an unfamiliar environment. At times their comments seem trivial, typical of travellers set in their ways — the language, customs, weather, food and servants were rarely adequate. But their comments also reveal profound preoccupations and anxieties over readjustment and change, ignorance of political and cultural dynamics, and pessimistic outlooks for the future in the face of self-preservation. These internal conflicts must be taken into account not only to grasp the significance of their correspondence with family back in England but also to understand Stefan and Lotte Zweigs' complex — at times endearing, at times frustrating — relationship with Brazil.

Brazil: Land of the Future

Any study of the relationship of Lotte and Stefan Zweig with Brazil must take into account his published travelogue *Brasilien: ein Land der Zukunft* (Stockholm, 1941). The Zweigs had a genuine appreciation for Brazil, but unlike his intensively researched biographies, *Brazil: Land of the Future* is essentially impressionistic. The book reveals that Zweig was caught between his hopes for the future and a longing for the past.

He had been an incessant traveller ever since his youth, and while he recorded impressions of his travels in numerous articles and letters, he had never written a book about France, England, India, the United States, Argentina — or anywhere else.

The book's title itself deserves some attention. Although Brazil is presented in the original German as 'a land of the future', the Portuguese translation, *Brasil: Pais do Futuro* (Rio de Janeiro, 1941), and the first English translation, *Brazil: Land of the Future* (New York, 1941 and London, 1942), dispenses with the 'a'. Thus, the Portuguese- and English-language titles turned the book into a celebration of an exceptional land, implying *the* land of the future. Zweig, who was in New York while James Stern (under the pseudonym of Andrew St. James) was working there on the English version, whenever possible reviewed translations of his books. Furthermore, as Zweig, with his New York publisher and friend, Benjamin Huebsch, thought very carefully about the titles of his books, it is unlikely that the omission of the 'a' was a mere oversight on his part, or a decision taken by the translator and publisher.[50] Only in 2000 did Lowel A. Bangerter add the 'a' to his English translation *Brazil: A Land of the Future* (Riverside, CA).[51]

There is no doubt that Stefan Zweig's work was intended to shed a positive light on a country that represented a peaceful model of coexistence to him, especially between different races, at a time when Europe was being torn apart by ethnic and religious hatred. Zweig first expressed his positive and often naïve ideas about Brazil in an essay published in 1936, against the background of the Nazis' rise to power in Germany.[52] In the introduction to *Brazil: Land of the Future*, Zweig explains that he wanted to return to Brazil in 1937, but reluctantly postponed the trip because of the war in Spain, then the *Anschluss* of Austria, the occupation of Czechoslovakia and Poland and, finally, 'the war of all-against-all in our suicidal Europe'.[53] Against these events, Zweig explained, he increasingly felt 'the desire to save myself for a while from a world destroying itself for another engaged in the progress of peaceful and creative development'.[54]

Although Zweig presents his book on Brazil as a travelogue, he explains that he is interested in the question 'what can we do to make it possible for human beings to live peacefully together, despite all the differences of race, class, colour, religion, and creed?'[55] Given his internal struggles and the suffering caused by exile from the idealized country and continent of his youth, when writing of Brazil Zweig identified what the translator Lowel A. Bangerter described as a 'spiritual utopia', reflected in his idyllic descriptions of the Brazilian people, especially the descendants of Africans.[56]

While *Brazil: Land of the Future* was a longing for an idyllic future, *The World of Yesterday*, published in the same year, was a nostalgic memoir about the Vienna of his youth.[57] Both books illustrate Zweig's unhappiness with his present situation. In *Brazil: Land of the Future*, Zweig nonetheless refused to make what he called 'definite conclusions, predications, and prophesies concerning the country's future . . .'[58] Moreover, Zweig claimed that 'the events of recent years had considerably changed our opinions concerning the meaning of "civilization" and "culture"', warning against equating these terms merely with 'organization' and 'comfort'.[59] Zweig's Brazil, based on official tours and introductions (alone or with Lotte) and his own personal quest for peace, was a mythical country, a land that to him represented 'future civilization and peace in our world, which has been destroyed by hatred and madness'.[60] The feelings that he expressed in his private correspondence are no less forthright. Writing to film director Berthold Viertel in 1940, Zweig foresaw that Brazil 'will be an example for the world . . .'[61] In the letters to Manfred and Hannah Altmann, his brother and sister-in-law, he consistently expressed similar views.

Travelling with his young wife surely influenced where Stefan Zweig went and how he was received. Yet nowhere in his Brazil book is there any acknowledgement that Lotte was a travel companion as well as his typist and translator with whom he discussed, clarified and edited his impressions.[62] This is true of most of Stefan Zweig's books, as few included acknowledgements. But in the epigraph to the German edition of the travelogue, Zweig implied that the idea of Brazil as a 'land of the future' was not originally his. He quoted a 1868 description of Brazil by the Austrian diplomat Count Prokesch-Osten:

A new place, a magnificent port, distance from shabby Europe, a new political horizon, a land of the future, and an almost unknown past that invites the scholar to do research, a splendid natural setting, and contact with exotic new ideas.[63]

While Lotte Zweig's voice and references are absent in the publications that she helped bring to fruition, in the letters to her family in London from Brazil and Argentina published in this volume, her spirited and earnest personality emerges, as do the couple's fears and anxieties as they face the challenges of a new existence away from Europe.

The letters from South America

Besides a few letters sent to Friderike Zweig by Stefan or Lotte, not many letters from Brazil and Argentina have been published — or are even known to exist.[64] This volume features both the only known series of letters written by Lotte Zweig and by far the largest series of letters written by Stefan Zweig while in South America. The letters were written to members of Lotte's family, almost all to Manfred and Hannah Altmann, her brother and her sister-in-law, generally at intervals of once or twice a week. In many of the letters Stefan expressed thanks to the Altmanns for handling his affairs in England — in particular caring for the house in Bath, but also for dealing with his London publisher and looking after financial affairs. But beyond these practical matters, the letters reveal sincere affection towards his brother- and sister-in-law that went far beyond gratitude. Through his young wife Lotte, Stefan Zweig had found a new family.

Despite the fact that the Zweigs were writing to Lotte's German-speaking family, they wrote all of the South American letters to the Altmanns in English. Following the outbreak of war, mail arriving in Britain was censored and the Zweigs recognized that letters in German would be much more likely to be subject to delays. Apart from being subject to normal random inspections by the Home Office's Postal Censorship Department, it seems unlikely that any special attention was paid to the Zweigs' letters. Had they been written in German, the Zweigs' and Altmanns' correspondence would certainly have been placed on the Department's 'watch list' and consequently would have suffered delays in delivery.[65]

In addition to crossing multiple national boundaries, Stefan and Lotte Zweig were constantly crossing linguistic borders. Although the Zweigs were both fluent in English, many of their letters (particularly those from Stefan Zweig) contain minor idiomatic, spelling or grammatical errors. It is important to emphasize that the Zweigs and the Altmanns were multilingual and their letters often include words or phrases in German, French and (occasionally) Yiddish — displays of what linguists call 'code-switching', typical of communication between individuals who understand many languages. Because language represents an evolving means of communication and of organizing knowledge, it is not surprising that the Zweigs, in their letters from South America, also included words in Portuguese and Spanish, their most recently acquired languages.

The personal nature of the correspondence adds much to our knowledge of both Stefan and Lotte Zweig — including their agonized attempts to secure places of refuge for friends and colleagues seeking to flee Europe, his pronounced mood swings, her asthma, the frustrations and emptiness of exile, the anxiety of coping with uncertainty, and the challenges of travelling, writing and working together. Twenty-seven years his junior, Lotte has a strong voice that conveys her own mental and physical condition and offers significant insights into her relationship to her husband. Occasionally optimistic, increasingly melancholic, but also often witty, revealing dry senses of humour, Stefan and Lotte Zweig's letters clearly portray the mood swings of the couple during their final years. From being fêted as celebrities as they toured Argentina and Brazil in 1940–41 to their self-imposed isolation in Petrópolis in 1941–42, the letters chronicle the Zweigs' gradual decline.

Stefan Zweig had always been an inveterate writer of letters, his correspondents including major European intellectuals, literary and artistic figures whom he counted as his friends.[66] Lotte Zweig also maintained her own correspondence, writing independently or alongside her husband to friends and family in England and the United States. Indeed the continued correspondence between Stefan and Friderike, his ex-wife, sometimes contained letters or notes from Lotte.[67]

The Zweigs wrote separate letters to Lotte's brother and sister-in-law that were usually mailed together, although occasionally a letter was sent from just Lotte or Stefan. Lotte once wrote — not without a measure of ironic truth — that '[o]nce in a while I must write a letter which Stefan does not "censor" before I send it.'[68] In the letters, Lotte and Stefan Zweig address their feelings of guilt for having fled Europe and for enjoying freedom in a country that they both love; they describe attempts to secure visas for colleagues desperate to escape to Latin America, their increasing concerns about finances, growing old and health, and their frustration at being separated from friends, family members and libraries. Everyday life is beautifully described: the struggle of learning Portuguese; an idealized image of the couple's black cook and maid; waiting for the postman to make his round and the disappointment if no letters were delivered; and other aspects of daily life in Brazil such as the addition to the household of Plucky, their much-loved dog.

Five general issues or themes help us to put the letters into perspective: the celebrity status of both Stefan and Lotte Zweig in Brazil and Argentina and their mutually supportive relationship; their concern regarding financial security, worries about the cessation of most royalty payments and excitement about lecture fees; the Zweigs' genuine preoccupation for friends and family in Europe and elsewhere due to the war; the Zweigs' naïveté, or lack of interest, towards the political situation in South America and cultural generalizations; and the couple's isolation and at times desperation, and their often poor mental and physical health.

The Zweigs as celebrities in South America

In South America, both Zweigs were fêted as celebrities not only because a small but growing middle class was reading Stefen Zweig's works, but also because they were European visitors who had taken a keen interest in the continent at a time in which Brazilians and Argentines still craved European approval. In 1936, Stefan Zweig was surprised and even overwhelmed by the attention he received during his South American visit. That attention was repeated in 1940, this time for Lotte as well as Stefan. While on board the ship to Rio de Janeiro, Stefan Zweig reported that he was anticipating having a very busy trip and that, 'friends expect us there in the kindest way and I have invitations for lectures from Uruguay, Argentine, Chile, Venezuela'.[69]

Although Stefan expected that his friends and the Brazilian press would pay him a great deal of attention, he was amused and surprised by the public's fascination with Lotte. On 23 August 1940, Zweig wrote, 'Unfortunately I am afraid that Lotte will loose her modesty here since she is always with ambassadors, ministers and photografed in all newspapers.'[70] Two weeks later, he again joked that 'Lotte behaves here like a great lady and presides [over] meetings, is photographed and to be seen in all the newspapers in all her beauty.'[71] And on 29 September, repeating his light-hearted tone:

> If it would be for Lotte, we would not leave at all Brasil, she is very changed and is pestering me every moment in her exalted way with exclamations. Is it not marvellous and so on and I have married her just because she has been formerly so discreet.[72]

Indeed, to Stefan's bemusement, his wife received floral tributes, some from anonymous admirers, and the photographers often seemed at least as interested in her as they were in him. Even if they initially enjoyed the attention directed at them, on 19 October 1940, Lotte expressed relief that '[f]ortunately the daily photographs have stopped and the papers only report, as they do with every person who is a little known to the public'.[73]

When, in late October 1940, the Zweigs travelled to Buenos Aires, it was clear that they felt guilty that they were living a pampered life compared to family and friends in Europe. On 27 October, Lotte Zweig described Buenos Aires as:

a new town, plenty of new people, plenty of telephone calls, plenty of delegations who insist on some more gratis-lectures, heaps of flowers, plenty of new things to eat, plenty of photos and interviews; a funny sort of life for me, and at the same time twenty times a day the thought: what is it like now in England, what are they doing in this moment?[74]

In her letter of 9 November 1940, Lotte reiterated how busy they were:

Only a short letter to day, for although I did not accompany Stefan to his lectures in Cordoba, Santa Fé and Rosario — from where he will return to-morrow — I have been rather busy, getting visas, tickets etc. of all kinds, answering the letters and the telephone, being invited although alone and getting rid of a cold . . .[75]

By the end of their trip, both Lotte and Stefan Zweig were writing about the need for 'rest and quiet', a theme that would constantly be repeated in the letters that were to follow.

Pacifism and activism: reaching out to friends and exiles from a place of security

Although Stefan had reclusive tendencies, and while Lotte lacked many independent connections, neither of them can, in fairness, be accused of not reaching out to the exile community. In England and wherever they travelled, the Zweigs were involved in helping family members, friends, and refugees in general. They both helped by writing letters, attending fundraisers, donating funds, providing work and using their contacts to try to secure visas for the United States, Portugal, Cuba, Mexico, Brazil and Argentina. On 23 October 1940, Lotte informed Hannah and Manfred about Stefan's plans at a 'Jewish charity affair'. In his letter dated 26 October 1940, Zweig wrote about his charitable activities on behalf of Jews in Buenos Aires but lamented the fact that there were so many conflicts among them:

The English, the Spanish are well arranged, but the great difficulty are the Jews. There are 250000 in this town and I have provided a lecture for charity-purposes — now they fight, who shall arrange the lecture . . . and I have the dearest hope that by this quarrel I shall escape . . .[76]

The Zweigs wrote regularly about the whereabouts of family members and friends, securing for them affidavits and visas, and ensuring that money was made available to those in need.[77] They were persistent in encouraging Hannah and Manfred to enjoy their property in Bath while at the same time lamenting that they could not do more for them and their friends. On 15 September 1940, Stefan wrote about how difficult it was for him to think of the troubles that many of his friends were facing, hoping that his efforts would assist some of them to secure American visas. In her 11 December 1940 letter, Lotte also commented on the difficulty in Brazil of helping their friends and family, even her brother Jan, a persistent cause for worry and frequently irritation:

> As to my dear Brother's letter: help him with money if you think he needs it and as you say yourself, he might be really at the end of his resources. As to the Brazilian visa, I do not think it will be possible. As they do not give visas now as a rule to Jews it would mean giving a personal guarantee and that is the only thing I cannot ask of Stefan in this case.[78]

Despite the demands of their itinerant lives, it is clear that the Zweigs were deeply concerned with the destruction of Europe by 'the monster' and for the wellbeing, wherever they might be, of friends and family. Stefan Zweig either made donations to Jewish communities in Portugal, the United States, England, Argentina and Brazil, or he offered them support through visits or lectures. He was particularly generous in helping other writers who were struggling in exile.[79]

The letters also express specific details of the Zweigs' domestic life as well as daily preoccupations, about Lotte Zweig's family in England and over the welfare of Eva in New York. These letters began on the ship bound for Brazil, when Stefan wrote, 'So do not worry too much: she will see a new world and nobody knows how such a connection with America can be valuable for her future', and these concerns would continue until their suicides. The Zweigs also insisted that the Altmanns should enjoy their property and possessions: 'I hope you will have there sometimes a good rest after the busy days in London', Stefan wrote in an undated letter shortly after leaving New York. These letters further illustrate that the Zweigs felt enormously guilty about their relative peace in a time when so many of their friends were suffering:

> To look out of our windows is simply a dream, the temperature is superb — a winter which is more June than May — the people spoil us in every possible way, we live quietly, cheaply and the most interesting life — really happy would it not be for you and all the friends and the great misery of mankind.[80]

Although Stefan was often criticized for not having been more vocal on the war and against Hitler, his generosity cannot be questioned. Even after their divorce, Stefan continued to assist Friderike, helping her and her daughters to escape Europe for the United States, ensuring that she had a pension, and maintaining a voluminous correspondence with her. Lotte, for her part, always treated Friderike cordially and genuinely took an interest in her welfare when she was seeking to emigrate to the United States. Their efforts went beyond family members. After the death in an airplane crash on 8 November 1940 of Alfonso Hernández Catá, Cuba's ambassador to Brazil, Lotte Zweig expressed profound sorrow at the loss of a man 'who in a short time has become one our closest friends' — and a vital contact in securing Cuban visas for friends, Cuba being a particularly attractive destination for people whose applications for visas for the United States were pending or who believed that it would be easier in Havana to obtain an entry visa for the United Sates.[81] Hernández Catá had promised to secure visas for the Zweigs' and Altmanns' friend Heinrich Eisemann, an antiquarian book and manuscript seller who had emigrated from Germany to London: 'I am afraid that the death of our friend Hernandez Catá will prove fatal to his Cuban visa,' wrote Stefan, 'as it was Catá who gave the guarantees for him . . .'[82] Similar thoughts are echoed in Stefan's letter of 15 November of the same year, although he later wrote that he would be following up with Hernández Catá's daughter about the visas for Eisemann.[83] Letters from the Zweigs attest to their continued efforts to help others and to find out what was going on in Europe, displaying minimal awareness of the political and social dynamics in South America.

Naïveté or convenience?

While the Zweigs may not have been aware of the intricacies of Latin American and Iberian politics, Stefan Zweig maintained contacts with members or representatives of the governments within these regions, including in Brazil, Argentina, Cuba and Portugal, allowing him to call on specific individuals for visas and other favours for friends. One of the most curious of these contacts was António Batista de Souza Pedroso, better known as the Visconde de Carnaxide, the representative in Brazil of Portugal's Secretariat of National Propaganda,[84] directed since its creation in 1933 by António Ferro, a confidante of President António Salazar, who played a role in helping Friderike in Portugal. Carnaxide arrived in Brazil in 1931. The Zweigs must have met him sometime during their trip in 1940, although Stefan may have previously met him during his 1936 tour. In letters to Hannah and Manfred in September and October 1940, Stefan referred to the viscount as 'our friend . . . who arranges all social things for us in splendid way', and he explained that his 'former wife has her visas to America and I believe also to Mexico, . . . thanks to the help of Ferro, who has been very kind to me, in Lisbon.'[85]

These comments indicate that although the Zweigs were personally against fascism in Germany and Austria and of course abhorred the Hitler regime, they were either unaware or uninterested in political developments in Portugal, or they were being pragmatic in accepting any help that they was offered at such a desperate time. This interpretation can also be applied to both Lotte and Stefan in Brazil, although the lack of awareness of the political, economic and social realities of their South American host countries is striking, particularly in the case of Brazil, a country where they chose to settle. In all their letters, there is only one mention of Getúlio Vargas, Brazil's dictator, and it is merely in reference to a book that Paul Frischauer, a fellow Viennese whom Stefan Zweig regarded as an opportunist, had been commissioned to write about him.[86] There are virtually no references to the Brazilian or Argentine political landscapes. One possible reason for this omission is the fear of censorship. But the Zweigs were not travelling or living in a vacuum, and their actions, their words and their publications had direct consequences and reactions, particularly in Brazil.

Stefan Zweig first arrived in Brazil six years after Getúlio Vargas became president following the so-called 'Revolution' of 1930 that shattered the oligarchical alliance that had controlled Brazil since the creation of the republic in 1889. The Vargas government co-opted populist programmes and politicians from the left and the right, communist and fascist, while Vargas outlawed, imprisoned or exiled many who opposed his rule. By 1937, the Vargas dictatorship had clearly emerged, euphemistically called the *Estado Novo* (the New State), with a constitution influenced by the more ruthless dictatorships of Portugal's António de Oliveira Salazar and Italy's Benito Mussolini. The *Estado Novo* actively co-opted the discourse on race, stymied independent civil voices and adopted anti-Semitic policies aimed at reducing Jewish immigration while promoting *brasilidade* or Brazilian-ness.

Ironically, Zweig's views seemed very much in line with the merging nationalism and patriotism attached to the concept of 'racial democracy', which espoused that Brazilians were either colour blind or did not harbour racial prejudice like their counterparts in North America, Germany or elsewhere. While promoting these national myths through education and through laws prohibiting discrimination based on race, gender or religion, the Vargas government relied equally on force and censorship. The *Estado Novo* banned all political parties, for example, and social and political groups based on one race were strongly discouraged.[87] Some in the Vargas government, as well as many prominent Brazilian intellectuals, were vociferous in expressing anti-Semitic or fascist views, highlighting the supposed links between Jews and Marxist-Leninist internationalism,[88] and arguing that Jews were essentially unable to assimilate into Brazilian society.[89] Vargas not only tolerated such positions by his supporters, but during the 1930s enacted laws and policies that aimed at severely restricting Jewish immigration. On 7 June 1937, with the authorization of Vargas, the Ministry of Foreign Relations issued the Secret Circular 1127, which prohibited the issue of visas to people of 'Semitic origin'. Although a memo of clarification confirmed a few exceptions for whom visas could be issued to — including 'well-known Jewish cultural, political or social figures' — the circular resulted in a 75 per cent drop in Jewish immigration over the following year and legitimized anti-Semitism.[90]

Although *Brazil: Land of the Future* was not published until 1941, Zweig had already formulated some of his opinions relating to the country, including those concerning race relations, following his brief 1936 visit there.[91] These views indicated a lack of awareness of the deep-seated anti-Semitism among the higher echelons of Brazilian society; indeed, Zweig made no mention of anti-Semitism in Brazil in any of his letters.

Many Brazilian intellectuals, particularly on the left, shunned Zweig's book on Brazil because they erroneously believed that it was commissioned by the DIP, the dictatorship's Department of Press and Propaganda, and because of its essentialism and its one-dimensional portrayal of Brazilians. Yet Zweig had few opportunities to discuss these issues with Brazilian intellectuals, particularly those on the left. At least initially, neither of the Zweigs could speak or read Portuguese well, although many Brazilian intellectuals would have been able to converse with them in French, while others would have been able to do so in English. In the midst of a whirlwind tour and travelling schedule and surrounded by adoring fans, it would have been difficult for the Zweigs to get a full understanding of the political and cultural landscape; it would also have been problematic as they were guests of the Brazilian government.

When Stefan and Lotte returned to settle in Brazil they seemed to prefer solace to social engagement. Indeed there is no evidence that they were interested in contemporary Brazilian literature any more than its politics. In his chapter on Brazilian culture in *Brazil: Land of the Future*, Zweig limits his praises to nineteenth-century figures, the novelist Machado de Assis, whom he calls the 'Dickens of Brazil', and compares the journalist and writer Euclides da Cunha's masterpiece

Os Sertões to the writing of the British archaeological scholar and adventurer, T. E. Lawrence. He does not mention any of the modernist writers nor indeed any other living Brazilian writer.[92] Neither Stefan nor Lotte Zweig seemed to have had much of an interest in the Brazilian cultural landscape or in the preoccupations of the national intelligentsia. Furthermore, when the Zweigs toured Brazil in late 1940 and early 1941, Stefan was dismissive of the provincial intellectuals he met.[93] Instead, he romanticized the common folk with their 'flexible intelligence, intuition, and the facility for expressing himself in speech', praising 'the whole young generation' for whom 'writing and literature have not been taken for granted as with the European, a heritage handed down through the centuries, but as something they have gained for themselves.'[94]

Jorge Amado, Carlos Drummond de Andrade, Ruben Braga and other well-known Brazilian writers criticized Zweig because of his connections to the Vargas regime.[95] Zweig was aware of their hostility and defended himself to the Brazilian weekly *Vamos Ler!* by saying, 'I wrote this book [. . .] independently, giving it all of the enthusiasm that I had within me when I observed and understood the present and future of this admirable country.'[96]

A note on exoticism

Whether the Zweigs were essentially naïve or whether they took advantage of their privileged position for their own benefit and the benefit of their friends, it is important to emphasize that as much as they enjoyed Brazil, they were in a completely new world and society, so different from the Europe that they had left behind. As was so typical of foreign observers, the Zweigs relied on generalizations about Brazilian society. In many of their letters, the Zweigs highlighted the exoticism and cultural differences. Nowhere are their exotic visions more apparent as in their descriptions of the landscape and slow pace of life: for example, during a visit in October 1940 to Teresópolis, a quiet mountain resort near Rio de Janeiro, Lotte sketched this picture:

> Everything else is perfect here, the landscape beautiful, we are right in the mountains, 3000 feet high and yet there is something tropical about it, orange trees, banana trees, bamboo, we have lovely rooms with a big terrace where we work, a swimming pool, dogs, food cooked by blacks but the mail from Rio takes several days and sometimes does not arrive at all.[97]

During the same visit, Stefan used an idyllic rhetoric reminiscent of the Brazilian anthropologist Gilberto Freyre in *Casa-Grande e Senzala*

(1933),[98] creating an image of contentment among the non-white Brazilian servants:

> I have seldom in my life seen a finer place, quiet, the town tasteful, the house people thinking the whole day what to do for us and our cooking all Viennese dishes we have not had since years. And peculiar charm in midst the tropical nature: the negros working in the same open like in the slavery days only happy and always smiling, fat pigs, horses, a really dream-hazienda. And what have we seen in Rio: the most perfect houses with gardens covering a whole mountain and on the other hand the popular life.[99]

Later in the letter, Zweig wrote that he was looking forward to going to Bahia, 'the most picturesque place and probably we will do it in a small steamer to see all the little towns on the coast — a glance on the street with all the coloured people in all possible mixtures is an inexhaustible delight.' In addition, on 3 December 1940, Zweig was not shy in sharing with Lotte's sister-in-law his flirtation and special liking 'for a certain half coloured girl, this charming type I admire so much . . .'[100] From Bahia, the theme continued, with Stefan Zweig equating black Brazilians with a Dionysian penchant for life:

> we are now here for three days and all what we have seen is most wonderful; it is the most colourful town I ever have met and today we assisted the great popular festivity, the Lavagem of Bom Fim — that means that a good part of the town, most negros, come to wash the church in honour of their saint and this washing which starts as a religious ceremony and finishes in orgie of thousand people who danse, cry, wash and become completely mad. I have never seen any thing of religious man-hysteria and all this in the brightest colours and without any artificial tricks — there come never stranger to see this and if would be in a theatrical production or a film the greatest "hit".[101]

Lotte Zweig, too, wrote about the simple but charming people around her, although the strain would clearly show when she had to rely on them in her own household, with her Brazilian domestic staff becoming more an annoyance than a delight.

Descriptions of weather also played a role in highlighting the exotic nature of Brazil, but it also charted the Zweigs' changing moods. As early as 23 August 1940, Stefan Zweig wrote that 'the only thing which prevents me to live here is the heat — we are arrived in full winter but it is warmer than in Bath in July and one shudders to think how it must be when spring commences (in October) and summer (in December.)'[102] And later, 'I would like to live nowhere except here would it not be for the heat which hinders my work.'[103] In a letter to her mother on 19 October 1940, Lotte Zweig reported that, 'it is only spring and the temperature ever agreeable, and anyhow as we lived through a heat wave in New York and stood it quite well, we are not afraid of heat.' This would change in January 1941 when Lotte described the Brazilian climate as 'anything else but invigorating'.[104] After the Zweigs settled in Petrópolis in late 1941, Lotte wrote of her health – complaining again of the weather:

> . . . I don't know whether it was the rush or the climate which I did not stand, the constant change of hot and cold, damp and dry, windy and close, in any case I got a cold and felt so dreadfully tired that I went to a doctor who made all possible tests without finding anything wrong . . .[105]

Both Zweigs linked the weather to their inability to work. Their letters repeatedly refer to the need for solace, good weather and time and space to work. Because they both believed that there was 'something in the atmosphere [in Rio] which makes you lazy',[106] in deciding to live in Petrópolis, they most likely thought that the cooler mountain climate would enable them to be more productive. Once there, they completed the work on *The World of Yesterday* and on Stefan's novella *Schachnovelle* (*Chess Story* or *The Royal Game*), but they could not work on other projects such as the biography on the sixteenth-century French essayist Michel de Montaigne because of lack of access to good libraries, to which they were accustomed. Moreover, in Petrópolis the solace and quiet they envisioned transformed into isolation, and the wet weather brought their despair to the fore.

Liminality and despair

At first glance, Lotte Zweig's letters seem to indicate that she felt more comfortable letting Stefan explain the cultural landscape. In addition to penning her own opinions, however, Lotte often wrote about her husband and pointed out his exaggerations. For example, referring to one of Stefan's earlier letters when he wrote of her bad health, Lotte wrote to her sister-in-law that, 'He somewhat exaggerates, I was not so very bad although there was a kind of relapse again when I came here, but this seems to be over and I am ready to climb all the mountains.'[107] In one of her longest letters from Petrópolis, Lotte also wrote about their work, the couple's life, and quite candidly about Stefan's depression:

Stefan begs to be excused if he does not write to you to-day, I shall meet him only in Petrop. and want to post this letter in Rio. — I am very happy that Stefan is feeling better and got over the period when he thought everything useless on account of the war and postwar and even lost the pleasure of his work. Thank God, this seems to be definitely overcome, his work interests him once and he even went to see some people to-day who might give him information and lend him some books he needs . . . I had learnt that Stefan's depression was not an isolated case but was attacking [. . .] the different European authors one after the other. This knowledge did not cheer Stefan but it helped me in a way, having understood why writers, owing to their imagination and on account of the fact that they are free to indulge in pessimism instead of their work, are more liable to be affected by these depressions than others . . .[108]

As holders of British passports and with access to financial resources, the Zweigs were able to continue their travels with relative ease, but it was becoming increasingly clear that travel itself had become its own sort of exile. Before deciding that he wanted to settle in Brazil, Stefan Zweig would articulate the condition of 'liminality' before anthropologists had even coined the term when he wrote, 'I belong nowhere, and everywhere am a stranger'.[109] Yet before returning to New York in January 1941, the Zweigs secured Brazilian residency permits giving them the option of returning to live in Brazil.

Return to nowhere: life in Petrópolis

On 15 August 1941, Lotte and Stefan Zweig left New York for the last time, sailing to Brazil aboard the SS *Uruguay*. With residency papers in hand they attempted to settle in Brazil, although they remained uncertain as to how long they would remain there. According to both Zweigs, Brazil would be a refuge from the war, and they would do all they could not to repeat the exhausting schedule of the previous year's South American lecture tour. Stefan wrote to the Brazilian publisher Abrahão Koogan that he wanted to avoid festivities and the hectic schedule of his last visit. In a letter from New York, Stefan informed Koogan that he had reserved a cabin on the *Uruguay*, and asked him not to tell anyone as he was exhausted and only wanted to rest in Rio de Janeiro and Petrópolis.[110] Two weeks later, Zweig repeated, 'I am very tired, I have worked a great deal and the idea of resting in Brazil is a great temptation.' But he also demonstrated a modicum of optimism and had perhaps overestimated his ability to accommodate to a new life in Brazil, planning to learn Portuguese and believing that, as he put it, 'because I read it without great difficulty [learning it] will not be very difficult'.[111]

Soon after moving into their new home at 34 Rua Gonçalves Dias in Petrópolis,[112] Lotte Zweig reported on their refuge and the privacy that they were hoping for:

> We have taken a house in Petropolis and will move up there some time next week. It is quite small, really only a bungalow and separate servants quarters as all the houses are arranged up there — I suppose still a remnant from the days of slavery — but we like it. It is built halfway up in a hill and has a beautiful view on mountains from a big covered terrace where I suppose Stefan will spend his days working. You walk up to it a number of steps through a nice little garden which the landlady promised will be full of hortensias in the summer. Behind the house immediately is the hill, but a few steps further up the gardens is just preparing a plateau and he promised to build a little summer house as well — so I shall take this as my residence during the day, and maybe later on, when the season begins, I shall change place with Stefan so as to hide him from unexpected visitors.[113]

If the Zweigs had lacked awareness or understanding of the political and cultural landscape surrounding them during their previous stay in Brazil, their decision to live full-time in Petrópolis isolated them further. Brazil was reaping the success of the cultural revolution of the 1920s and 1930s; outcasts, intellectuals, musicians and singers intermingled in the theatres, cafés and cabarets of downtown Rio de Janeiro, where music and dance and Brazilian avant-garde were becoming more important.[114] As Stefan explained to his former wife, it was simply a relief to be back in Brazil, to not be travelling and to have a house — '[a]s primitive as it may be here, I will be free from hotels and without looking at suitcases.'[115]

Already in late October, however, after the Zweigs had moved into their home in Petrópolis, there were signs that their refuge was increasingly feeling like a place of isolation, as they attempted to balance the banalities of daily life with their worries about friends, family and the war in the wider world. At first they seemed content. Stefan began to work, play chess and enjoy the landscape. Had the Zweigs finally found paradise on Rua Gonçalves Dias? In their first letters from the house the Zweigs describe the natural beauty and appealingly simple life of Petrópolis. '[T]he neighbourhood', wrote Stefan on 3 October 1941, 'is very primitive and therefore pitroresque, the poor people are so nice here as you cannot imagine.' In another letter he claimed:

we feel extremely happy here, the little bungalow with its large covered terrace (our real living room) has a splendid view over the mountains and just in front a tiny cafehaus, called "Café Elegante" where I can have a delicious café for a halfpenny and enjoy the company of black mule-drivers.[116]

At the same time as they marvelled at how inexpensive everything was, they felt guilty in such a wonderful environment knowing that many of their friends were suffering through war. Stefan, in particular, saw the irony in the fact that he was living in a resort town, of the sort he had enjoyed visiting for decades, tucked away and isolated from his world as his sixtieth birthday approached:

I would not have believed that in my sixtieth year I would sit in a little Brazilian village, served by a barefoot black girl and miles and miles away from all that was formerly my life, books, concerts, friends, conversation.[117]

The Zweigs had always worked on projects that rarely required forging local contacts, but in Europe and in the United States, friends and associates were always nearby and he could readily consult his personal collection of books or libraries. In Brazil this lack of contacts was pronounced. It would be misleading to describe the Zweigs as reclusive; they lived in a social enclave as many Brazilians did, but as foreigners the alienation was accentuated due to cultural and linguistic barriers as well as psychological ones. In Petrópolis and Rio de Janeiro the Zweigs socialized with a small number of Brazilians and foreigners. Alfonso Hernández Catá, the Cuban ambassador to Brazil,[118] whose death deeply affected the Zweigs, was one of their closest friends.[119] Gabriela Mistral, the poet and Chilean consul in Petrópolis, was another significant contact, as were the German journalist Ernst Feder and the Brazilian historian Afonso Arinos de Mello Franco. In his biography on Stefan Zweig, Alberto Dines lists, from the Zweigs personal telephone book, 32 contacts in Rio, São Paulo and Curitiba, indicating their potential for socializing beyond Petrópolis.[120] 'I see strictly *nobody* for weeks', wrote Stefan in his letter of 10 November 1941 to Hannah and Manfred, an affirmation that seems more like a choice than an imposition, a reflection also of the fact that the Petrópolis social season was summer, in particular from January.

When they chose to, the Zweigs travelled down to Rio de Janeiro and visited cultural centres such as the downtown neighbourhood of Lapa and the cinema and theatre district of Cinelândia. When in the city, however, although the Zweigs sometimes saw friends and acquaintances, socializing was not a priority.[121]

Social opportunities were always available and the Zweigs sometimes received guests in their home in Petrópolis, but they felt they needed peace and tranquillity more than anything else. In their isolation, however, their states of depression became acute. This seemed particularly true of Stefan, although Lotte, who had followed Stefan in his travels, was not immune to her husband's mood swings while she faced her own challenges in a foreign environment away from her family.[122]

Stefan and Lotte, nevertheless, continued to work on their European projects and, when possible, corresponded with their widely scattered friends. Their letters show a continuing ignorance of, or lack of interest in, the South American political situation. This became even more apparent now that they were actually living in Brazil. The letters to Hannah and Manfred from August 1941 to February 1942 are devoid of any cultural, political or economic detail related to Brazilian society, apart from brief mentions of Brazil's possible involvement in the war:

> We write to you under the impression of the Japanese war declaration which isolates us perhaps somewhat more from home and you; there is not yet clear if Brazil will declare war to Japan as well but in any case the life here is not so influenced by the war as the country is self-sufficient.[123]

Their observations — often strikingly ethnocentric in nature — were related to their day-to-day activities. The generalized comments on the exotic Brazil of the previous letters gave way to tension and disbelief in some Brazilian customs. Nowhere is this seen more than in the comments about their domestic help.

As part of the middle- and upper-class milieu they did not attend to their own household chores, nor did they take care of their own garden. This had been the case in Austria, in Bath and in New York as well. Because the Zweigs led an almost reclusive life while in Petrópolis, the only Brazilians with whom they had daily contact were their maid and cook (Ana de Oliveira Alvarenga) and their gardener (Antônio Morais) and his wife (Dulce Morais). With this limited exposure to the lives of ordinary Brazilians, they marvelled and admired the way that Brazilians could be happy with so little. Yet their reactions and descriptions of daily life and the challenges of the so-called 'servant question'[124] also reveal a deep longing and sense of loss and sometimes a collective fear and melancholy which had less to do with the Brazilians than with the Zweigs' inability to change and embrace Brazil and Brazilian customs.

Lotte's comments about Ana de Oliveira Alvarenga, for example, reveal her own insecurities in a foreign land and her angst over having to explain the basic household tasks in Portuguese. Although Lotte was frustrated with her maid, she 'did not send [her] away the first day', because she did not have the 'courage to interview another one and face the task of introducing her to our foreign ways and to my strange Portuguese'.[125] After one month, however, Lotte was reservedly optimistic:

> In any case the worst of my household troubles are over, and after the hard beginning of teaching a maid who did not know anything in a language which I could hardly understand and had never spoken before, things which I did not know well myself, I am not afraid of anything any longer. My maid is adequate now although she will never become perfect, and I have little to do with the household.[126]

By the beginning of the year, Lotte was expressing pleasure with her maid's progress as well as her own, vowing to make a 'tablecloth now that we have decided to keep the house for a longer period and now that the maid's cooking is fair enough to invite occasional informal guests.'[127]

Both Stefan and Lotte were not only 'astonished by the poverty', but also idealized it. In one letter Stefan highlighted the lack of sanitary medical conditions and birth control while also romanticizing it, comparing the simplicity of Brazilian life with the unnecessary opulence of old times in Europe:

> One is always astonished by the poverty of the people here and one learns how many things of our life are superfluous — if I remember René Fulops[128] child with all kind of sterilizations and protektions; here a black midwife does (and not very cleanly) all the work and the children grow nevertheless here like strawberries — our black maid has no less than five. Living here means to get knowledge of life, all is here (except in the Frischauer luxurious quarters . . .) like two hundred years ago and this gives life here a great charm; people live the old family life and are happy to have a dozen children without to worry how to feed them and God helps. It would be strange for us to return to European and Northamerican ideas after all this experiences — the one big advantage is that one is not more so afraid to become poor. In such countries one could live with very few if one would forget his former standard.[129]

Such psychological tensions are present in every letter from Petrópolis: between the old and the new, between loss and discovery, and between pessimism and optimism. As the letters progress, the sense of isolation and desperation intensifies. At times the Zweigs' moods and physical health are directly influenced by the uncomfortable weather.

In a letter written in Petrópolis in early 1942, Stefan Zweig wrote about the unremitting rain and its impact on their moods and health:

> We had not very good weather here; since 40 years it did not rain so much in Brazil but we make every good moment our long walks . . . Alltogether we are very happy to be here instead of Northamerica and Lotte feels somewhat better — I am not yet satisfied completely, but I hope that she will stop soon her night-music.[130]

Although the Zweigs found the cooler climate in the mountains more bearable than Rio de Janeiro's often oppressive heat, the heavy rains that characterize summers in the mountains were problematic for both of them. Lotte's 'night-music' was not music at all but instead referred to the sounds that she made because of her asthma. Asthma had been a health concern for Lotte ever since she was a child, although in Europe she had usually been able to manage it. The stress of travel combined with the hot and humid climate in South America and then intense cold, followed by intense heat and humidity, in the United States seemed to have exasperated her condition and its symptoms, including uncomfortable breathing and wheezing. Even before returning to Brazil, Stefan complained about the New York weather and Lotte's asthma and his depression. To Ben Huebsch he wrote that he felt extremely depressed and that he could not 'imagine that we will ever see peace again . . .',[131] while to Abrahão Koogan he explained that Lotte was not in good health and that they wanted to return to Brazil.[132]

From Petrópolis, perhaps recalling how awful she felt in the United States, Lotte wrote to Friderike that she was now feeling much better and that their 'life is just the opposite' of what it was in New York, and that they were now 'living isolated', and 'working, reading, walking a lot'.[133] In early October 1941 Stefan wrote light-heartedly to Hannah and Manfred about Lotte's work and health, and their marriage:

> Lotte is busy; you would not believe it as we make very few walks and see no people that the day passes so quickly away, that we are quite supossed to be here already three weeks. I am happy that Lotte likes this kind of life as much as I do; I am only not quite satisfied with her health. She has cheeted me first in having no dowry, now in loosing weight by her damned asthma, which is somewhat better but every night there are one or two dialogues between her and a dog in a house far away. Whenever she begins to cough the dog begins to bark as the air is quite still and transmits every sound in a great distance. I insist that she now makes a cure . . . because here life is

so quiet and easy that I wish she should take provisions for her bad times which are expecting us in the future . . .[134]

Stefan also wrote that he and Lotte needed rest and stability to regain strength in the face of his 'psychic depressions' and Lotte's asthma.[135] 'It was really necessary for us to stabilise for longer time', he reported, '. . . we were both frightfully tired'. He continued, 'Lotte more by her asthma and myself by psychic depressions; here in the solitude we hope to get new strength also alas, we will want much strength.'[136] Initially Lotte also wrote about her health with exasperation, but she wrote about her hope for a calmer time as well. In January 1941, she wrote that she was considering a possible experimental treatment that would hopefully relieve some of her symptoms:

> . . . a nose and throat specialist whom we met in Buenos Aires made me an interesting proposition for an asthma treatment which he said had success in about 80 percent of the cases in Argentine and in France where he has studied and learned the process . . . The treatment consists in touching a Sanglien in the upper part of the nose with a needle with some kind of liquid which reduces the oversensitivity and after repeating this about a dozen times in an interval of 2–3 days each, the asthma should be cured. It sounds phantastic to us . . .[137]

Despite the persistent rain in Petrópolis, Lotte's letters give the impression that she often felt quite well. Some three weeks before committing suicide Lotte told her family that her asthma had not 'all been bad recently and I even gave Stefan the pleasure of a few quiet nights.' Since arriving in Petrópolis, she reported, she had only a single asthmatic episode, 'one very slight, just strong enough to get an injection and to allow myself the luxury of a day in bed.'[138] On 21 February 1942, however, the day before the suicides, Lotte repeated her sense of anxiety and desperation, and referred again to her health problems as she tried to convince her sister-in-law that suicide was the only solution:

> Going away like this my only wish is that you may believe that it is the best thing for Stefan, suffering as he did all these years with all those who suffer from the Nazi domination, and for me, always ill with Asthma.[139]

In Stefan's last letter to Friderike, he also explained that he and Lotte were yearning for rest and quiet:

when you get this letter I shall feel much better than before . . . You have seen me in Ossining and after a good and quiet time my depression became more acute. I suffered so much that I could not concentrate any more . . . I was too tired . . . and poor Lotte had not a good time with me, especially as her health was not the best . . .[140]

In choosing a place to live, Stefan and Lotte did what millions of immigrants have done: they sought out an area that most reminded them of home and tried to first recreate, if not preserve, their customs and habits in the new environment. At the same time, many Jewish immigrants and refugees quickly integrated into Brazilian society, learned the language and generally adapted to Brazil. For the Zweigs this was more difficult, since their lives revolved around his publications in German, a market that was all-but extinguished. When the Zweigs returned to Brazil, they had lost all contact with his German publishers, and there were no guarantees that he would be published in England or in the United States.

Despite the fact that both were multilingual and had made progress in Portuguese by the end of 1941, their alienation was also related to language. Neither Stefan nor Lotte enjoyed Portuguese. Earlier Lotte had lamented the fact that Brazilians did not speak Spanish, a feeling that never really changed.[141] On the other hand, Stefan communicated mostly in French and Spanish. Moreover, he regretted that he was obliged to think and write in the same language as Hitler yet his livelihood depended on it, or so he believed.

Gerhard Metsch, a fellow German-speaking immigrant to Brazil who visited the Zweigs in Petrópolis in 1941 and 1942, gave three reasons why he believed they were unhappy in Petrópolis: the wet climate, the absence of a library, and the lack of friends.[142] Along with frequent mentions in the Zweigs' letters of the weather and the severed connections with friends and family, Stefan cited the lack of access to books in Petrópolis as a major problem. In a letter to José Kopke Fróes, the director of the municipal library in Petrópolis, for example, Stefan lamented that he did not have his library in Brazil since it was the most important resource for his work.[143] Add to these factors, the anxiety over the war and the loss of their homelands and it is easy to understand why the Zweigs felt physically and mentally isolated and depressed, never finding the solace that they so badly wanted.

Making sense of the suicides

The letters clearly express Stefan's and Lotte's sense of isolation and depression but they also show that they were lucid when they decided to take their lives. Furthermore, the planning and consideration underscore an eerie sense of calm and righteousness. On 18 February 1942, five days before the suicides, Stefan Zweig wrote to Abrahão Koogan, making him the executor of his property in Brazil, and apologizing for leaving him such tasks. In a letter dated 21 February 1942, Lotte Zweig also wrote that 'should I die in Brazil', either Dr Samuel Malamud (the Zweigs' Brazilian lawyer) or Abrahão Koogan, 'alone or together', could handle her affairs in Brazil. She bequeathed her modest collection of jewellery and the money that she had deposited in her account at the Banco do Brasil to her brother Manfred. She also asked that her clothing, shoes, and personal belongings be given to the needy.[144]

At the end of January 1942, Stefan had completed his *Schachnovelle* (translated into English as *The Royal Game* and *Chess Story*), which takes place on board a ship en route to Buenos Aires and is the only work of fiction that he wrote in Brazil. It is also his only work of fiction that deals directly with Hitler's moral destruction of Europe and presents a protagonist, like himself, who must flee Europe. On 21 February 1942, he mailed copies of his completed novella to his translator and publisher Alfredo Cahn in Buenos Aires, and to his publishers Ben Huebsch and Gottfried Bermann Fischer in New York. (He also left a copy for Abrahão Koogan.)[145]

Both Zweigs also took time to write letters to several friends and acquaintances, as well as to the municipal library. On 21 February 1942, they wrote separate farewell letters to Hannah and Manfred. Lotte's letter, addressed only to her sister-in-law, is deeply apologetic, although it offers advice on the future of her niece Eva. Lotte ends the letter thanking Hannah and asking for forgiveness, but explaining that what she was about to do 'is best as we do it now'.[146] Stefan goes further, explaining that they had made a mutual decision because of the suffering exasperated by Lotte's asthma and their 'nomadic life which did not allow me to do my work efficiently'. He is also apologetic, feeling a 'responsibility', but insisting that they had lived a happy life together. 'You know', he wrote, 'how perfect we two have lived together these years and that there was not a moment of disagreement between us.'[147]

Stefan wrote farewell letters to many others, including Friderike Zweig, Ernst Feder, Afonso Arinos de Mello Franco, Victor Wittkowski, and to Margarida Banefield, his landlady, to whom he apologized for the problems that their suicides would cause. He also composed a public declaration: the word declaration ('Declaração') is written in Portuguese, but the words that followed, which are written in German, begin by explaining that he had decided to take his life of his own free will, offer thanks for the hospitality that he received in Brazil, and end with a farewell to all of his friends. Lotte is eerily absent in all of these farewells, although as we have shown, she did write to her family.[148] While Lotte refers to the turmoil of Europe as a cause of her husband's feeling of hopelessness — 'suffering as he did all these years with all those who suffer from the Nazi domination',[149] no such direct political references are found in either Stefan's private letter to Hannah and Manfred nor in his 'Declaração'.

We glean a sense of Lotte's own motivation and decision to commit suicide from Stefan's last letter to Hannah and Manfred, stating that her health was poor. The treatment that Lotte underwent for her asthma was not helping, while the anxiety that often accompanies asthmatic attacks — or fear of attacks — is likely to have exacerbated her depression and may even have made the attacks worse.[150] Gerhard Metsch, a local German friend, was less equivocal. When he visited the Zweigs, he saw a woman who was depressed and overwhelmed by her husband's depressive state. Moreover, Metsch claimed that 'Without a doubt, she [Lotte] did not want to commit suicide. She liked him, as we now know, and she suffered because she had to follow him from one country to the other'.[151] Lotte's last letter casts some doubt on this assertion, however.

We know that Stefan Zweig took his life first. He poisoned himself on the bed facing the ceiling, dying with his hands crossed. Did they say goodbye to one another? We do not know. We do know that Stefan was already dead before Lotte took her own life. She embraced him by lying on her right side and putting her left hand over him as he lay facing towards the ceiling.

Biographers claim that, in the build-up to the execution of the suicide pact, Lotte was simply too weak, and lacked the strength of character, to control or resist her husband's depression.[152] These South American letters, however, show that Stefan and Lotte Zweig had a much more balanced relationship than is claimed, one that ultimately was overcome by severe depression and profound feelings of despair. With the Europe that he loved destroyed, Stefan Zweig found himself leading 'a poor, a shabby, a undignified individual life' but while he was hopeful that the Nazis would be defeated, he questioned whether after the war he would still have 'strength and sense enough to enjoy life.'[153] Lotte Zweig's own sense of isolation, aggravated by her failing health and the sombre mood of her husband, led her to conclude that suicide, or as she put it in her last letter to her family, 'going away like this', was 'the best thing . . . for Stefan . . . and for me'.[154]

The letters from South America chronicle the life, times and deaths of Stefan and Lotte Zweig in Brazil and Argentina. They not only shed light on the couple's preoccupations and aspirations after their decision to leave Europe, but they also give us a unique view on to the domestic and familial life of the Zweigs in the midst of World War II, when so many families were being torn apart. The letters also give readers an intimate view of Stefan Zweig — the man, refugee and immigrant — while providing the first comprehensive portrayal of his wife, companion and assistant Lotte Zweig.

The organization and presentation of the letters

Part I of this volume begins with a letter that was written on 14 August 1940 on board the SS *Argentina*, the ship that carried the Zweigs on their first voyage from New York to Rio de Janeiro. The correspondence continued regularly — ranging from twice a week to fortnightly — until 21 or 22 January 1941, the last letter having been written on board their flight from Trinidad to Miami. The Zweigs then travelled back to New York, where they remained between January and August 1941. Although the Zweigs sent letters to Hannah and Manfred Altmann from the United States, these are not included in this collection as their central focus was on the practical details for the care in New York of Eva, the Altmanns' daughter. Nonetheless, some of the letters also provide invaluable insights into why the Zweigs decided to return to Brazil. Thus, Part II describes the Zweigs' time in New York and New Haven. Part III covers the Zweigs' second joint visit to Brazil, with letters from 24 August 1941 aboard the SS *Uruguay*, until 21 February 1942, the day before the couple committed suicide in Petrópolis. Part IV is an account of Stefan and Lotte Zweig's final days that Ernst Feder, a friend of the Zweigs in Petrópolis, sent to Manfred Altmann.

We have reproduced the original letters verbatim, including printed addresses or other details that appeared on the original paper. So, for example, when the Zweigs used stationery of a ship or a hotel, the printed information is provided in italics. The only sections of letters that are not included are some of those that specifically concern arrange-ments for the care and welfare in New York of Eva. In reproducing the letters, the original spelling, grammar, punctuation and paragraph breaks have been maintained. In most cases the language is fluent, and where there are errors in spelling or grammar, they do not inhibit the reader's understanding.

Notes

1 See reactions in *Aufbau* (a journal for German-speaking Jews established in New York in 1934). A special edition was dedicated to Zweig: 'In memoriam', *Aufbau*, 27 February 1942.

2 Thomas Mann, 'Nachruf', *Aufbau*, 27 February 1942.

3 In some official documentation, including her German passport, she used the name 'Lieselotte'.

4 Thomas Mann to Erika Mann, 24 February 1942, quoted in Klemens Renolder, 'Stefan Zweig and Austria', in *The Cultural Exodus From Austria*, ed. by Friedrich Stadler and Peter Weibel (Vienna: Löcker, 1993), p. 241. Mann is referring to Zweig's suicide note in which he writes of the difficulty of reconstructing his life.

5 Zweig's life has been thoroughly treated by biographers including Elizabeth Allday's *Stefan Zweig: A Critical Biography* (Chicago: J. Phillip O'Hara, 1972), Donald A. Prater's *European of Yesterday: A Biography of Stefan Zweig* (Oxford: Oxford University Press, 1972), Alberto Dines' *Morte no paraíso: A tragédia de Stefan Zweig* (Rio de Janeiro: Nova Fronteira, 1981 and Rocco, 2004), Hartmut Müller's *Stefan Zweig* (Hamburg: Rowohlt, 1988), Dominique Bona's *Stefan Zweig: L'ami blessé* (Paris: Plon, 1996), Serge Niémetz's *Stefan Zweig: Le voyageur et ses mondes* (Paris: Belmond, 1996), Gert Kerschbaumer's *Stefan Zweig, Der Fliegende Salzburger* (Salzburg: Residenz, 2003) and Oliver Matuschek's *Stefan Zweig: drei Leben — Eine Biographie* (Frankfurt: S. Fischer, 2006). As far as Lotte Zweig is concerned, neither biographies exploring her life nor volumes of her correspondence have been published.

6 The biographers have taken the description from 'Die schweigsame Frau' ('The Silent Woman'), an opera in three acts by Richard Strauss, with libretto by Stefan Zweig. See Prater, *European of Yesterday*, op. cit., p. 226, where Lotte Zweig is referred to as a 'silent woman'. Dines, *Morte no paraíso* (2004), op. cit., p. 225, refers to Lotte Zweig as 'uma silenciosa mulher'. The same adjective is employed in French in Niémetz, *Stefan Zweig*, op. cit., p. 555.

7 LZ to HA&MA, Rio de Janeiro, 7 December 1940.

8 Victor Turner, *The Ritual Process: Structure and Anti-Structure* (Chicago: Aldine Publishing Co., 1969), p. 95.

9 *New York Evening Post* (10 November 1928).

10 *Atlantic Bookshelf*, CLVI (October 1935), p. 10.

11 *Books* (25 August 1935), p. 3.

12 Donald A. Prater, 'Stefan Zweig and England', in *German Life and Letters*, vol. 16, issue 1 (October 1962), pp. 4–5.

13 'Stefan Zweig: Jews in the World of Yesterday', in Hannah Arendt, *The Jewish Writings*, edited by Jerome Kohn and Ron H. Feldman (New York: Schocken Books, 2007), pp. 317–28; originally published as 'Stefan Zweig: Juden in der Welt von gestern', in *Sechs Essays* (Heidelberg: Schneider, 1948), pp. 112–27, based on an earlier English version appearing under the title 'Portrait of a period', *Menorah Journal* 31 (1943), pp. 307–14.

14 See Stefan Zweig, *The World of Yesterday* (Lincoln: University of Nebraska Press, 1964), pp. 326–28. Stefan Zweig's open suicide letter (his 'Declaração', dated

22 February 1942) laments the destruction of Europe, which he calls his 'spiritual homeland'. The original of what has become a much-reproduced document is held by the Department of Manuscripts and Archives of the Jewish National and University Library, Jerusalem.

15 SZ to H. G. Wells, 18 November 1939, HO282/4, National Archives (London).

16 Jean-Michel Palmier, *Weimar in Exile: Exile in Europe, Exile in America* (London: Verso, 2006), pp. 11–14.

17 Lieselotte Altmann: naturalization application, 14 July 1938, HO282/4, National Archives (London).

18 Lotte Altmann's other brother, Richard, had left Europe in the late 1920s, settling permanently in Egypt.

19 Lieselotte Altmann: naturalization application: conditional landing card 14 May 1934, HO282/4, National Archives (London).

20 Lieselotte Altmann: naturalization application: conditional landing card 14 May 1934, HO282/4, National Archives (London).

21 Otto M. Schiff to R. E. Gomme (Ministry of Labour), 19 February 1936, HO282/4, National Archives (London).

22 Friderike Zweig, *Stefan Zweig* (London: W.H. Allen, 1946), pp. 225–26. See Dines, *Morte no paraíso* (2004), op. cit., p. 235; Matuschek, *Stefan Zweig*, op. cit., p. 274; Prater, *Stefan Zweig* (1972), op. cit., pp. 225–26.

23 Friderike Zweig, *Stefan Zweig*, op. cit., pp. 225–26; Prater, 'Stefan Zweig and England', op. cit., p. 6; Lieselotte Altmann: naturalization application: conditional landing card, 14 May 1934, HO282/4, National Archives (London).

24 Klemens Renoldner, Hildemar Holl and Peter Karlhuber, eds, *Stefan Zweig: Bilder, Texte, Dokumente* (Salzburg: Residenz, 1993), p. 149.

25 Vivian D. Lipman, 'Anglo-Jewish attitudes to the refugees from central Europe', in *Second Chance: Two Centuries of German-speaking Jews in the United Kingdom*, ed. by Werner Eugen Mosse et al. (Tubingen: J.C.B. Mohr, 1991), p. 520.

26 Otto M. Schiff to R. E. Gomme (Ministry of Labour), 19 February 1936, HO282/4, National Archives (London).

27 Joseph Roth, *Briefe, 1911–1939* (Cologne: Kiepenheur and Witsch, 1970), p. 334.

28 See Dines, *Morte no paraíso* (2004), op. cit., p. 236.

29 Dominique Bona, *Stefan Zweig: Uma biografia* (Rio de Janeiro: Editora Record, 1999), p. 275.

30 August 1934, quoted in Donald A. Prater, *Stefan Zweig: Das Leben eines Ungeduldigen* (Munich and Vienna: Carl Hanser, 1981), p. 312. Original quote in German: 'Du bist kein Emigrant, mach Dich nicht freiwillig dazu! Verlaß den Acker nicht, aus dem Dir alles gewachsen ist'. Following the *Anschluss* in 1938, Csokor himself fled Austria, first for Poland, then Romania and finally Yugoslavia where he was arrested and interned until 1945.

31 Niémetz, *Stefan Zweig*, op. cit., p. 568.

32 Bona, *Stefan Zweig*, op. cit., p. 273.

33 Stefan Zweig, *Briefe 1932–1942* Vol. IV, ed. by Knut Beck and Jeffrey B. Berlin (Frankfurt: S. Fischer, 2005), pp. 143–46.

34 SZ to FZ, 26 August 1936, Stefan Zweig/Friderike Zweig, 'Wenn einen Augenblick

die Wolken weichen', Briefwechsel 1912–1942, ed. by Jeffrey B. Berlin and Gert Kerschbaumer (Frankfurt: S. Fischer, 2006), p. 307.

35 Stefan Zweig, 'Kleine Reise nach Brasilien', in *Länder, Städte, Landschaften* (Frankfurt: Fischer Tagebuch, 1981), pp. 153–84. The essay was originally published in the Budapest German-language newspaper *Pester Lloyd* from 17 October to 8 November 1936 and then in Zweig's collection, *Begegnungen mit Menschen, Büchern, Städten* (Vienna: Reichner, 1937).

36 SZ to FZ, 21 August 1936, Stefan Zweig/Friderike Zweig, 'Wenn einen Augenblick die Wolken weichen', op. cit., p. 306.

37 SZ to FZ, 26 August 1936, Stefan Zweig/Friderike Zweig, 'Wenn einen Augenblick die Wolken weichen', op. cit., p. 307. SZ to FZ, 21 August 1936, Stefan Zweig/ Friderike Zweig, 'Wenn einen Augenblick die Wolken weichen', op. cit., p. 306.

38 Koogan later donated his correspondence with Stefan Zweig to the Biblioteca Nacional in Rio de Janeiro.

39 SZ to FZ, Buenos Aires, 12 September 1936, Stefan Zweig/Friderike Zweig, op. cit., pp. 309–10.

40 Applicants were required to show that they had resided in the United Kingdom or one of its territories for one year immediately preceding the date of application and a total of four years within the previous eight years. Lotte Altmann submitted her application on 14 July 1938 and Zweig submitted his on 13 December 1938; see HO282/4, National Archives (London).

41 Stefan Zweig to H.M. Chief Inspector, Immigration Branch, Home Office, HO282/4, National Archives (London).

42 Certificate of Marriage between Stefan Zweig and Lotte Altmann, HO282/4, National Archives (London).

43 SZ to Siegmund Warburg, 6 September 1939, *Stefan Zweig: Briefe 1932–1942*, op. cit., p. 258.

44 *Stefan Zweig: Briefe 1932–1942*, op. cit., p. 276.

45 Herbert Smith & Co. to Mrs Lotte Zweig, 21 February 1940, HO282/4, National Archives (London).

46 See the testimony of Hermann Zesten in *Stefan Zweig Bilder Texte Dokumente*, op. cit., p. 168.

47 Franz Werfel, 'Stefan Zweigs Tod', in Hans Arens (ed) *Stefan Zweig: Sein Leben-Sein Werk* (Esslingen: Bechtle, 1949), p. 185. See also Fred Uhlman, *The Making of an Englishman* (London: Collancz, 1960).

48 SZ to Abrahão Koogan, 22 July 1940, *Stefan Zweig: Briefe 1932–1942*, op. cit., p. 278.

49 The film was eventually produced and first screened in 1950.

50 SZ to HA&MA, New York City, 31 March 1941; SZ to Ben Huebsch, Ossining, late July 1941, Stefan Zweig, *Briefe 1932–1942*, op. cit., p. 310.

51 Stefan Zweig, *Brazil: A Land of the Future* (Riverside, California: Ariadne Press, 2000).

52 Stefan Zweig, 'Kleine Reise nach Brasilien', in *Länder, Städte, Landschaften* (Frankfurt: Fischer Tagebuch, 1981), pp. 153–84.

53 Stefan Zweig, *Brazil: Land of the Future* (London: Cassell and Company, 1942), p. 4.

54 Zweig, *Brazil: Land of the Future*, op. cit., p. 4.

55 Zweig, *Brazil: Land of the Future*, op. cit., pp. 6–7.

56 Zweig, *Brazil: A Land of the Future*, op. cit., pp. 255–59.

57 First published in Stockholm, 1942, as *Die Welt von Gestern*. An English translation was published in 1943.

58 Zweig, *Brazil: Land of the Future*, op. cit., p. 6.

59 Zweig, *Brazil: Land of the Future*, op. cit., p. 11.

60 Zweig, *Brazil: Land of the Future*, op. cit., p. 13.

61 SZ to Berthold Viertel, 11 October 1940, in Zweig, *Briefe an Freunde*, op. cit., p. 289.

62 See LZ to HA&MA, Rio de Janeiro, 23 October 1940. Lotte wrote of her responsibilities while travelling: 'In between Stefan dictates a lecture in English, that is to say I shall translate it and he will revise it, another lecture for the refugees in Buenos Aires and revises his other lectures in French which he might have to give, and sometime I shall have to pack — and pack carefully because we fly and I have to select what to take.'

63 Quoted in Zweig, *Brazil: A Land of the Future*, op. cit., opening page.

64 We have cited from those rare published letters in this introduction. They come from Stefan Zweig, *Briefe 1932–1942*, op. cit., and Stefan Zweig/Friderike Zweig, 'Wenn einen Augenblick die Wolken weichen', *Briefwechsel 1912–1942*, op. cit.

65 During the war, all overseas mail to or from Britain passed through the Postal and Telegraph Censorship Department's depots in Liverpool and London; in 1940 censors randomly selected for inspection 20 per cent of letters arriving from South America, while in 1941, 50 per cent were inspected. See *History of the Postal and Telegraph Censorship Department 1938–1946*, Volume 1 (London: Civil Censorship Study Group, 1996; first published by the Home Office, London, 1952).

66 Many of these letters have been published; see, for example: Stefan Zweig, *Briefwechsel* (Frankfurt: S. Fischer, 1987) and *Stefan Zweig: Triumph und Tragik: Aufsätze, Tagebuchnotizen and Briefe* (Frankfurt: Fischer Taschenbuch, 1992). Zweig's letters have also been published in works by many other intellectuals including Sigmund Freud, Rainer Maria Rilke and Arthur Schnitzler.

67 See the letters from Lotte Zweig to Friderike Zweig included in the correspondence between Stefan and Friderike Zweig in Stefan Zweig/Friderike Zweig, 'Wenn einen Augenblick', op. cit.

68 LZ to HA, Ossining, 21 July 1941.

69 SZ to HA, SS *Argentina*, 14 August 1940.

70 SZ to HA, Rio de Janeiro, 23 August 1940.

71 SZ to HA&MA, Rio de Janeiro, 10 September 1940.

72 SZ to HA&MA, Rio de Janeiro, 29 September 1940.

73 LZ to Therese Altmann, Rio de Janeiro, 19 October 1940.

74 LZ to HA&MA, Buenos Aires, 27 October 1940.

75 LZ to HA&MA, Buenos Aires, 9 November 1940.

76 SZ to HA&MA, Buenos Aires, 26 October 1940.

77 Many names are referred to in the Zweigs' letters, but most go unmentioned. In a lecture on Stefan Zweig broadcast on the radio in California on 23 April 1950,

Camille Honig (see p. 198) explained how Stefan Zweig had provided him — and countless other struggling writers and artists — with research work, paying ten times the rate a research assistant would normally command.

78   LZ to HA&MA, Rio de Janeiro, 11 December 1940.

79   Palmier, *Weimar in Exile*, op. cit., p. 246.

80   SZ to HA&MA, Rio de Janeiro, 15 September 1940.

81   LZ to HA&MA&TA, Buenos Aires, 9 November 1940. On Cuba and the plight of Jewish refugees, see Robert M. Levine, *Tropical Diaspora: The Jewish Experience in Cuba* (Gainesville: University Press of Florida, 1993) and Gordon Thomas and Max Morgan-Witts, *The Voyage of the Damned* (London: Hodder and Stoughton, 1974).

82   SZ to HA&MA, 15 November 1940.

83   See SZ to HA, Rio de Janeiro, 11 December 1940.

84   Secretariado Nacional de Informação, Turismo e Cultura Popular.

85   SZ to HA&MA, Teresópolis, 6 October 1940 and SZ to HA&MA, Rio de Janeiro, 15 September 1940.

86   See SZ to HA&MA, Petrópolis, 3 October 1941.

87   Alfonso Henriques, *Vargas o maquiavélico* (São Paulo: Palácio do Livro, 1961), pp. 223–26. Thomas Skidmore, *Politics in Brazil: Experiments in Democracy, 1930–1964* (New York: Oxford University Press, 1967), pp. 28–30. For a general view of Vargas' populist policies, see Robert M. Levine, *Father of the Poor? Vargas and His Era* (Cambridge, Cambridge University Press, 1998).

88   One tragic case was that of Olga Benário, a German-born communist activist of Jewish origin. In 1935 Benário accompanied the Brazilian Communist Party leader, Carlos Prestes, from Europe to Brazil, travelling on false papers. By the time Prestes and Benário arrived in Brazil they were married. Following a failed insurrection against the Vargas regime in November 1935, Prestes and Benário were arrested. In January 1936 — the same year as Zweig's first visit to Brazil — Benário was deported to Germany where she was held in Ravensbrück concentration camp. She was murdered in 1942 at the experimental hospital in Bernberg. See Fernando Morais, *Olga: Revolutionary and Martyr* (New York: Grove, 1990).

89   Jeffrey Lesser, *Welcoming the Undesirables: Brazil and the Jewish Question* (Berkeley: University of California Press, 1995), pp. 83–105. Robert Levine, 'Brazil's Jews during the Vargas era and after', *Luso-Brazilian Review*, vol. 5 no. 1 (Summer 1968), pp. 45 58.

90   Lesser, *Welcoming the Undesirables*, op. cit., pp. 92–93. For a contrasting view of Jewish immigration to Brazil, see Marcos Chor Maio, 'Qual anti-semitismo? Relativizando a questão judaica no Brasil dos anos 30', in *Repensando o Estado Novo*, ed. by Dulce Pandolfi (Rio de Janerio: Editora FGV, 1999), pp. 229–56. Maio argues that the number of Jews entering Brazil actually rose following the imposition of official restrictions.

91   Stefan Zweig, 'Kleine Reise nach Brasilien', in *Länder, Städte, Landschaften* (Frankfurt: Fischer Tagebuch, 1981), pp. 153–84.

92   Zweig, *Brazil: Land of the Future*, op. cit., pp. 134–65.

93   SZ to HA&MA, Bahia, 16 January 1941.

94   Zweig, *Brazil: Land of the Future*, op. cit., p. 157.

95 Dines, *Morte no paraíso* (2004), op. cit., pp. 388–92.
96 See *Vamos Ler!*, 23 October 1941, pp. 18–19, 52–53.
97 LZ to HA&MA, Teresópolis, 10 October 1940.
98 Gilberto Freyre, *Casa-Grande e Senzala: Formação da família brasileira sob o regimen de economia patriarchal* (Rio de Janeiro: Schmidt, 1933); the book did not appear in English until 1946 (as *The Masters and the Slaves: A Study in the Development of Brazilian Civilization*) or in German until 1965 (as *Herrenhaus und Sklavenhütte: Ein Bild der brasilianischen Gesellschaft*). There is no evidence that Stefan Zweig read Freyre's work. In fact, according to Alberto Dines, Freyre, who met Zweig, reported that Zweig had not been familiar with his work. See Dines, *Morte no paraíso* (2004), op. cit., p. 326.
99 SZ to HA&MA, Teresópolis, 10 October 1940.
100 SZ to HA, Rio de Janeiro, 3 December 1940.
101 SZ to HA&MA, Bahia, 16 January 1941.
102 SZ to HA, Rio de Janeiro, 23 August 1940.
103 SZ to HA&MA, Rio de Janeiro, n.d. (after 29 September 1940).
104 LZ to HA&MA, Rio de Janeiro, 12 January 1941.
105 LZ to HA&MA, Petrópolis, 12 January 1941.
106 SZ to HA&MA, Petrópolis, 10 February 1942.
107 LZ to HA, Petrópolis, 10 November 1941.
108 LZ to HA, Rio de Janeiro, 2 December 1941.
109 Zweig, *The World of Yesterday* (1964), op. cit., p. 6.
110 SZ to Abrahão Koogan, 1 August 1941, Stefan Zweig, *Briefe 1932–1942*, op. cit., p. 311.
111 SZ to Abrahão Koogan, 15 August 1941, Stefan Zweig, *Briefe 1932–1942*, op. cit., pp. 311–12.
112 Appropriately, the Zweigs settled on a road named for the poet Antônio Gonçalves Dias (1823–64), who is known for his tribute to exile, 'Canção do exilio' (Song of Exile), which he wrote in Portugal in 1843.
113 LZ to TA, Rio de Janeiro, 13 September 1941.
114 For a view of the cultural developments during the 1930s and 1940s in Rio de Janeiro see Daryle Williams *Culture Wars in Brazil: The First Vargas Regime, 1930–1945* (Durham and London: Duke University Press, 2001). For issues related to race and the Vargas regime see Darién J. Davis, *Avoiding the Dark: Race, Nation and National Culture in Modern Brazil* (Aldershot: Ashgate International/ Centre for Research in Ethnic Studies, 2000).
115 SZ to FZ, Petrópolis, 10 September 1941, Stefan Zweig/Friderike Zweig, 'Wenn einen Augenblick', op. cit., pp. 371–72.
116 SZ to HA&MA, Petrópolis, n.d. (c. late October/early November 1941).
117 SZ to HA&MA, Petrópolis, n.d. (c. late October/early November 1941).
118 SZ to HA&MA, Rio de Janeiro, 4 November 1940.
119 SZ to HA&MA, Rio de Janeiro, 9 November 1940.
120 Dines, *Morte no paraíso* (2004), op. cit., p. 325.
121 Dines, *Morte no paraíso* (2004), op. cit., p. 401.
122 Gerhard Metsch, 'Briefe aus Petropolis', in *Die letzte Partie* (Bielefeld: Aisthesis, 1999), pp. 51–67.

123 SZ to HA&MA, Petrópolis, 10 December 1941. Brazil did not declare war on Japan until 6 July 1945, although on 22 August 1942 it declared war on both Germany and Italy, with an expeditionary force consisting of 25,000 men taking part in the 1944 Italian campaign.
124 LZ to HA, Rio de Janeiro, 4 September 1941.
125 LZ to HA&MA, Petrópolis, 21 January 1942.
126 LZ to HA, Rio de Janeiro, 2 December 1941.
127 LZ to Martha Kahn, Petrópolis, 10 January 1942.
128 René Fülöp-Miller, see p. 197.
129 SZ to HA&MA, Petrópolis, 21 January 1942.
130 SZ to HA&MA, Petrópolis, n.d., but before letter of 21 January 1942.
131 SZ to Ben Huebsch, Ossining, n.d. (July 1941), in Stefan Zweig, *Briefe 1932–1942*, op. cit., p. 308.
132 SZ to Abrahão Koogan, New York City, n.d. (c. 15 August 1941), in Stefan Zweig, *Briefe 1932–1942*, op. cit., p. 311.
133 LZ to FZ, Petrópolis, 16 December 1941, Stefan Zweig/Friderike Zweig, 'Wenn einen Augenblick', p. 387.
134 SZ to HA&MA, Petrópolis, 3 October 1941.
135 SZ to HA&MA, Petrópolis, n.d. (c. late October/early November 1941).
136 SZ to HA&MA, Petrópolis, n.d. (c. late October/early November 1941).
137 LZ to HA&MA, Rio de Janeiro, 12 January 1941.
138 LZ to HA&MA, 1 February 1942. There is a very high incidence of asthma in Petrópolis, the main allergen being mites that feed on mould that is endemic in the area's warm and humid climate.
139 LZ to HA, Petrópolis, 21 February 1942.
140 SZ to FZ, 22 February 1942, Stefan Zweig/Friderike Zweig 'Wenn einen Augenblick', op. cit., p. 394.
141 LZ to HA&MA, Rio de Janeiro, 13 September 1941.
142 Gerhard Metsch, 'Briefe aus Petropolis', in *Die letzte Partie* (Bielefeld: Aisthesis, 1999), pp. 51–67. This essay contains responses to two interviews conducted by Ingrid Schwamborn in September 1994 and January 1995.
143 Niémetz, *Stefan Zweig*, op. cit., pp. 732–36.
144 Partial copy of letter from Lotte Zweig, 21 February 1942, Abrahão Koogan Personal Archive, I-45, 10, 9, Biblioteca Nacional, Rio de Janeiro.
145 Ingrid Schwamborn, 'Aspekte des Spiels in Schachnovelle', in *Die letzte Partie*, op. cit., p. 265.
146 LZ to HZ, Petrópolis, 21 February 1942.
147 SZ to HA&MA, Petrópolis, 21 February 1942.
148 The historian Leo Spitzer referred to Lotte's 'voicelessness', pointing out that she had apparently left 'no note, no declaration, no word' and commenting that the suicide pact and Stefan Zweig's 'Declaração' were a dramatic case of a woman as a 'submerged subordinate partner to her famous but despairing mate.' Leo Spitzer, *Lives in Between: Assimilation and Marginality in Austria, Brazil, West Africa 1780–1945* (Cambridge, Cambridge University Press, 1989), p. 172.
149 LZ to HZ, Petrópolis, 21 February 1942.
150 See E. Chen and G. E. Miller, 'Stress and inflammation in exacerbations of

INTRODUCTION

asthma', in *Brain Behavior, and Immunity* 21:8 (2007), pp. 993–99 and Melissa
Opolski and Ian Wilson, 'Asthma and depression: a pragmatic review of the
literature and recommendations for future research', in *Clinical Practice and
Epidemiology in Mental Health*, 1:18 (2005).

151 Gerhard Metsch, 'Briefe aus Petropolis', *Die letzte Partie*, op. cit., pp. 51–67.
152 See, for example, the biographies by Friderike Zweig, Serge Niémetz, Alberto
Dines, Dominique Bona and Oliver Matuschek.
153 SZ to HA&MA, Petrópolis, 21 December 1941.
154 LZ to HA, Petrópolis, 21 February 1942. In the German edition of his Zweig biography, Alberto Dines reproduces the two most famous lines of Antônio Gonçalves
Dias' poem 'Canção do exílio' ('Song of exile'): 'My homeland has palm-trees /
Where the thrush sings.' Dines intuits that exile and paradise pervaded the road in
Petrópolis where the Zweigs lived, although the couple was apparently oblivious
to the connection. See Alberto Dines, *Tod im Paradies: Die Tragödie des Stefan
Zweig*, tr. by Marlen Eckl (Frankfurt: Büchergilde Gutenberg, 2006), p. 485.

PART I

Letters from Brazil and Argentina
14 August 1940 to 22 January 1941

VIA AIR MAIL
ON-BOARD
S.S. Argentina

[c. 14 August 1940]

Dear Hannah,

We start this letter on board of the ship[1], the rest will follow from Rio where we hope to find your news. I am sorry to say it but we are frightfully spoiled here on the ship and it is the most wonderful voyage one can imagine. — I wish you had only one day out of our twelve. The air warm and a marvellous brise all day, sunbaths and waterbathes, nice people, Brasiliens, Argentines, Suisse, Dutch which all are good and old readers of my books. — From tomorrow (after Barbados) I shall get a state cabin to work in. It was really necessary and a rest after the hot days of Newyork, where poor Lotte nearly broke down.[2] — I have done there hard work to make some money, minor but amusing work and we had to see many people. Unfortunately just the last two days; when you called about Heiner[3] were the worst, I had to see a doctor on behalf of an attack of sciatica and some other thing. Lotte lost a filling and had to rush to a dentist, then we had to go to the Custom House and when our ship left Lotte was so weiry that she remained the whole next day to bed. But what a splendid rest cure we have and I suppose that Brasil will not remain below our expectations. Our friends expect us there in the kindest way and I have invitations for lectures from Uruguay, Argentine, Chile, Venezuela; I suppose all we so all right and we would be perfectly happy as seldom in a voyage would not the idea of the war destroy much of our feelings. We get on the ship nearly no news, just a few lines — the Americans are terribly indifferent to all what happens, they help but they have not the right compassion and not enough foresight — we were glad to leave New York because we could not stand longer this "jolly news" in such a time. We have charming people on board, all the ambassadors of the Havana conference[4] are my chess partners. Now Lotte will write you more. Kind regards

Stefan

1 The SS *Argentina* belonged to the Republics Line, a subsidiary of the Moore-McCormack Line, established under President Franklin D. Roosevelt's Good Neighbour Policy. The *Argentina* served on the United States–Caribbean–South America route and carried up to five hundred passengers.
2 A reference to Lotte's asthma attacks.

3 Heiner Mayer, see p. 200.
4 At the Second Consultative Meeting of Ministers of Foreign Affairs (the so-called 'Havana Conference') of 21–30 July 1940, the United States agreed to share with its neighbours the responsibility of protecting the Americas from external aggression, a marked change from earlier interpretations of the Monroe Doctrine.

VIA AIR MAIL
ON BOARD
S. S. Argentina

14.8.40

Dear Hanna and Manfred,

While in New York I had one single letter from you, one from the children and one from Mama[1] and now it is again a long time without news- but I hope that everything is allright with you, that Eva gets over safely and in good company and that she feels happy in her new home. I am afraid my last letters from Newyork were rather confused and incoherent, it was a terrible rush those last days as we worked with Viertel[2] every afternoon and sometimes in the evening [. . .]

As to Heiner[3] I have written to Mr. Berner, Rose's brother-in-law and asked him for an affidavit. Unfortunately, your cable arrived at a moment where also the last Americans of our acquaintance had left New York and so we could not arrange anything for him. Also Mr. Berner is away until the end of the month, but I feel sure that he will do it if he possibly can, I have asked him to answer me by air mail to Rio and I would then cable you to inform him about the dates and names so that he can fill out the affidavit. Of all the persons we know Mr. Berner seemed the most likely to do it.

As to Ursel[4] I did not try anything as in her case the British re-entry permit would be required should she not come in under the quota. And I heard from people trying in similar cases without success.

I hope to find long letters in Rio — you did not say anything about yourself and Manfred's work. Is Alice[5] still with Horngrads?[6] Did I understand right that Marta could stay, what will you do with Ursel when Eva is gone, can you leave her in Bath with the people who moved in, and will you go back to London then? Do just as you feel is best for your own sake, don't think of our house, it is more important that the arrangements are suitable for you.

50

[The end of the letter above has probably been lost. Although it was written by Lotte Zweig, she did not sign it.]

Dear Hannah, a postscript. We have had lunch with Mr. S.[7] and I will tell you frankly our impression — they are nice people, she not too intelligent but surely of good temper; they seem to have a good income, perhaps they are "new riches" who enjoy still her being wealthy but not "protzig"[8] and very good-hearted. I have the impression that Eva will be quite happy there — of course the fact of being far away from you will spoil a little her happiness and if you are sincere to yourself you would not wish that it were otherwise. My sister in law will also be interested in her and Anita Cahn[9] is also ready to expect her at the pier. So do not worry too much: she will see a new world and nobody knows how such a connection with America can be valuable for her future. As to Heiner[10] I will do my best. Unfortunately all people I know here are away — perhaps we find something in the last moment and then we would ask you to cable us all dates (birth date etc) which are necessary for the forms.

Yours
Stefan

1 Lotte's mother, Therese Altmann, see p. 194.
2 Berthold Viertel, a film director and screenplay writer (see p. 203).
3 Heiner Mayer, a brother of Lotte, see p. 200.
4 Ursel (Ursula), the daughter of Alice and Heiner Mayer, see p. 200.
5 Alice Mayer, the wife of Heiner Mayer, see p. 200.
6 The Horngrads made corsettes and Alice had worked for them in the past.
7 Eva Altmann's first hosts in New York. Members of the host family are here referred to by the initial 'S'.
8 Show off (boastful).
9 Anita Cahn, a friend of Lotte Zweig's in New York; possibly Anita Cahn Block (1882–1967) a noted American theatre critic, newspaper columnist and socialist.
10 Heiner Mayer, see p. 200.

[Undated — on board S.S. *Argentina*]

Dear Hanna, for Eva all is now well prepared as you have heard by our cable — they are wealthy people in a large house in an elegant suburb of Newyork and they are really <u>eager</u> to have a good educated child. We see them today for lunch. All was more difficult than we expected as everybody is away from Newyork and this is also the major difficulty for the affidavit for Heiner[1] — I cannot ask one from Huebsch[2] as he has given already too many and I do not know if we can find anybody in those last two overcrowded days. Till now I could not have anything behind here for my former wife, I am trying now to get Mexican visas for her whole family.

Thousand thanks that you have settled all about the house in Bath, I hope you will have there sometimes a good rest after the busy days in London.

We have here a hard time, as I have worked a good deal merely small things, but we will have read during the twelve days on the ship. I have offers for lectures in Argentine, Uruguay, Chile, Venezuela, more than I will probably do and you need not worry about us. Don't be too economical and send us cables to Rio (from where we send immediately our Hotel address) — I do not rely on airmail. In great love and hurry yours

Stefan

We arrive in Rio the 21. August.

1 Heiner Mayer, see p. 200.
2 Benjamin W. Huebsch, Zweig's American publisher, see p. 198.

Rio 23. Aout 1940

Dear Hannah, we have been so glad to get your letter from 8 August so quickly, the others have not arrived yet except the first one. Rio is as marvellous as ever, nothing in the world to be compared with it. Unfortunately I am afraid that Lotte will loose her modesty here since she is always with ambassadors, ministers and photografed in all newspapers. But we have plenty of time for us, take three times a week Spanish lessons as I have my lectures in the other countries to deliver in Spanish — I do not know what to accept, in Chile I am invited officially with the obligatory visit to the President, in Uruguay

I have only two lectures and about three in Buenos Ayres, provided I will do all this. Personally I would like to stay here, we live here in a delightful little hotel[1] with all the comfort in a nice appartement and very cheap — what a contrast with New York, where one always has the feeling to be a "Hochstapler"[2] and where I have a good pretext for not shaving every day to go with dirty looks. On the ship it was delicious, 12 days of perfect weather with swimming baths and a choice of the most interesting and cultivated people. You cannot imagine how refined and cultivated the upper classes here are — a small élite but a wonderful one: culture in houses, in manners and of a politeness, which even overshadows my own. Lottes room is full of marvellous flowers, we have autos for drives and in the same time they are not insistent. The only thing which prevents me to live here is the heat — we are arrived in full winter but it is warmer than in Bath in July and one shudders to think how it must be when spring commences (in October) and summer (in December.)

The strangest thing is that I get quite indifferent what happens with my books, that I do not care to get no letters. I have got for my former wife a visitors visa to America and possibly one for Portugal but do not know if she will leave without her children.[3] All correspondence with France is nearly impossible and I cannot cable — by the way, cables from here are frightfully expensive but do not hesitate to cable us as often as you can. We shall stay here in any case till to the first weeks of October and possibly even longer as we have to go then to the other American countries which are somewhat cooler in summer (winter for you.) Here we can follow all the events much better and are much more confident; the sympathies in South America for England are very great and all is much more European-minded than the United States. We hope you have a good time, a relatively good one at Bath and you know that our best wishes are with you all. Stefan.

23.8.40

Dear Hanna and Manfred,

Yesterday we received your letter of the 8th Aug. and on our arrival we found one of July 12th, both air-mail, and that is all what we had from you so far except that one Clipper[4] letter in London. It will be best if in future you number your letters and I confirm which one we receive. It is an event for me to hear from you, and you can't write often and long enough. For instance, I do not quite know whether Marta was able to stay with Manfred after all and if Rosa is still with him — also what you will do when Eva leaves, go back to London? Please yourself entirely and don't think too much of the house except as a place of rest and enjoyment for you and Manfred. I know it will be hard for you to be without Eva, but I hope that it will not be for too long and that she will be happy with the S. family. They are kind, friendly people and I believe not quite as rich as I first though, just comfortably off, earning well and as all Americans spending freely. About Heiner's affidavit. I cabled from here that it would be sent from America soon by Jacob Landau.[5]

Jacob Landau has travelled with us from New York. He is director of the Jewish Telegraphic Agency[6] in New York and has cabled from here to his wife to send the affidavit either herself or through his office. It is a bit more complicated from here to arrange it, but Mr. Landau feels confident that the affidavit can be sent in his absence. He is a very decent man and will certainly see to it – although by correspondence only — that the matter is not neglected. I certainly have learned from the affair with Eva's affidavit. Let us hope that it helps Heiner[7] to get over and if Alice[8] is willing to work in a household she will easily find work, and then she can slowly build up a business for herself.

As to us: we had a beautiful crossing with very nice South-Americans and are being spoilt here. I must admit that in spite of all the events and in spite of the fact that I always feel a little homesick for you, the former Bath-family and Bath itself, we really enjoy it here. Rio is just as beautiful as Stefan promised, the people just as nice as he said and the winter not hard, one feels just right in a light summer dress and I need not have brought my winter things for this Brasilian winter.

We were glad to get your cable on the ship and to learn that Manfred spent the weekend of Eva's birthday with you. I wish we could have been with you. I hope you are all well. Please give Mama my love and tell her about my letter, I shall writer her soon and perhaps enclose a few photos made on our arrival.

Kindest regards to all, especially to Lizzie[9] who seems to have developed into your caretaker,

Lotte

Also cable when Eva is sailing so that we can also inform our sister-in-law in New York.

---

1   The Paysandú, a fashionable, yet discrete art deco-style hotel located directly across from the beach in the primarily residential suburb of Flamengo.

2 Con artist.
3 Friderike Zweig (see p. 204) and her daughters Alexia Elizabeth and Susanne Benedictine von Winternitz.
4 Airmail letter, in this context a 'clipper' being a Pan American World Airlines sea plane.
5 See p. 199.
6 The Jewish Telegraphic Agency, established by Jacob Landau in 1917, collected and distributed news relating to Jewish communities worldwide.
7 Heiner Mayer, see see p. 200.
8 Alice Mayer, the wife of Heiner Mayer, see p. 200.
9 Litzie Philby, see p. 201.

Hotel PAYSANDÚ

6.9.40

Dear Hanna, dear Manfred,

I have just written a long letter to Mama and do not feel energetic enough to write you as well especially as I wrote you at length a few days ago. Just one little thing about Mama: She wrote me that she was going to change over to the small single room and I asked her in my letter to keep hers. You have plein pouvoir[1] to settle the one-pound-difference from our account, and more, if necessary. — I hope you are still all well and as cheerful as your last letter from Bath indicated. I am waiting to hear about Eva. Has Manfred much work and must he go out at all times? — We are well and happy here and have equipped ourselves for the summer which we will have here and in the other countries until December. We continue to work in the mornings, go out in the afternoon, learn Spanish,[2] meet quite a lot of people, I am concentrating hard on names and faces and feel very proud that I recognize most people, even in other surroundings. I am reading the war reports every day and learn a lot of Portuguese thereby. Although these reports are very long I do not think they say any more- or perhaps not even as much- as you read in the English papers. — From common acquaintances we met Huyn's.[3] They feel quite well here but he has not yet found anything. — We will be here until middle of October and then inform you by cable. But the postal address will remain Editora Guanabara.[4]

Kindest regards for everyone, love and kisses for you,
Lotte

1 The authority.
2 Lotte was studying Spanish as she was going with Stefan on his lecture tour of Argentina. Despite their great love of Brazil, they did not seem to enjoy the Portuguese language.
3 Count and Countess Huyn. Until the *Anschluss*, Count Huyn served as press attaché at the Austrian Embassy in London. In 1939 he became a newsreader with BBC radio's German Service.
4 Stefan Zweig's Brazilian publishing house.

––––––––––––––

Your letter of Aug 26th arrived this morning.

Until middle of October

FLIGHT POST

Hotel PAYSANDÚ, Rio
then c/o Editora Guanabara
132 Rua Ouvidor, Rio
who will forward letters

Rio, 10.9.40

Dear Manfred and Hanna,
Thanks for your cable that Eva has sailed. I hope she has a very good journey and will feel happy in her new surroundings. I asked S. to cable me her arrival and I hope you will do so as well. We are of course very anxious to have news from you, and please write often. I was surprised that our letters had not yet arrived because we wrote at least once a week from here. We only write by air from here, and I expect you get a few letters at once. We address them to your London address. I hope that you are all well at once. We address them to your London address. I hope that you are all well when this letter arrives. And if you think it better that Mama leaves, tell her not to worry about the cost and I hope she will get permission to leave and go wherever she wants as I do not think that she may go to Bath. — We are perfectly well in these wonderful surroundings and shall be sorry to leave in the middle of October. But Rio is getting very hot in November, and so Stefan will give a few lectures in Uruguay Argentina and Chile. There is a possibility that we travel from Buenos Aires to Chile through the straits of Magellan, but that is yet uncertain. We expect to be in Chile in December and in January in

New York — we got our visas, visitor visa for lectures, today. — Here in Brazil Stefan will go to Sao Paulo for a day for a lecture, and then we are invited by the Governor of Minas Geraes to see his Province where there are interesting old towns like Ouro Preto and Mariana, a gold mine etc. As we will go by air we will be away from Rio not more than 2 or 3 days.

Kindest regards and love,
Lotte

We would be perfectly happy here would it not be for you. Lotte behaves here like a great lady and presides meetings, is photographed and to be seen in all the newspapers in all her beauty. In the evening we feel always completely confused by speaking in quick turns English, French, Spanish, German, Yiddish, Portuguese; you will see in our letters, that we are not more able to write correctly any language. Next week I have a full program and we confuse all people on behalf of their endless names (everyone has at least three names) and at least three languages and it is difficult to retain only a single one if one meets every day a dozen of them. I have asked S. to let Eva cable frequently at our expense because I understand that you will be anxious for news from her. Yours

Stefan Zweig

FLIGHT POST

Rio

Sunday, 15.9.40

Dear Hanna and Manfred,

Just now I got a telegram that Heiner's[1] affidavit has been cabled. I do not yet know any details besides this and shall phone Mr. Landau to Sao Paulo to-night in order to hear more and then I shall send you a cable. Within the next few days I also hope to get a cable informing me of Eva's arrival in USA. I believe I confirmed already your letter of Aug 26th. I am glad that you still enjoy Bath and I hope you will have a relatively calm time and if possible with Manfred. What about Mama? Did you try to get permission that she leaves London? I am afraid she will not be allowed to go to Bath, but perhaps she can go with some friends. Yes,

Manfred is right, we follow with great concern all the newspaper reports, and I really wish sometimes that I could be with you in order not to have to wait so long for news. On the other hand, I cannot deny that we enjoy our stay here enormously. We have today changed over to other rooms looking out on the bay, and this little detail will make it more difficult for us to leave Rio. Up to now it is not yet very hot, and the weather is just perfect for strolling around and making excursions. Friday Stefan has a lecture in Sao Paulo and as I was invited as well. I shall accompany him although I do not expect too much from this town except a visit to the snake farm where they make Serum against snake bites.[2]

I hope to have another letter from you within the next few days and wish that it contains good news.

All the best wishes to all of you,
Lotte

Dear Hannah and Manfred, it is not at all easy for us to write to you, we read in the newspapers about the furious attacks on England unhappily also that they are rebuked/and we feel ashamed to have here such a perfect life. To look out of our windows is simply a dream, the temperature is superb — a winter which is more June than May — the people spoil us in every possible way, we live quietly, cheeply and the most interesting life — really happy would it not be for you and all the friends and the great misery of mankind. I will do everything to prolong our stay here as Lotte will absoluly not leave, but I have to fulfil my duties. I have a lecture in San Paolo this week, very well paid, 250 dollars and hotel and plane for us both, this covers alone one whole month and I have no material worries as the lectures in Uruguay, Argentine, Chile are equally well paid and we are invited in Uruguay and Chile as guests of the government, which will pay railway and hotels. Next week we are going to the old towns in the interior of Brazil as guests of the Government, poor Lotte will be photografed abundantly and here you could see her in all the cinemas. Finally we go back to Newyork we have already our visas and shall see (and let us hope so) and fetch Eva, you may be both sure that we will look after her and bring her back grown-up and perhaps with a Yankee -accent.

It is terrible for me to remember all the friends there over. I hope that Robert Neumann[3] and Kormendi[4] could leave, we have done all for an American visa during my stay. Friedental[5] I cannot help from here except if he would like to go to Brazil or to Cuba — in January I will try all possible. My former wife has her visas to America and I believe also to Mexico, she is thanks to the help of Ferro,[6] who has been very kind to me, in Lisbon. But all the others. You will understand how ashamed we feel here and I should be glad to know that you can enjoy Bath in these days of wrath. Please be generous with money, nobody knows what the next years will bring and I should be so glad to be of any help to you, to your family and our friends. Yours

Stefan Zweig Till 15. October Hotel Paysandú, Rio, after that we cable next address

1 Heiner Mayer, see p. 200.
2 The Zweigs visited the Instituto Butantan, a biomedical research centre. Established in 1901, Butantan soon became internationally renowned for its research on venomous insects and reptiles, in particular snakes. The serpentarium was an important attraction for visitors to the city.
3 See p. 201.
4 Ferenc Körmendi, see p. 199.
5 Richard Friedenthal, see p. 196.
6 António Ferro, see p. 195.

---

c/o Editora Guanabara
132 Rua do Ouvidor
Rio de Janeiro

22.9.1940

Dear Hanna and Manfred,

I have not had a letter from you last week, and I have not received the cable of Eva's arrival either, but I hope that both will arrive to-morrow, and that you will be able to inform me that you have a quiet time in Bath and that Manfred is not too worn out. I write a letter to mama to-day which address to Woodstock Road[1] also as I hope that she has been able to leave London, and if not for Bath, at least for the country with a friend.[2] — We have, as in the last weeks always, only to report a lot of social life, invitations, receptions, presents of flowers and books, and the only drawback — besides the fact that these masses of people and their kindness is somewhat confusing and also tiring — is that Stefan does hardly find any time for his work. The free time he has had during the last week has mostly been taken by the preparation of his lectures, translations into English, French and Spanish, revisions, retranslations and the Spanish lessons. But at least Stefan understands now Spanish and Portuguese quite well and talks Spanish, if necessary, and I am also able, although with some difficulty, to follow a conversation in Spanish as well as in Portuguese, and I manage to make myself understood by the porters in the hotel of whom only one speaks English and the others no foreign language at all. — We have just returned from Sao Paulo where Stefan gave a lecture, the first in Brazil. We have flown there Friday in 1 ½ hours, attended a luncheon in our honour with all the obligatory flowers, photographers and speeches, were taken for a sight-seeing tour in the town and found very little to see, and in the evening after the lecture went to another reception where we stayed until after midnight. The next morning Stefan went to see the building of the newspaper who had invited him for the lecture, and I was visited by Roselotte and Yorg[3] who send their kindest regards and say that they had thought of inviting Eva for the duration[4] and are willing to take her even now should you so desire. At two we were again taken to the airport, and after a half hour of polite conversation with all the people who had come to see us off, flew back to Rio, and today we are firmly determined no to accept any visitors and invitations and to have a very quiet day. Tuesday morning we are flying to Minas Geraes to visit some old and interesting towns in that province, Ouro Preto, Mariana etc. and we intend to be back on Thursday. We shall probably also go to Bahia* for a few days, and we have invitations to go to a hazienda[5] in the interior, for a lecture in Santos, and to travel on the rio San Francisco. Whether we shall be able to do all that, is still uncertain. Stefan is not yet quite decided whether he shall really go to Chile and whether we shall not instead remain in Brazil a little longer and then return to USA directly from here or perhaps from Buenos Aires. In any case the postal address will remain c/o Editora Guanabara, and the telegraphic address we will cable you always. Kindest regards to you all, keep well and write frequently. I intended to write to Lizzy[6] for a long time, and I shall do so soon. I hope that she is still with you in Bath, and I would not be surprised to hear that you have some more friends out there now. I hope you have received the affidavit for Heiner.[7] I was only informed that it had been cabled, without any details, and although I asked for more detailed information I have not yet received it. We had a cable from Eisemann[8] that he is back home. Kindest regards from Marta, we should like to hear from her.

Best love and kisses,
Lotte.

* Bahia is as far from here like Paris from Moscau — we are really great travellers.

All is perfect here, we see the best and nicest people and would love only to have a day without our photos in the newspapers and the stories where we have been and what we have done. Anyhow I will see as much of this fascinating country as possible and it will give together with my former notes a nice little book. Lotte has become very talkative in society and is in great love with Rio like myself — why has this country only five month in the year temperate climate!! I have met Kenneth Grubb[9] from the Ministry and will in Buenos Aires give a little lecture also for the English circle in English — developing in a kind of lecturer in four or five languages. If only we were not anxious about you we would call this the happiest times of our life! Why does Manfred not give lectures and why does he study Greek[10] instead of the language of the future countries. Stefan Zweig

I am glad to know you settled again in a comfortable warm flat, and that you can even stay there at night, and I can hope for nothing better than that you will be able to remain there until the end of the war. It is still a strange thought to me when I think of you in London to place you in Regency Lodge and no more in Woodstock Road[11] and I found lots of memories to unite me to the old house, I also thought of you at Christmas time, how different it was for all of us this year. But the main thing is that you spent a good time here and that Manfred had a real rest. I am sure he needed it as well as you, Hanna after the removal. — Your friend Paul[12] suddenly appeared last week, he arrived on a cargo liner with wife, child, Lubitrea and few cases of books and manuscripts, and Stefan became jealous, and we admired them because they immediately took a furnished flat while we are living in one hotel room. He came as chairman of the United Correspondents[13] and seems to be getting on well because he did not phone the whole week. When we met him, they were still a little bewildered and hardly told any stories.

I am afraid I must stop, I see Stefan has written a lot and otherwise the letter gets too heavy.

Kindest regards and kisses,
Lotte

1 The Altmann family's home — and Manfred's medical practice — was at 55 Woodstock Road, Golders Green, London NW11. Hannah, Manfred and Eva Altmann lived there with Martha Kahn (Hannah's sister), Lotte (until she moved

in with Stefan Zweig) and a constant flow of refugee friends.

2 Lotte and Manfred's mother, Therese Altmann, moved to Harrogate, Yorksire, to escape the wartime bombing of London.

3 Though married to each other, Roselotte and Georg Altmann were cousins; they were also cousins of Manfred and Lotte Altmann. They moved to São Paulo well before the war.

4 The duration of the war.

5 In Spanish, *hacienda*. In Portuguese, *fazenda*, which basically means a large farm.

6 Litzi Philby, see p. 201.

7 Heiner Mayer, see p. 200.

8 Heinrich Eisemann, see p. 195.

9 See p. 197.

10 According to his obituary in the *British Medical Journal* (13 November 1954), during the air raids on London, and while doing military service from 1944 to 1946, Manfred studied ancient Greek to be able to read Plato in the original.

11 Manfred and Hannah moved from Golders Green to Swiss Cottage.

12 Paul Frischauer, see p. 196.

13 United Correspondents was created in February 1940 by Paul Frischauer, financed by Britain's Ministry of Information. As the principle shareholder and sole correspondent, Frischauer appointed himself United Correspondents' 'South American Representative'. By early 1941 funding had been withdrawn and the organization was wound up.

FLIGHT POST

Rio 29. Sept. 1940
Hotel Paysandú

Dear Manfred and Hannah, you write that you want long letters — alas, it is the only thing we can do for you. I am ashamed to say that all is perfect here, the climate delicious (now in winter time) the people wonderful and all sympathies on the side of England. We just came back from the interior, where we were invited by the Governor of the province Minas Geraes; we were taken to the capitol in a plane, had an autocar with a charming secretary of the ministry all the time at our disposition and were brought back in two days auto-travelling through the country. By that we have seen a lot and the real life of Brasil. Next week we will go somewhere in the mountains to have a rest — we are not tired, not in the least, but I want to do some work before we leave and here we are bombarded with invitations, interviews and I am looking forward for a few days without speaking in five languages to two hundred people and not to have our picture in the paper. If it would be for Lotte, we would not leave at all Brasil, she is very changed and is pestering me every moment in her exalted way with exclamations. Is it not marvellous and so on and I have married her just because she has been formerly so discreet. But I have to do my duty and we will leave about the 22 October. I have two lectures in Montevideo and will give two at Buenos-Aires and two in the Universities of Cordoba and Rosario. They had made me a programme of six lectures in Buenos Aires, but I have enough. The lectures are well paid and we can make easily our living from it, so I do not want to make a profession out of it. Later on I should afterwards go to Chile and Venezuela and Cuba, I have from everywhere urgent offers, I think however I will not accept them and you will understand it if you look on the map, what enormous distances that means. But all the receptions in all these little countries, the noisy publicity are against my conception of life. It is good to know, that I could make my living for months and months going around as a lecturer but we prefer a more quiet way and it is impossible to write in midst of such travelling. Thank God, I am not greedy neither for money nor for honours. By the way, please dispose of my accounts for you and your family as if it were yours and I would be grateful if you would send to friends like Friedenthal[1] or Fleischer[2] something to relieve their situation, I feel somewhat guilty that I have here all honours and a decent living through my work while you are disturbed in your profession and have anxious days and nights. Please believe me that I do not care at all for the house and the property; we are all reduced to the minimum of what men can ask from life — life itself and this is already much in these days. [. . .]

Please send us often cables, it has no sense to be on your side parcimonious and perhaps you can send them even with paid really so that you may be sure that we are always able to give you notice about our whereabouts. Dear Hannah and Manfred, I know it is a hard moral test for you not to envy us who can continue our work quietly and in a beautiful surrounding but I feel that your good wishes are with us as ours are always with you.

Stefan

postal address from now on, even when we have left Brasil:
c/o Editora GUANABARA, 132 Rua Ouvidor, Rio de Janeiro

Dear Hanna and Manfred,

Today we got your and Mama's letter of the 12th Sept. after two weeks without news except the cable about Eva's arrival. Please do not forget that I wait just as impatiently for your letters as you for ours and write regularly and as often as possible, if only a few lines. If I cannot be with you, I want at least to know everything about you and our friends. I hope you had a few days rest in Bath. We had a letter from Ingram[3] yesterday and write him and Mr. Orchard[4] by airmail today. I am glad that you can rely upon their advise and help if necessary. Has Lorle[5] been alone with Ursel[6] in the house all the time, except for Griffith? I was sorry to hear that Mr. Miller[7] is ill, I hope he will recover again, he belongs to my memory of the house just as much as you and the children and Marta.[8] Is Alice[9] still in Baker Street. I hope the affidavit for Heiner[10] has arrived by now. Mr. Landau assured me that it had been cabled but he had himself no detailed news about it, as he was travelling about and got no letters himself but only cables. — I cannot tell you how glad I was that you cabled me Eva's arrival. I got your cable Sunday afternoon and I read the news about the ship disaster in the Atlantic about an hour before S.'s cable arrived. What a shock it must have been for you and what a relief that she was not only on the other ship but already safely arrived. I have not yet a letter from her, but I suppose it is on the way. I wrote her last week and am writing her again today so that she does not feel all alone, even though I feel sure that she is already on the best of terms with Mr. and Mrs. S. She will just have arrived in time for the new term in school and Mr. S. assured me that there were excellent public schools in New Rochelle, and that they knew plenty of children in the neighbourhood. My sister-in-law was already in touch with Mrs. S. before Eva's arrival and will certainly have visited her by now, and I suppose Rose[11] will go to see her too, so that I will have reports from them soon. — I hope that you are all in good health and that you are not too much exhausted by the lack of sleep and the continuous excitements. I am glad that you have a good shelter at last and that you are even able to sleep there. Has Manfred to go out a lot or has his practice gone down with the latest events? I could also imagine that he has a lot more to do and I only hope that he has not to go out during an attack. We think of you more often than you imagine and the people here too are very sympathetic to the cause of England. — From ourselves I can only repeat that we have a much too good time, that everybody is extremely nice and that the only drawback is that they are even too nice. We have so many invitations and the newspapers are so interested in what Stefan does that we consider going to a small place in the mountains nearby at the end of this week so that Stefan can work quietly at least for a few days and that our brains can have a rest from the continual change of faces before us and of the change of languages in the conversation. Last week we have been in the province of Minas, as Stefan wrote, and it was very interesting to travel through the country.

Kindest regards to you all,
Lotte

1 Richard Friedenthal, see p. 196.
2 Victor Fleischer, see p. 196.
3 Arthur Ingram, Zweig's solicitor in Bath.
4 Another solicitor in England.
5 Lorle was a niece and adopted daughter of Martha Kahn, see p. 198. Lorle came to England in late 1938 or early 1939 with the Kindertransport, the rescue mission of Jewish children from Germany, Austria and Czechoslovakia. After the Zweigs left Bath, she spent most of the war at Rosemont.
6 Ursel, the daughter of Heiner Mayer, see p. 200.
7 Mr Miller was the Zweigs' gardener at Rosemount and continued to work there in their absence from Bath.
8 Martha Kahn, see p. 198.
9 Alice Mayer, the wife of Heiner Mayer, see p. 200.
10 Heiner Mayer, see p. 200.
11 Rose Wohl was a friend of the Altmann family in New York City. She initially arranged for the care of Eva Altmann in New York when she was evacuated there from London.

[Rio de Janeiro, undated]

Dear Hannah and Manfred, as Lotte is lazy and writes only short letters it is to the "Hausknecht"[1] to write all what happened — we like the city and the people enormously and we are delighted how much of sympathy in all the important quarters exists for England, how much pity for France; the newspapers are in contrast with the Northamericans absolutely partial for England and express openly the hope that Hitler's attacks will fail, English ships come from time to time but one does better to write by air over Newyork, it takes sometimes only 10 days. My plans are not quite definite, I have a lecture, well paid, in San Paolo and here I will therefore speak only for some charitable purpose,[2] then Uruguay 2 lectures and Buenos Aires and Chile; our expenses will largely be covered and I have time to write meanwhile. I admire Rio every day more, it is the most colourful, the most fascinating town I know, full of surprises and new beauties; it develops with a rapidity which seems unbelievable — we went to day in the town just an hour (for two American cents) and had not passed half of the city. Today we had two receptions Lotte had not less than four ministers for conversation (and with the former ambassador Corbin[3] five) first at the reception for the Uruguay minister, where she sat at the side of the foreign minister than in a party given in her honour (or ours) at the minister of communications — charming house in the midst of gardens with views one only can dream. Yesterday we had long nightly auto driver along the ocean and over the mountains, tomorrow we have the minister of Cuba[4] for tea and mean while short visits and talks, — often too much because I want to explore this town and there are so many parts we have not yet inspected I would like to live nowhere except here would it not be for the heat which hinders my work as I was able to see in Newyork — but they are already constructing air conditioned houses here. We read the news from England every day and you may imagine that we do not forget you a day in our good days here and feel somewhat ashamed. Kindest regards to you all

Yours Stefan Zweig

1 Male servant.
2 This is an example of Stefan Zweig faltering in his use of English; the phrase should more accurately read as: 'I have a well-paid lecture in São Paulo and in Rio I will only speak for charitable purposes'.
3 Charles Corbin (1881–1970), French ambassador to London from 1933 to 1940.
4 Alfonso Hernández Catá, see p. 197.

FLIGHT POST

Teresopolis, 6.10.40

Dear Hanna and Manfred,

I write rather in a hurry for we have just arrived here for a weeks' rest, and Stefan's editor[1] and his wife who brought us in their car, are still with us and waiting to take us round and show us the town or village, whatever it is. I hope that you are all well, that Manfred has not too much work and was able to take a few days rest in Bath with you, Hanna. How I wish we could be there together, soon! [...]

Kindest regards and kisses,
Lotte

Dear H. & M. We are looking every days through all newspapers for good news and follow all the events — we hope the best for you. We regret very much to leave Brazil for Argentine the 26. October — we had here an excellent time. We have seen the most wonderful houses, my publisher brings us every where we like in his car, our friend the Viscount Carnaxide[2] arranges all social things for us in a splendid way, the Ambassador of Cuba[3] sends me nearly every week a box of Havanahs and on every corner are coffee houses. We live very cheaply here and see a lot — all would be perfect without the anxious thoughts about you. I suppose we will leave out Chile and Venezuela, I am not willing to travel too much as I have no time to work and one has to do his work even in these times. I heard that Robert Neumann[4] is back again, I wish I knew his address as I would like to let him know that we so not forget him. Yours,

Stefan

1 Abrahão Koogan, see p. 198.
2 Viscount Carnaxide was the representative in Brazil of António Ferro (the Portuguese government's director of culture and propaganda).
3 Alfonso Hernández Catá, see p. 197.
4 See p. 201.

---

c/o Editora Guanabara
132 Rua Ouvidor, Rio de Janeiro

Teresopolis, 10.10.40

Dear Hanna and Manfred,

I was very happy to get your letter of the 24th Sept. to-day and to without too much difficulty. Of course we are always anxious about you when we read the news of air-attacks in the paper and therefore we asked you to cable, if at all possible, once a week. It was not quite clear from your letter, Hanna, if Manfred was still with you in Bath — I hope he was able to stay a few days and have a good rest. I would like to know about his work and whether he, as a doctor, has to go out also during an air-raid or whether perhaps he is now also employed in a hospital. I hope that Mama has by now been able to leave London. I can understand the difficulties and that in a way she prefers to stay, but on the other hand there is no point in her staying where she is if she has a possibility to go to a quieter place. I cannot tell you how happy we are to know Eva safe and settled. [. . .] We had the first letter from her to-day, saying that she is very happy there, that school is very nice and that S.'s have a huge Alsation dog. Mr. S. added a note how happy he is to have her and that they are already very great friends. Eva also writes that my sister and brother-in-law[1] have been there. The shock of reading in the paper the news of the disaster[2], was as great for us as it was for you, and I can understand how you feel about it. That thought haunted us for days. Fortunately your cable had arrived the night before, because S.'s cable only arrived hours after we had read the news in the paper. Well, at least she is safe at S.'s, apparently quite happy about everything. I am sure my letters, mostly air-mail, which were forwarded to us from Rio, have been lost. That is the great drawback of this place where we are staying. Everything else is perfect here, the landscape beautiful, we are right in the mountains, 3000 feet high and yet there is something tropical about it, orange trees, banana trees, bamboo, we have lovely rooms with a big terrace where we work, a swimming pool, dogs, food cooked by blacks but the mail from Rio takes several days and sometimes does not arrive at all. Now we have found out that there visits a tradesman who comes up from Rio every day- it is 3 hours by car and that's why your letter was not lost. And this gives Stefan courage to consider coming here again for a fortnight after he has done his duty and went to Argentine and Uruguay for the lectures. According to our present plans we fly to Buenos Aires on the 26th (six hours), stay there a fortnight to 3 weeks, go for a few days to Montevideo, then come back up here to Teresopolis for a fortnights rest which will be necessary after a few weeks continuous receptions, lectures and whole-day politeness in various languages, This place where we are staying is ideal for working and rest, and as the lights' often is still a little medieval — the light depends on the water supply and it has not rained for a few months and so it is rather sickly and weak — we go to bed very early and get up at 7, so that the morning is enormously long and leaves us a lot of time for work and walk and a swim if we feel like it. Although it is only Spring now, it is already very warm and while you will be glad with some kind of heating (by the way, can you heat the shelter, and which room do you use in Bath for it?) we will have a rising temperature until we get to New York. Fortunately we found out in the New York heat wave that we both support it well, and up here in Teresopolis the nights are always cool. So this problem does not worry us, even if we should have to stay in South America longer than we intend to now.

You do not write, Hanna, how long you are staying in Bath. In any case I am glad that you have filled the house with friends and that it helps a few people to get some rest, and it will be good company for you and for the children. Ursel[3] and Lorle[4] must feel very grown-up with all the smaller children. Please thank Ursula[5] for her letter. Is she going to school as usual? I am sorry to hear that Alice[6] lives in such a menaced district and more sorry that apparently again something is wrong with Heiner's[7] affidavit which should have arrived long ago. I hope you will cable us soon as this is settled for him although it would be a more anxious thought than ever to know them on the ocean. Do continue to write often and in detail. There is always a possibility of a letter getting lost, especially in South America, and I am always impatiently awaiting for the weekly letter. [. . .]. Give my kindest regards to all the inhabitants of Rosemount[8] and Woodstock Road. I am glad that they still remember us and I wish nothing better than to refresh this memory in person very soon together with my lawful wedded husband.

Best wishes and kisses to you both,
Lotte

Dear H. & M. I cannot tell you how happy I am that the house in Bath is of such a good use and we can be helpful to your friends. You will understand how we feel all the difference of fate; that I by my duty and work have to be in the most fascinating surrounding while you live out the menaces of our common enemy. I have seldom in my life seen a finer place, quiet, the town tasteful, the house people thinking the whole day what to do for us and our cooking all Viennese dishes we have not had since years. And peculiar charm in midst the tropical nature: the negros working in the same open like in the slavery days only happy and always smiling, fat pigs, horses, a really dream-hazienda. And what have we seen in Rio: the most perfect houses with gardens covering a whole mountain and on the other hand the popular life. Now I have to pay for all that with a gunfire of lectures, two in Rio next week (in French) three then in Buenos Aires (in Spanish and one in English) two in Rosario and Cordoba, two in Montevideo; they pay very good and all our expenses are largely paid. We live here in our normal way with everything we want, avoiding carefully the luxury hotels and you can not imagine the kindness of the people. Instead to go to Chile and Venezuela we will return here to Brasil, I have still to go to Bahia, the most picturesque place and probably we will do it in a small steamer to see all the little towns on the coast — a glance on the street with all the coloured people in all possible mixtures is an inexhaustible delight! Pardon my English. By reading Portuguese, speaking French and Spanish I have lost the orthografy and do often not know what language I use or misuse. I have not forgotten the house but since I know that it is such a good shelter for our friends (kindest regards to all) I feel much less remorse; on the contrary! Sometime I wish I could change with you for a week not to have all this lucky time for us alone and to share your harder life . . . I see there is no justice in the world. Roundabout the new year we hope to be with Eva. You understand that we cannot give approximate days as our plans depend from work, invitations, obligations, ship departures and not in the least from the development of things in the world. If you hear from Friedental let me know it, I would like so much to help him[9] — in the United States is no possibility but perhaps here. Love to you all

Stefan

1 Alfred and Stephanie Zweig, see p. 204.
2 The sinking, on 17 September 1940 by German submarine torpedoes, of the *City of Benares*, a Canada-bound ship carrying 406 crew and passengers, including some ninety evacuee children. Two hundred and forty-eight lives were lost, including seventy-seven children. The tragedy ended the British government's Children's Overseas Resettlement Board.
3 Ursel (Ursula) Mayer, the daughter of Alice and Heiner Mayer, see p. 200.
4 Lorle was a niece and adopted daughter of Martha Kahn, see p. 198. After the Zweigs left Bath, she spent most of the war at Rosemont.
5 Ursula (Ursel), the daughter of Heiner Mayer, Lotte's brother, see p. 200.
6 Alice Mayer, the wife of Heiner Mayer, see p. 200.
7 Heiner Mayer, see p. 200.
8 The Zweigs' house in Bath.
9 Richard Friedenthal (see p. 196) was interned as an 'enemy alien' in Shropshire and the Isle of Man.

c/o Editora Guanabara
132 rua Ouvidor, Rio de Janeiro

Rio, 16.10.40

Dear Hanna and Manfred,

There is not much to write today. We had a very pleasant and extremely quiet week in the mountains where Stefan got all his favourite dishes, where he could work quietly and where we had nice people to talk if we wanted to. Now we try to accustom our ears again to the noise of Rio and think of the noise you must endure. We expect to have a very lively week before going to Buenos Aires and will probably have a rather hectic time there. In the middle of November we intend to be in Montevideo and by the end of December in New York where Eva is the only attraction.

We hope that you all have not too bad a time and could good wishes help, England would have won already. Stefan is trying to get a visa for his friend Friedenthal[1] here and maybe even a modest job, but he does not know how to communicate with him, and then visas have become almost as difficult here as in America, or even more so as there are no rules but only silent restrictions.

Kindest regards to all, kisses to you both,
Lotte

Mr. Landau wrote me from Buenos Aires this week that he had sent the signed affidavit forms for Mr Mayer[2] by registered air-mail. They should arrive before this letter — I do not know at which address and I hope that this will remove the last difficulties as apparently the ablest affidavits were not accepted.

Dears, please tell Eisemann[3] that I will speak with my friend — as far as I know he has not such power from the distance and he would have offered spontaneously his help seeing how we get every day cables and letters to procure visas for South America. Till now I have not been able by the constant travelling to come in touch with the right people and we had to get our own for Argent. And the States. — all becomes more difficult every day and one must reserve the best strength for those who are the nearest to you. Please do not be unhappy that your child is far away we are glad she is safe and would be happy to know you both nearer to us.

Yours
Stefan

From Friedental[4] I hear nothing and do not know his address; it would be important to know it.

1 Richard Friedenthal, see p. 196.
2 Heiner Mayer, see p. 200.
3 Heinrich Eisemann, see p. 195.
4 Richard Friedenthal, see p. 196.

EDITORA GUANABARA
WAISSSMAN KOOGAN LTDA.   Rio, 19th October 1940
LIVREIROS E EDITORES
RUA DO OUVIDOR, 132
TELEPH 22–7231
RIO DE JANEIRO
END. TELEG.: EDIGUA — BRASIL

Dearest mother,[1]

I got to-day your letter of Oct 1st, addressed to New York, and I hope that you live now in a quieter place. As I wrote you already, do not economise now, I shall be glad if at least our money can be of some use now and if I know you at least as comfortable as it can be. I often try to imagine what life must be in a town so acutely at war as London, but my imagination fails me and I can only admire and pity those who continue to work and live under such a strain. When we meet people who have lived in England and who have still communication with it, we invariable sit together and exchange bits of information and feel somehow homesick although we know of course how lucky we are not to live through the war night and day. I expected already before your letter arrived that you might leave London and my last letters to you I addressed to Manfred. I am afraid that he, as a doctor, cannot help going out under any conditions, and I suppose that he told Hanna to remain in Bath. At any rate they will be glad to know Eva safe, and I believe quite happy in her new surroundings. I suppose we will see her at the end of December — I repeat our next plans: 26th by plane to Buenos Aires (in 6 hours), about a fortnight in Argentine where Stefan has about half a dozen lectures, also a little in the country universities, then a few days

Uruguay with one or 2 lectures in Montevideo, and then a few weeks more in Brazil, presumably in Teresopolis where it does not get so hot. Now it is only spring and the temperature ever agreeable, and anyhow as we lived through a heat wave in New York and stood it quite well, we are not afraid of heat. We regret to leave Brazil and it is only out of sense of duty, to fulfil his promise, that Stefan decided to give all his lectures in Argentine and Uruguay. We have made a few real friends among the hundreds of people we met, and that gives one a little a feeling of belonging to a place. We still enjoy the beauty of Rio, and although lately we did not find much time for excursions, every walk or drive in the tram- there are buses as well, but we prefer the old-fashioned, open trams- is a pleasure as regards natural beauty and local colour. Stefan is trying hard to work regularly, but in Rio itself it is very difficult with all the engagement, invitations and now the practical travel arrangements. Besides this people have a lot of time here and there is still the good old habit that the men drop in for a little chat in the afternoon, and three times a week Stefan had his Spanish lessons as he will speak in Spanish in some of the places in Argentine and Uruguay. I have given up attending his lessons. It is impossible for me to keep Spanish and Portuguese apart as I hear and read both languages at the same time, and I have made up a language of my own which combines both and somehow is understood. With all our invitations we have not been in a concert, theatre or film the whole time except once at a first night of a Portuguese play. Last night I heard the radio also for the first time since we are here, and it was the English news service from the BBC, and a strange feeling to hear it so far away. As we were all people who had lived in England a long time, we became quite sentimental about this fact. I hope that you have in the meantime got the photos which I sent a long time ago. Fortunately the daily photographs have stopped and the papers only report, as they do with every person who is a little known to the public what we do and what we are supposed to do. On the whole we have had a quieter time lately and met mostly people we know at the various places we went to, and as a special treat our friends invite persons which keep one occupied the whole evening by the effort to remember with whom one was talking. Altogether we have had a time here which would have been absolutely perfect if it were not for the thought of all the people in Europe which is continually in our mind. Stefan could not have had a nicer reception here, and if the too great publicity was sometimes a nuisance, it was in itself well-meant. In any case we both love Brazil very much, and should we be forced to choose, we would prefer it greatly to USA. But I hope this choice will no be necessary and that everything comes to a good end quicker than we all dare to hope now.

Kindest regards and kisses,
Lotte

Best wishes from Stefan

Kindest regards to Manfred and Hanna I await their next letter before
I write to them.

1 Therese Altmann, see p. 194.

FLIGHT POST

Address now:
c/o Editora GUANABARA   Rio, 23. X. 40
132 RUA OUVIDOR, Rio
(Letters will be forwarded)

Dear Hanna and Manfred,

I just got your letter from Bath (30.9. and 2.10.) and I write immediately
although we are again feeling like in a madhouse — leaving Saturday
for Buenos Aires, to-day Stefan's conference in French "Vienne d'hier",
since two hours a phone call from Buenos Aires announced without
name and not yet come through, urgently some books to sign for people
who are leaving Rio to-day, to-morrow a Jewish charity affair where Stefan
has to speak an introduction, a men's luncheon to-morrow and the last
rehearsal of the Spanish lecture on Friday. In between Stefan dictates a
lecture in English, that is to say I shall translate it and he will revise it,
another lecture for the refugees in Buenos Aires and revises his other
lectures in French which he might have to give, and sometime I shall
have to pack — and pack carefully because we fly and I have to select
what to take. I sign the form of the Westm. Bk[1] and Stefan will decide
soon about the other authorisation and send it, I suppose, when we will
again have a free moment. — It gave me quite a shock that you had to
transfer part of your furniture, but please always write about everything.
I fear nothing more than to have to think that you hide anything that has
happened. About the cables: we prefer that you send them every week
or fortnight. Letters are so irregular, sometimes a fortnight nothing and
then English air-mail twice a week. And we shall be only happy to hear
that nothing has happened. I can imagine that it is hard for you to have

strange children around you instead of Eva, but in any rate she is safe in a friendly and carefree atmosphere. [. . .] Excuse the hurry, the lecture is at 5, it's now 3 and I have to post the letter before. Kisses to all. Lotte

1 Westminster Bank.

DIRECCIÓN TELEGRÁFICA
"CITY HOTEL"
BUENOS AIRES

26 October [1940]

Dear Manfred & Hannah, this only to tell you that we are safely arrived in Buenos. Lotte was sufficiently photographed and we could open a flowers-shop with the flowers are tossed in our apartment here. Then we went straight away (leaving behind all the people in the hall) to the opera where we had tickets for a marvelous ballet and now I have to pay for all that with lectures in all languages. The English, the Spanish are well arranged, but the great difficulty are the Jews. There are 250 000 in this town and I have provided a lecture for charity-purposes — now they fight, who shall arrange the lecture, the Zionists, the refugees, the Spanioles[1] and I have the dearest hope that by this quarrel I shall escape, because they will now have finished her discussions during my stay here. We go also to Cordoba, Rosario and after that to Montevideo. The seven hours in the plane were a bit shaky but we arrived without any trouble except that in the unique 20 minutes stay at Porto Alegre[2] I could not get a coffee and smoke a cigar because we had there a reception. In these countries a foreign writer is still a rare and appreciated beast and the curiosity takes much of our time, poor Lotte is hanging constantly on the phone and explaining in five different languages that we do not accept invitations. All this will be over in a fortnight and than I can finally work a month or six weeks before going for Newyork. We have no news from Eva who is not likely to become ever a great writer but I knew through my sister in law that she is happy and I wish you could be with her. We speak every day how injust it is that you have to suffer all the difficulties — don't believe that we forget you. For Friedental I have already tried something but it will take some time. And poor Heiner,[3] — one cannot help him but materially. Kindest regards to all from yours

Stefan Zweig

1 Zionists in Buenos Aires came from a mix of backgrounds but were largely of recent Eastern European origin; the refugees were predominantly German-speaking Jews; the 'Spanioles' can be identified as Jewish-Argentinian, including liberal and leftist writers who were introduced to Zweig by his publisher, translator and friend, Alfredo Cahn and through the local branch of PEN.

2 Porto Alegre, the capital of Rio Grande do Sul, Brazil's southernmost state.

3 Heiner Mayer, see p. 200.

DIRECCIÓN TELEGRÁFICA   Buenos Aires, 27.10.40
"CITY HOTEL"[1]
BUENOS AIRES

Dear Hanna and Manfred,

We are now already a day in B-A. — a new town, plenty of new people, plenty of telephone calls, plenty of delegations who insist on some more gratis-lectures, heaps of flowers, plenty of new things to eat, plenty of photos and interviews; a funny sort of life for me, and at the same time twenty times a day the thought: what is it like now in England, what are they doing in this moment? I hope that this is one of the rare weekends where Manfred is with you in Bath, and that Mama has left London. Lotte Sch[2] still is at Raeburn's[3] house and I again wrote her to address herself to you if she needs something. — Between meeting people Stefan is busy putting the finishing touch to his various lectures and I am typing the last one. The Spanish lecture will be "Unité spirituelle du monde",[4] the English address will have the cheering title "Hope in the Future" and the other charity lecture will be about Vienna and its culture. Needless to mention that every lecture means a cocktail party before and a dinner party after. In a week's time we leave for Cordoba, Rosario and Santa Fé who get a Spanish lecture each — the one about spiritual unity and the other about Artistic Creation. This trip will take 5–6 days and will, I hope, be interesting as well as entertaining. Mr. Cahn[5], Stefan's translator will accompany us (for his own pleasure, for our Spanish is, although bad, sufficient to get along) About Uruguay Stefan has suddenly decided to leave it out. It is a little out of the way and he will have enough lecturing these two weeks here. Perhaps we stay a few days longer here in Buenos Aires and then return to Brasil where we will first try to remain in Rio (but in a different hotel where we could have a room with terrace which gives more air) and then, when it gets too hot, go up to a place in the mountains, we do not yet know which.

Kindest regards and kisses, keep well,
Lotte

1 The City Hotel was a state-of-the-art hotel opened in 1931. Built in an imposing vaguely neo-Gothic style, the hotel was located at Bolivar 160, half a block from the southwest corner of the Plaza de Mayo, long a focal point of political life in Buenos Aires.
2 Lotte Schiff, a close friend from Frankfurt of Lotte Zweig.
3 The Raeburns were neighbours in Bath.
4 The spiritual unity of the world.
5 Alfredo Cahn, see p. 195.

---

address remains: Buenos Aires, 1.11.40
c/o Editora Guanabara
132 Rua Ouvidor, Rio

DIRECCIÓN TELEGRÁFICA
"CITY HOTEL"
BUENOS AIRES

Dear Hanna and Manfred,

Enclosed a long letter for Mama which you please forward and which tells you nearly all the news. I got your letter, Hanna, with Mama's, dated 5th Oct, posted Bath 16th and forwarded from Rio, already yesterday — it could hardly have been quicker. But you write something about a letter which Manfred wrote; it was not inside, and we have not had a letter from him for a long time. I can easily understand that he lost a number of his patients in the last months but why doesn't he come and stay with you completely, is this not possible? It would seem so much more natural than to give up the rest of your own house and move still further into town. I am glad that Mama is now with her sisters, it will be one worry less for you and Manfred. I am sorry that professor M. and his wife had to leave you and I can only hope that the new solution works out satisfactorily and wish for you that your maid could join you in Bath so that you had less work. I thought, Clara Joss and Barbara[1] were coming — how did you get Erwin[2] instead? Perhaps it is the better thing because I remember that he was a clever little boy, and I hope he does not bother you by being religious, and helps you instead in house and garden. If you still convert the stables into living rooms — I thought Mr.

Orchard wanted to keep a cow in them — and take more children, you must beware of not becoming a second Mrs. Lewin.[3] But if it is not too much for you — for us it is a good thought that our house is being useful at least and I am glad that Mr. Miller[4] is able to work again — give him our kindest regards as well as to Mr. Ingram and Mr. Orchard. — From Eva and S.'s you have apparently had good news since your best letter and from what my sister-in-law writes you can be completely reassured about her. She has had Eva for a week end, she saw Mr. S. and phones to Eva every week and she wrote that there was no doubt that Eva was happy there, that she had a lot of friends already and that S. like her very much. If they don't write often, it does not mean anything. They are very American, kind, gay and without any imagination beyond their own scope, and as somehow the life of the average American is allways a rush they probably do not realise that a child's letter is not enough for parents. But I can absolutely rely upon my sister-in-law who is rather inclined to critisize, that she immediately informs me if anything goes wrong, but so far she wrote completely satisfied. — I shall write once more from here before we leave for the provinces and I can only wish that you and Manfred shall have no major troubles in the times to come.

Kindest regards and kisses,
Lotte.

Kindest regards. You may imagine how we expect your news. I wished Manfred would go to Bath it has no sense to continue this double life and don't worry about the practis as long as I have still a penny there over — please be reasonable in these times of folly. — We have here very interesting but very strenuous times. I am, as it seems a splendid lecturer but I do not like to remain it and am longing to do some real work. Love for all of you Stefan

1 Clara Joss, an Austrian refugee and wife of the cartoonist Fritz Joss, and their daughter Barbara. They were part of the Altmanns' circle of friends that included Peter Smollett (see p. 202) and Litzi Philby (see p. 201).

2 Erwin was a nephew and adopted son of Martha Kahn (see p. 198); he came to England in late 1938 or early 1939 with the Kindertransport, the rescue mission of Jewish children from Germany, Austria and Czechoslovakia. After the Zweigs left Bath, Erwin spent most of the war at Rosemont.

3 A reference to a 'Mrs Lewin' who was a head of a home for children brought to England with the Kindertransport.

4 The Zweigs' gardener in Bath.

DIRECCIÓN TELGRÁFICA   Buenos Aires, 9. 11. 40
"CITYHOTEL"
BUENOS AIRES

Dear Mama, Hanna u Manfred,

Only a short letter to day, for although I did not accompany Stefan to his lectures in Cordoba, Santa Fé and Rosario — from where he will return to-morrow — I have been rather busy, getting visas, tickets etc. of all kinds, answering the letters and the telephone, being invited although alone and getting rid of a cold. Stefan is still away and will return to-morrow about lunchtime. At 6 we have promised to go once more to the Opera to see a ballett and Hansel & Gretel, arranged by old friends from Salzburg, at 10 two men are coming who want to see him about something, Monday he has a lecture at La Plata, one hour from here, Tuesday he has to see a doctor who wants to clean his ears (nothing more, only that hurt a little) Wednesday we fly over to Montevideo where we will be received, offered lunch and a reception after the lecture and a short radio talk, Thursday afternoon we will be back here, in the evening while I pack Stefan will give a radio talk here, Friday at 6 in the morning we leave for Rio where we hope to arrive in the afternoon. In Rio we will go to another hotel this time, where we get a room in the 6th floor with a large covered balcony so that it is cooler and more agreable. There we will stay until it becomes too hot and then either go directly to the States or somewhere in the mountains near Rio — we have not yet decided which. [. . .]

We shall not be sorry to leave and look forward to returning to Rio — although our joy is rather spoiled by the sudden death through a stupid and tragic accident of our best friend there, Hernandez Cata, Minister of Cuba, who in this short time had become one of our closest friends.[1] — Here we have had a hectic time and did not like it too much in spite of the wonderful reception Stefan has had and which surpassed even that of Rio. But we prefer the Brazilians and the beautiful landscape of Rio, and maybe for that reasons our impressions were somewhat biassed and prejudiced.

I do hope from all my heart that you all are well and it is a relief to read in the papers that the attacks on London are diminishing in force. Let us hope that they will soon be stopped altogether. Also here we have found a spontaneous pro-British sympathy.

Kindest regards and kisses, also to Manfred included,
Lotte,

Letter address: c/o   Editora GUANABARA
132 rua OUVIDOR
Rio de Janeiro.

1 Alfonso Hernández Catá died on 8 November 1940. The plane that was carrying
   him, together with fifteen other passengers, had just taken off from Rio de Janeiro's
   Santos Dumont Airport bound for São Paulo when it collided with another
   aircraft over Botafogo Bay. There were no survivors. According to *Time* magazine
   (18 November 1940), crash investigators described the event as an 'impossible
   accident'.

DIRECCIÓN TELGRÁFICA   12. Nov. 1940
"CITYHOTEL"
BUENOS AIRES

Dear Hanna, I did send you to day a cable asking you to inform
Friedental[1] that I was informed today that the Argentine Consulate
in London has been instructed to deliver a visa for him. I was here in
private audience with the minister of the Exterior Roca[2] to ask him for
three visas, one for Friedenthal[3] and he was so kind to grant it to me and
as his secretary told me the cables have gone already to London. Please
help him for money for the passage and as much as he wants; here in
Buenos Aires I have instructed my friends to be useful to him and also
in Brazil he can have opportunities. For the United States I could not
help him for the moment.

I have just returned from the tour in the province which was as
strenoous as successful — I am glad, Lotte remained in Buenos Aires,
she would not have stand this strain, lectures, nights in the train, and
drives from 7 in the morning, receptions, photographie. It was a sort of
sensation, an author of Europe who speaks Spanish and now it goes to
Montevideo where I have to speak in a hall for 4000 — 5000 people,
leaving behind our flower garden — even the W.C. and bidet are full
of flowers for Lotte. But how happy we shall be to have again a quiet life
and not to rivalise with cinema-stars. We have refused, Chile, Paraguay,
Colombia, Cuba, we have enough for the moment — enough of
success, fees, flowers, people and refugees. How we are longing to sit
quietly again in Bath!

A sad news was that our best friend in Rio, Hernandez Catá the
ambassador of Cuba has been killed in an stupid aeroplane-accident.
Three days after his death a letter had reached me here, saying, that he
would wait with his car on the aerodrom, when we arrive — and he

lost his life meanwhile in a plane excursion. He was the kindest man I have met since years and he garanties for Eisemann[4] in Cuba — I hope they did send the visa to Eisemann from Havanna. You understand that the only way to be grateful for the preference and happiness which we enjoy is that we try to use here our influence to help to others. It is frightfully difficult for there exists a secret order not to give any more visas to Jews and only the minister of the Exterior could personnaly break this iron rule. What times, — and how often, you can not imagine it, so our thoughts to you and what we have too much of happiness here would be due to you all. Now I have to work for two month on my book on Brazil and then we will think over if we go to Newyork — my sister in law is in contact with Eva and we get always notices through her — not Eva herself, who seems to be too happy to write. Yours

Stefan Zweig

My dears,

I am terribly busy, tired and still upset about the news of the death of Catá, and that is the only thing which spoils the pleasure of returning to Rio to a normal working life and a beautiful landscape. I shall write you at length immediately we arrive in Rio. In the meantime kindest regards and kisses

Lotte

1 Richard Friedenthal, see p. 196.
2 Julio A. Roca Jr., a pro-Allies Argentine foreign minister who resigned office in 1941.
3 Richard Friedenthal, see p. 196.
4 Heinrich Eisemann, see p. 195.

FLIGHT POST

On the way from Buenos Aires to Rio 15. Nov. [1940] Dear Hannah and Manfred, now in the aeroplane we have the first moment since three weeks. The strain was hard, yesterday at 1030 I read still broadcast, we came home at midnight where a cinema agent was waiting for me.

In the morning at 5 we had to get up and found at six the same agent waiting, now we are on the way, after having been photographed for the thousands and last time. I had altogether ten lectures instead of four in these three weeks and we have doubled the fees of the last ones except the one in English and one in German I gave for charity purposes. And then the table speeches, the interviews, the cine photos, the travels — I have at least made the tour round the world — yesterday still Uruguay, going and re turning by plane: poor Lotte was frightfully tired even without having accompanied me in the more strenous voyages in the province. But now it is over. I have earned enough in three hard weeks that we can now pass the next three month in our relaxed way and do some work. I am longing to have some quiet time without publicity. And whenever I want to take up again lecturing I can do it, I have invitations to Paraguay, Cuba, Columbia, Chile and I do not know how many countries and of course here and in Uruguay again. But we will stay for two months at least in Brasil and see how we can stand the climate in summer, probably we shall retire in the mountains (the only difficulty is to find a hotel there with a little comfort and quietness, as all in Rio moves at the same time to these places).

As to Friedental[1] I wrote you, that I had a private audience at the Minister of Foreign Affairs who at my request granted me three visas, two for my former publishers[2] in Holland and one for Friedental; as I hear the cables have gone already to the respective consulates. I am nevertheless not quite sure, that all will go smoothly as every time we ourselves had to do with visas there were always delays and sometimes forgotten; if it should not be delivered to him, please cable that I may remind here. I remember how complicated it was to transform our visitors visa to Brasil in a permanent one and you may imagine that all was well prepared for us, but always there is some thing forgotten or a detail wanting in these burocratic times; now all is in perfect order for us and we want no more special permissions to go in and out of Brasil and can ever stay as long as we want.

All what you write about our home in Bath is very recomforting; please do not forget that you can make me personally a great pleasure and that is in disposing of all my belongings for you and your family as if it were yours. It is a great satisfaction for me to know that it is useful to somebody — and especially to people like you — while it is totally useless to me. Please remember this always. And Manfred have from time to time a rest. Who knows what still expecting is all our only one thing is really wise for the future — to keep fit, to have his body and his brains in good order. As to Eisemann[3] I am afraid that the death of our friend Hernandez Cata will prove fatal to his Cuban visa as it was Cata who gave the garanties for him and now the only man who could urge if there was some hindrance or delay is gone. I am sorry for Eisemann that it did not work immediately as Cata and I had hoped, but perhaps there will be another opportunity. A bookseller in Buenos Aires wired him for books and they are already in touch — here is a lot of wealth but the people in Argentine have not yet learned to spend it in cultural things, they begin now smoothly. The country is not very inspiring and both Lotte and I prefer Brazil which is pittoresk and has a great charm in the landscape and in the people. I hope you will know it a day. And now I leave the sheet to Lotte, who is again allright and will write you all I have forgotten to tell you about Argentine and Uruguay (where the abundance of food and the quickness of life has for us Europeans somewhat exciting) Yours

Stefan

Dear Hanna u Manfred,   We received yesterday both Hannas' letter with the copy of Eva's first letter and yours, Manfred which was very interesting. I am happy and grateful to know her safe and well, and if she does not like my family-in-law, she exaggerates perhaps but is not altogether wrong.[4] I was glad to know that you were both all-right so far, but I would feel better if you were both away from London. When do you give up Woodstock Road? — We are glad to return to Rio and we are determined to live quietly there and work. I am only sorry that I did not bring a new Royal Portable Typewriter with me, mine is beginning to wear out, although still incomparably better than your brother's. Has Heiner[5] got all the papers for his affidavit now? You did not mention it and I only had information from Newyork that he had sent a cable confirming the receipt of the affidavit and that the forms had been sent by registered airmail from Buenos Aires. Stefan's first wife and most of his collegues have been able to get out of France and are now in Newyork. In South Am. There are few new comers as visas to all the countries are almost impossible to get. About our journey to Argentine I shall write more later on when my impressions have settled down. For the moment I only remember that the meat portions were enormous, the weather continually changing from hot to cold, the telephone continually ringing, Stefan giving one lecture after the other and little speeches in between, myself continually dead-tired and our time taken by all sorts of things from early morning to late at night. From Uruguay my principal impressions were the first flight by hydro-avion and the fact that we did not speak anything but Spanish and that fortunately ladies were excluded from the banquet after the lecture.

Best wishes and kisses and kindest regards to the Rosemount — and Woodstock inhabitants.

Lotte

1 Richard Friedenthal, see p. 196.
2 In addition to a visa for his friend Richard Friedenthal (see p. 196), Zweig was seeking visas for Herbert Reichner, a former publisher of his in Austria, and Fritz Landshoff (see p. 199), the German co-founder in Amsterdam of Querido Verlag, the German-language exile publisher.
3 Heinrich Eisemann, see p. 195.
4 Alfred Zweig and his wife Stephanie, see p. 204.
5 Heiner Mayer, see p. 200.

---

c/o _EDITORA GUANABARA_   Rio, 19.11.40
(WAISEMAN KOOGAN LTDA.
LIVREIROS E EDITORES)
RUA DO OUVIDOR, 132
(TELEPH. 22–7231
RIO DE JANEIRO
END. TELEG.: EDIGUA — BRASIL)

Dear A. & M. we cannot tell you anything about Eva, as she did not write to us — [. . .] Anyhow we hope to see her in February. For the moment we have but one desire: to sit quietly and not to move. I have done enough with travelling by air and auto and trains and hydroplanes in those 16 days — more than another in a lifetime and the idea to travel 14 days to Newyork is for the moment a ghastly one for me. I am very worried about Manfred. I do not understand why he must just now start a new profession as a Xray specialist — after the war his practice will flourish again and he would better do to take a rest. Don't think too much about the future and remember always that you have a child who wants you. Don't worry about money, you should know already that one of the very few pleasures I have now left is to know that you have not to think about and may freely and largely dispose of all I have — we have a duty one against the other in such times. I told you that I had to give ten lectures instead of four and am invited to give more in Spanish and in all possible countries of South America — so we have at least something useful to do and I am glad that I am physically still fit to stand the great strain. Ever yours, Stefan Zweig

Friedental's[1] visa will soon be confirmed if there should be difficulties — I had a formal promise.

1 Richard Friedenthal, see p. 196.

Rio, Central Hôtel

Rio, 22.11.40

Dear Hanna u Manfred,   Just now your telegram about the next address — [. . .] About the new living arrangement of Manfred's I send my best wishes, all included in the one that he may be able to live there for the duration without having to change, and that he can keep up quiet long weekends at Bath. — About Fr's[1] visa we cabled you again yesterday. The explanation is that the second person for whom Stefan had also secured (or thought to have secured) a visa to Argentina from England, had cabled about difficulties in getting it in spite of telegraphic instructions from Buenos Aires, and that led to the second cable from thee, ordering the Arg. consul in London to give at least a tourist visa to those two. But maybe Fr. owing to his protestant faith had less difficulties than the other, the former editor of Querido[2] in Amsterdam who is now in England. You did not write anything about your brother, so I am afraid it is not yet settled. Tell him, if he likes, to take Stefan's manuscript case for the journey. It is always useful and I am sorry I did not insist on taking it. — Our plans keep on changing. The newest idea is to stay here in Rio for 3 months instead of packing up again in a few weeks to go to the mountains. Until now it is not at all hot in spite of splendid weather. Stefan wants me to apologise to Mama because I wrote her that it is now the rainy season — we have a large room with a big covered terrace and no sun after 10 a.m., overlooking down directly on a bathing beach, and the room even has a real writing-table. So I think we shall stay here and see how long we like it. If it gets very hot in the end, we think of going to the USA, stopping first in Bahia and Pernambuco, then a boat to New Orleans and from there continue by train to Newyork, where we would look for a hotel or small furnished service flat somewhere near the town but not in the town itself, as there are too many friends and colleagues of Stefan's now in Newyork to allow him quiet working hours. Needless to stay that I shall then see much of Eva and give detailed reports, but

I am convinced already now that she feels very much at home at New Rochelle as I take her silence for a sign of being pleasantly occupied all the time. I suppose it will be by the end of Jan. middle of Febr. that we get to Newyork. — I hope that in Bath all goes smoothly in spite of the many people and that none of the children or adults gives you any trouble. Please tell Lizzy[3] and Mannheim[4] that for a long time I intended to write them and that I have not given up the idea. — It will soon be time to congratulate you and Mama to your birthdays. I am sorry I cannot send any presents, I can only say that it would give me pleasure if you get a beautiful present for yourself or for each other in my name.

Kindest regards, also to Smolletts[5]
and kisses, wishes and best love,
Lotte.

[Pages 1 to 3 of the letter below are missing]

Continuation of page 3 shall go to Newyork. Personally I hate the idea of changing and packing and further more the enormous family of Schnorrers[6] who expects us there will make the stay not restful. I want to work and that has been nearly impossible through my lecture tour and the perpetual voyages. Time goes on, a few days and I shall have been for the last time in the fifhieth and I not believe that I shall ever write a book a life begins at Sixty! Must I say that we think continually on you and that all our wishes are over the ocean this same ocean which lies so blue and peaceful before our windows, while you have to stand against all forces of this devil who wants to destroy our life. Yours ever

Stefan Zweig

1 Richard Friedenthal, see p. 196.
2 Fritz Landshoff, see p. 199.
3 Litzie Philby, see p. 201.
4 Karl Mannheim, see p. 200.
5 See Peter Smollett, p. 202.
6 Yiddish for 'beggars' or 'spongers'. In German the word has come to mean 'freeloaders'. A certain chutzpah is required of a 'schnorrer', with money often being solicited for supposedly religious purposes.

AEROGRAMMA
VIA PANAIR
c/o Editora Guanabara
132 rua Ouvidor

Rio de Janeiro   Rio, 27.11.40

Dear Hanna u Manfred,

We have not had any letter from you last week and so far not this week, and I am glad we had at least the cable giving us your new address. From us there is little to report. We have had a quiet week, did not see many people, enjoyed our balcony and the fact that it is not yet hot. Our plans are still uncertain. We intend to stay here in the Hotel Central[1] as long as it does not get too hot, and then — by the middle or end of January — we would like to go to Newyork during the hot season here. But it is a very expensive journey and therefore it would be good if you could enquire at the [–?] Lloyd by phone perhaps about the possibility of sending the ticket from Engl[2] or to pay it there and give instructions to Cook[3] here to make it out for us. Perhaps you or the travel bureau could wire us whether this can be done without difficulty and how it is to be done. — Stefan wants still to add some lines, so kindest regards only and the information that we had at last a letter from Eva, a fairly long one. We hope to see her in February. Best love

Lotte

Dear Hannah and Manfred, we do not yet know what we shall do in January. Till now the weather is very agreeable and if it does not get worse we shall stay here in our very airy hotel. As to our voyage to Newyork we have not yet decided anything. It is at least 13 days voyage, perhaps even more and rather expensive. Perhaps you could once ask at the travel-office where we bought our passage, if we could buy from them the passage from here to Newyork at the MacCormick line and they could cable the passage over here — this would facilitate very much our intention and we are then nearer to England. Should this be possible please do it and inform us by cable. We had a lot to do here with formalities as our permit expires soon and to facilitate matters and voyages in the future we took an illimited one which is of course a sort of garantie not to repeat always on their applications, but what formalities we had to fulful, fingerprints photos with attestations, papers and papers now it is done and we have never to worry about delays, difficulties and so on. As to further lectures I am rather reluctant, the voyages from country to country in this enormous continent take days and days; I prefer to sit quietly and to work — till now the heat has not yet arrived and the beauty of this town fascinates us after weeks more and more. If we could have you here for a fortnights rest you would forget all the hard days and recover physically as morally. [. . .] We are here very glad to have finished with our lectures — only yesterday I have still one in the Foreign Office in honour of our friend, the Cuban minister, whom we lost in an air accident. Lotte feels allright and I repeat we should be happy, if we would know you in safety — I hope you will have both a few days rest at Bath, at least at Christmas. We would have liked to send you some coffee, sugar and similar Brasilien samples as a Christmas present but we will ask first, if it is possible and if there are no special permissions — one is already expecting formalities everywhere and I would have liked so much to show you that we don't forget you and remember well our last Christmas in Bath. Let us hope, that such good and cordial hours will come again.

Yours
Stefan Zweig

1 Built in 1915 and demolished in 1951, the Hotel Central was located on Flamengo Beach (Praia do Flamengo) in Rio de Janerio. It has a spectacular view on the Bay of Guanabara.
2 England.
3 The British travel agency Thomas Cook, which had offices or representatives worldwide.

_____

Hotel Central   Rio, 3. 12. 40

FLIGHT POST

Dear Hanna u Manfred, No letter from you or Mama since more than
2 weeks, and I am glad we had at least your cable. But I do not want
to wait longer, as this letter shall convey to you, Hanna, our heartiest
congratulations and best wishes for your birthday, and many happy
returns –, let us hope the next will see us all united again. I cabled you
that at least one letter of Eva was on the way and that we had one. She
seems to be quite well and happy there, also my sister-in-law wrote lately
that she had again spoken to her on the phone, and if all goes according
to plan I hope to see her in February. In the meantime we are trying
out the Brazilian summer. It is gradually getting warmer, but our room
is very airy, Stefan, as you know, enjoys perspiration, and so all is well
so far. – and we often try to imagine your life which in every respect
must be the opposite of ours. I hope that at least Manfred takes a long
Christmas holiday at Bath although I am not sure whether it is still as
quiet as it was the last months. Do all the families in Rosemount use
the sitting-room?[1] And is Clara[2] with child out there now? And how is
life in Regency Lodge? Was the removal difficult or didn't you take your
furniture there? Marta will be busy there, I suppose, and glad of it. I do
not know whether I wish your brothers things were settled or not, I would
like the idea of his travelling now. Paul,[3] contrary to your letter, has not
yet arrived and Stefan is glad about it. We lead a very quiet life now. As
long as the family of our friend Catá[4] who died in that stupid accident,
was still in Rio we were kept busy visiting them and Stefan spoke at a
commemoration. Now they have left and we see few people, do not go
out much, but sit on our balcony and work and read. We have made
one or two excursions and are always delighted to discover still more and
more unknown things.

Once more many happy returns, and best wishes,
Lotte.

Dear Hannah kindest wishes for your birth day; my own was somewhat
spoiled; at one of the innumerous registrations a nice, half coloured girl,
this charming type I admire so much, wrote in the register under hair:
"grey".[5] As I said it was the first time in my life she was so kind to alter
it into "brown", but I am afraid, it was the last time. Do not follow this
bad example. You can imagine how we read the newspapers — with all

good feelings and you know how hopeful I was from the first day; we try to imagine all our friends and where they may be. I have myself no news and do not know where to write, as most of them have without any doubt left London. Often — no, daily we are ashamed to enjoy such a glorious summer here, the heat is not so great as we feared and we hope to stand it through. I am glad to have a rest from my lectures, I hate to be from morning to evening a public person and enjoy now our privacy. We have only one room here but with a very big terrace so that it makes nearly two — what I miss are books as I cannot store them here. Of that I shall have in the States with her marvellous libraries — I dream to go to a place (university or other town) about two hours from Newyork to have a quiet life and notwithstanding the possibility to "go to town" — about the distance of Bath to London, which was agreable in peace time. So Lotte could see from time to time Eva and I my brother[6] and a few of the friends, but I have to avoid the innumerables which are now there. How much will you have to tell us, I do really not know how you divide your life between all those who want your care and your help, but more you have to do less you will be anxious about Eva who really seems to enjoy her new life and even our rather harsh letter, that she may write you at least once a week, will not spoil her the privileged stay. I think we better direct the next letter to Bath as I hope from all my heart that Manfred will take there a holiday; one must nowadays seize every good moment and enjoy it — let us not think too much, it doesn't help. Give my love to your sister, to all our friends if you see them — I would like to describe how peaceful and even without imagination of all our fate this Southamerican world is but you would not believe it. Yours ever

Stefan Zweig

1 Rosemount was inhabited by refugee friends and relatives of the Altmanns and by people working for the Admiralty which, during the war, had been relocated from London to Bath.

2 Clara Joss, an Austrian refugee and wife of the cartoonist Fritz Joss. She was part of the Altmanns' circle of friends that included Peter Smollett (see p. 202) and Litzi Philby (see p. 201).

3 Paul Frischauer, see p. 196.

4 Alfonso Hernández Catá, see p. 197.

5 Stefan Zweig was being increasingly anxious over his impending sixtieth birthday and saw the reality of his age in his changing hair colour.

6 Alfred Zweig, see p. 204.

FLIGHT POST

7 XII 1940   Dear Hannah and Manfred, we have a letter from Eva today that she has for 4 weeks no news from you. I am afraid that letters have been lost. We wrote to you both every week regularly and now being anxious we have tried to make an arrangement with the Western Telegraf that all the telegramms we send could be paid by you as we want to inform you regularly about your daughter and are somewhat short of money. You will understand that and I hope it will be possible so that you may not have to all your other anxious times the worry about your child. Please send us like before cables from time to time — we are in such enormous distance that letters are not sufficient as they seem to take much time. Eva writes quite happy, she is some what disappointed that we arrive later than we proposed but I want badly a few weeks without travelling. From us there is nothing new to relate. We live a retired life and till now we could stand the heat very well, only one wants more sleep and feels his energy a little diminished. We ourselves have no letters from you all now for three weeks but your cable reassured us at least that you are allright. Kindest regards to all and love to you

Rio, Hotel Central   Stefan Zweig

Dear Hanna u Manfred, — There seems to be an all-round shortage of letters just now — we have no letters from you since 3 weeks, you have no letters from Eva for 5 weeks and she has no letter from you since 4 weeks. But I hope that all these letters which certainly have been written are not lost but only delayed and will arrive as a nice Christmas surprise. In any case I repeat our birthday wishes which we expressed in our last letter. — We are all-right, it is not yet so very hot and I have not even started bathing. We are continuing to work and to see few people, and my only activity consists in taking Spanish lessons, in order to change my Esperanto into real Spanish. From Eva we had another letter today telling that she has seen Rose Wohl[1] and her sister and brother-in-law and that they are "very sweet". But I have had no word from Rose herself — it seems to be a general defect of the American character, this not-writing — although I feel sure of her friendship and I am beginning to appreciate it very much. She wrote a few days ago that she had again spoken to Eva by phone and that everything was allright and that she was going to see her soon. I am looking forward to seeing Eva in Februay. Even if we do not remain in Newyork, we will not be more than two hours away at the most, and I shall be able to see her frequently for at least 2 or 3 months.

To make plans or even to think ahead for more than 4 or 5 months one does not dare although I always hope for pleasant events and sometimes even have rather premature dreams about being at home again with you. I am surprised to find myself so much more sentimental than I thought, but I discover more and more deeply this habit of living with you for so long, has grown and how much I miss you. My only consolation is that at least our house is useful to you as a place for rest and I do wish it will remain it. How are Rauman's[2] fitting in that Rosemount-life? Give them my kindest regards, also to all the others especially to Lorle[3] and Ursula[4] to whom I want to write since a long time.

Best wishes, kisses and souvenirs,
Lotte

1 Rose Wohl was a friend of the Altmann family living in New York City.
2 The Raumans were an Austrian couple who lived near Manfred and Hannah Altmann in Golders Green, London. At the Altmanns' invitation, they stayed at the Zweigs' house in Bath in order to escape the worst of the Blitz and to help look after Rosemount.
3 Lorle was a niece and adopted daughter of Martha Kahn, see p. 198.
4 Ursula (Ursel), the daughter of Alice and Heiner Mayer, see p. 200.

Rio, 11.12.40

FLIGHT POST

Dear Hanna u Manfred,

Finally we had a letter of 6.11 from you after more than 3 weeks without mail. In the meantime you seem to have moved into your new flat, and I hope you can stay there for as long as you like. What did you do with your maid, could you take her to Bath? Whom are you going to take instead of Mrs Youngman[1] and her children? I am very glad, Hanna, that you wrote about yourselves, because I want to know as much as possible about your life, and there are still lots of questions which I could put you. For instance, who is Frank? I thought you had Ewin there and I cannot think of any Frank I know.[2] From your brother[3] we had a letter, thanking us, but I hope he does not travel now during the cold season. Should he go, one of Stefan's tweed suits might be useful. As to my dear Brother's[4] letter: help him with money if you think he needs it and as you say yourself, he might be really at the end of his resources. As to the Brazilian visa, I do not think it will be possible. As they do not give visas now as a rule to Jews it would mean giving a personal guarantee and that is the only thing I cannot ask of Stefan in this case. I shall write him next week, should you see him before tell him we think it over and give him something if you think he needs it. I think I shall also write to mama, and don't you worry too much about it. I know what it means beginning to help him, but we were not surprised — it had only come one day. — Forgive if I do not write more to-day, it is already late for posting, and it is hot. I hope for a thunderstorm to-night and then I shall write more at length. Keep well and induce Manfred to stay as long as possible with you in Bath.

Yours, Lotte.

FLIGHT POST[5]

I join a few lines on this famous paper which would be more convenient for other purposes.[6] Rio is and will always remain the most beautiful town of the world, even such a unenthusiastic being as Lotte finds it wonderful. All would be ideal here without the heat in summer and as there are already flats with aircooling I think it over if it should be necessary for my health to go to a southern climate. And how far is this world from yours and from America! One can write only by air mail and that would mean for me never to send manuscripts and for Lotte to write still shorter letters than usual. My Spanish makes good progress and I like the language enormously — the easiest perhaps of all Latin ones and I wonder what they will say in Buenos Aires when I am lecturing in Spanish. Here we live a very quiet live, I do my best to continue this retirement after having seen so many people and if I am giving a lecture I will do it on the last days. I have not heard a word from Europe since months except your letters and also from America I hear nearly nothing, but I do not complain, all personal things being quite indifferent now. For Friedental I can do nothing from here except if he would like to live here, all correspondence has no effect in America, one has to phone and phone every day and to run. A few weeks ago it would have been much easier, but he never mentioned this intention. Thanks for all

Stefan Zweig

1 Mrs Youngmann.
2 Frank, who was a son of Mr Miller the gardener, helped around Rosemount from time to time. Ewin was either a son or grandson of Mr Miller.

3 Heiner Mayer, see p. 200.
4 Hans (Jan) Altmann, p. 193.
5 This letter was found attached to Lotte's letter above. It appears, however, that Stefan Zweig wrote this before their visit to Buenos Aires.
6 By 'famous paper' Stefan Zweig probably meant 'infamous', jokingly suggesting that its quality was better suited to be used as toilet paper.

---

11. XII 1940   Dear Hannah, We have today a card of my sister in law who was visiting Eva — I must admit that she takes it seriously and is already affected with all the responsibility-complex of the Zweigs. In this case it is very good and you can rely upon her better than others. Don't worry if there come no letters regularly; we also got yours with a long delay. — We do not know exactly when to go and how, finally we want to combine it with a trip to Bahia and the Northern Brazil, which would pay us half the fare and the fares for such enormous distances are frightfully high. The disagreable thing is that you have to book three weeks before as there are few places and we have then no ship from the North of Brazil on the other hand I want to finish a little book on Brazil, which will be very helpful to us and perhaps to others in the future. We are now in plain summer, but I find the heat still tolerable, only you want more sleep and eat less. What is perhaps an advantage for my point. Now to you. I implore you again and again, dispose freely and without scruples of all I have, help your family and also your brother-in-law as I believe that there is very little chance to get him now a visa. I have always tried my best for others and I hope, that Catas[1] daughter will now see in Cuba for Eisemann[2] after the death of her father — here we are in a particular situation because we have here the personal responsibility for any person and would try to get over and we know how small the chances are for a newcomer. As to Victor[3] I wrote him but had no reply, give Koerner[4] and all others my kindest regards, we must try for Hermann Neisse[5] all immediately in the States. In no case we shall stay in Newyork, I have to work and could not have a quiet life there — probably we go somewhere to a small university or near town so that we could come to Eva from time to time. All is so very obscure in these times — as to you I repeat, do not worry about the material side of things and try to keep yourself fit. I hope you will stay the whole Christmas here in Bath and I wish Manfred and you would not return to London but after a good rest. Yours Stefan Zweig

1 Alfonso Hernández Catá, see p. 197.
2 Heinrich Eisemann, see p. 195.

3 Victor Fleischer, see p. 196.
4 Stefan Zweig's stock broker in London.
5 Max Herrmann-Neiße, see p. 197.

Hotel Central   Rio, 15.12.40

Dear Hanna u Manfred, Just a few lines to-day to tell you that we remember you and that hope you are well. We are beginning to feel rather warm, go out little and work a lot instead. I have begun bathing and shall make it a habit to do so every morning before breakfast. At night it is good to be with friends who have a car to take us a little further out — 20 minutes from here it is already much cooler and refreshing. In January I suppose we will still go to the north of Brasil, to Bahia, Recife and Belem and from there probably continue to USA — we may decide to fly as Belem is already a third of the whole distance and there is no connection by boat to Newyork. — I hope you have had a very quiet and restful Christmas and that Manfred spent already your birthday in Bath and remained until after New Year.

Kindest regards, kisses, best wishes,   yours, Lotte.

Dear Hanna and Manfred, there is not much to tell about us. We support the heat better than we supposed and I continue to work regularly but without enthusiasm (for whom does one write to day?). We have no news from all our friends and are glad to be in touch with you. As to our voyage we do not enjoy it to much, we would like to have a few month without packing and wandering around, but who has not this wish to have a quiet life in these terrible times and we all must learn to dream of things which once were the most natural. But let us keep form. we are with you with all our thoughts and wishes

Stefan

95

Hotel Central   Rio, 16. 12. 40

Dear Hanna,   This morning I got your letter (No1 to Rio) from
Nov. 16th as well as one from mama. In the meantime you will have had
letters from Eva and I hope long ones. We will be there in February and
then I will tell you all I can about her and her life. I wrote to S's about a
fortnight and got a very friendly and polite letter asking them to see to it
that Eva writes regularly and explaining what it means for parents to be
without news. The Americans have not much imagination, and also my
friend Rose whom Eva visited weeks ago, has not written me a single line
although she should know that I would be glad to have a report about the
child. Meanwhile we had a Christmas card from Eva together with my
sister-in-law[1] who has visited her again and who writes that everything is
all-right. — I am very glad your brother does not have to travel now, it is
the worst possible season now. About Ursula's[2] future it seems too early
to worry. I suppose the best will be if her parents keep her with them
later. Even if her mother should go out to work, she could do part of the
household, and as the public schools are free (Eva is visiting one) and in
some districts very good, that should be no problem. Should we be in the
USA when they arrive — I don't think they will be able to travel before
several months — we will of course advise them as much as we can, and
even should we have left, I would try and recommend Heiner[3] as well as
Alice[4] to people which I think might be useful to them. — You will have
moved into your new flat now, I suppose, and be very glad to be settled
again. Did you get part of the furniture to Bath already? You are quite right
in all you do to improve the house I wish Manfred would frequent it even
more. A pity he has to take that X-Ray course in London. I am glad that
you have Raumans[5] with you and that you get on so well together. Give
them my kindest regards. — Here is great joy everywhere about success
of the Greek and of the English offensive, and the great number of jokes
that are in circulation about the Italians, is a good expression of this state
of mind — Who are the fastest runners in the world? The Greek, because
they even catch up with the Italians. — The Italian colony in Sao Paulo
is supposed to have asked for police protection because two Greeks have
landed in Santos. — A man orders spaghetti in a restaurant and when
he gets them asks for English Worcestershire sauce. When the sauce is
brought the spaghetti have disappeared, — etc. etc.
        The other day you asked how we get along with our things. As a matter
of fact, I had often been on the point of writing about it, but at the last
moment I always thought — I cannot write you about such ridiculous
things now; you would not be in the mood for it. Stefan had a second
tropical suit made and always wears one while the other is being cleaned.

The tails he did not need yet. The invitations, although numerous and often big receptions, were never so formal and smoking and evening dress we have only worn once on the boat and once in Rio. I had to buy 3 more summer dresses, washable simple things, and for invitations I ware alternatively all my black dresses, and the dresses I bought in Poland years ago, did very good service. For afternoon receptions, — if the day was a little cool, — I used my black woolen dresses, the one from Poland with short sleeves or the one from May Fair which I bought last year. And as the invitations were at so many different places, I got round beautifully. Black is the great fashion this year — in Newyork even for summer wear, ridiculous as it looked in the hot streets — and the materials of my dresses in wool as well as silk is so much superior to all what you get here that I was quite well dressed as a rule. Now the mania of invitations has died down somewhat. The heat makes the people inactive and lazy, and most families are preparing to leave for the summer. We stand the heat very well so far although at times one gets a little fed up with it. Most of the picture houses and casinos are air-conditioned and the sea or near, one can always get some fresh and cool air, and in the own room one dresses not much better than Adam and Eve and gets refreshment from the douche and the ventilation — You will have got an enquiry from the Western Cables whether you are willing to pay for our telegrams and I am glad you said you would. I think it is less trouble for you that way than sending reply paid. As to the Middle safe[6] I will see whether I can send you a letter with certified signature, otherwise an authorisation would have little value.

Kindest regards to you and Manfred, Smolletts and Raumans and all the children,
Lotte

1 Stefanie Zweig, Alfred Zweig's wife, see p. 204.
2 Ursula (Ursel), the daughter of Heiner Mayer, Lotte's brother, see p. 200.
3 Heiner Mayer, see p. 200.
4 Alice Mayer, the wife of Heiner Mayer, see p. 200.
5 Neighbours in Bath.
6 A safe-deposit box held at the Midland Bank.

Hotel Central (next address will come by cable) 27. XII 1940

Dear Hannah and Manfred, as you see we are preparing already our next voyage and we have not yet quite decided, how to do so it, by boat or by plane. All is complicated as I have to visit the cities in the North of Brazil, Bahia, Olinda, Pernambuco, the isle of Maranhao[1] — it will be no pure pleasure to visit equatorial countries just in the summer time but we are "Kammer quo"[2] we know already what a Brazilian summer has in store and support it quite well. The advantage is that by this half the travel will cool us nothing — the other half from the frontier to the States is still expensive enough. Great difficulties means the costume. On the plane we can have not much luggage, in North Brazil it will have 40 degrees over zero and in Newyork 20 degrees under zero three days later. But Lotte stands all this through much better than I thought and we work every day, eating very little during the heat and sleeping much. All the trouble of Brazilian summer-life could be averted with expense of an air conditioned room, an "anticentralheiting" — then one could live even in summer-time here and we love even now this wonderful city very much. Now about you. Please have often a weeks rest in Bath, do spend freely and do not worry, be sure that we shall look after Eva and give you more news about her. You can thoroughly rely upon us. I hope Friedental[3] got his visa, the Argentine Consul makes it a speciality to make difficulties; he had the telegrafic order for Landshoff[4] and Friedental in the first days of November and as he did not deliver it (to our astonishment) to Landshoff who immediately applied, the Foreign Minister called a second time to deliver tourist visas to both, I cabled you the date of the second cable. Give my love to Martha[5], to all friends, tell Fleischer,[6] that I had never a reply on my letter to him and believe me yours sincerely and faithfully

Stefan Zweig

Only a few words to-day as it is time to post the letter. We are feeling hot but well and Stefan is glad of the good chance to lose-weight. Nevertheless, winter weather will be a pleasant change, and I am looking forward to it and to seeing you again.   Yours, Lotte

1 São Luís, the capital of the Brazilian state of Maranhão.
2 Accommodations are paid for.
3 Richard Friedenthal, see p. 196.
4 Fritz Landshoff, see p. 199.
5 Martha Kahn, see p. 198.

6 Victor Fleischer, see p. 196.

Dear Hanna & Manfred   Rio, 31.XII.40

We very much hope that you have spent not only Christmas but also the following week until at least New Year in Bath and that you both had a thorough rest. I have heard that the winter is very cold in Europe this year, and I hope there is a good livable shelter in your new apartment. We are living just the extreme of your live. It has now become very hot- exceptionally hot, as we are told — and we have taken an attitude of defense against the heat. The days are not too bad, although to-day where the temperature inside the house has been 33° Celsius at 11 in the morning, we sought refuge in the air-conditioned bar (which usually does not open before nightfall). The evening and nights which are hot and airless are a little hard to bear sometimes but the thought of you all over there does not allow us to complain as the others do. On the whole we stand the heat very well and Stefan is grateful to it as he is losing weight without any special effort. We have again thought of going away to the mountains, but decided that it is not worth while and that we better leave a little earlier than we originally intended. About our plans I do not want to tell you too much because we may change them again. We intend to go first to the north of Brazil and visit Bahia, Recife and Belen. It will not be much hotter than here, and as this journey will not cost us anything — except receptions, signatures and innumerable photographs — we will already be half the way up to the States.

Kindest regards and New Year wishes,   Lotte.

Rio 3 January 1941

Dear Hannah and Manfred, your letter from the 24 December has just arrived, you see, it takes sometimes five weeks and you may be sure that we have written every week to you and even sometimes twice a week. We have really the feeling that we must talk to you even by distance and if one or the other letter is belated or lost, it will never be our fault.

[Stefan Zweig — not signed; possibly a page is missing]

[Rio de Janeiro, undated]

FLIGHT POST

Dear Hannah and Manfred, thanks for your cable, I hope our friend will get the Argentine visa as the minister in [–?] was so kind to cable twice to London; should he go to Argentine he has to [–?] for Brasil and I shall see him there and give every help, also in Buenos Aires my friends will be useful to him. It is now quasi impossible to get any visas; for Eisemann I will try again in Cuba about a fortnight when Cata's daughter will arrive there. We will have in the great hall of the Foreign Office here a memorial celebration for him on Monday, presided by the Minister of Foreign Affairs and I will speak there in the name of his European friends — (in French naturally.) So we are always busy and we have to defend us against too many invitations; I personally would like not to leave our room from where we have the most marvelous view in the world and till now the weather is splendid and not at all hot so that I have even not yet worn my tropic clothes. — About Eva you have the news from Lotte, that we have no news at all directly by her. I am nearly convinced that the S. do everything to let her forget her family and to cut off al visits. I am not a great admirer of my sister in law and would cheaply exchange her against one like you but I must admit that she has tried her best, to look after her. Also our selves had never a line from S. it seems that they like Eva so much that they will not give her back. In any case we wrote her a energetic letter. Please do not worry about [Eva]. She is safe, that's what matters. And all post-war things are so obscure that we better do not to think about — we have to live this time through and the most important remains to live and to keep fit for all the nice surprises which are expecting us. — From all our London friends we have not heard a word, Frischauer[1] has not yet arrived here and the only thing he would be useful to me would be to hear about you and your daily life. I hope that Manfred and you will after the days of work retire to have some rest at Bath, I cannot repeat too often, that we want to see you not only in good health but also with good temper and unshaken nerves. I know how Manfred likes his duty as a doctor, but a doctor has not only to render healthy his parents but also himself. Now we have more than one month or two to make our plans, if we about our next plans, Lotte has already written you, and if all goes right we shall be end of January in Newyork but when this letter arrives you will have our address — and you can always write also to my publisher c/o Viking Press, 182 East 48 Street. The voyage will be a hard strain as we have to be back in Bahia, Recife, Belem on the Amazons — look at the map and you will see the distances. From there we will fly to Miami and from there go by train, 30 hours because I prefer not to change the climate too quickly from 40° plus to 20° minus. Yesterday I was surprised by Frischauers visit. He is here with wife and child and a "nurse". I have not spoken [to] him but by telephone and see him tonight. I am pleased that he did not come earlier — now we are leaving already and he can tell his stories to others. He came in the last moment as I hear that all visas will be stopped. I hope Friedental got his; the consulate must have not only one cable about him but two; as the consul refused it first to Landshoff[2] who was mentioned in the same cable, he cabled again the order for both. All what you say about the new summer house beauty in Bath has created mixed feeling in us, pleasure and the doubt, if we will ever be able to enjoy our quiet life. But let us not worry about the future — all I hope is to find a quiet place for the next two or three months to work and you will have a word about your daughter. Mail is much quicker from the States than from here. To America you better send cards with paid reply as we still are short of cash but I hope that like in Argentina I will by lectures and articles find easely my way. About a second lecture tour to South America I shall decide there. Kindest regards to you all from yours Stefan Zweig

1 Paul Frischauer, see p. 196.
2 Fritz Landshoff, see p. 199.

Rio, 11.I.41

Dear Manfred and Hanna,

Today we had your letter of Dec 18th, and we are sorry that you are worried about Eva. Obviously S's determined silence towards you and us is strange and that Rose Wohl behaved in the same manner does not make the matter any more agreeable. But you need not worry any longer. By the letters of my sister-in-law you can be assured that Eva is well and apparently quite happy there, and when you get this letter we will already have seen her — and S! I'll see to that — and decide what is best for her and take her away if it should seem advisable. That we should love to have her with us I need not emphasise, but that we cannot yet decide so long as our own plans are only made from three months to three months. But you can rely upon us that we shall not leave Eva at S's if the surroundings are not right. As to the school I cannot say anything until I have been there. But I am afraid the American curriculum is somewhat different from the English, and should we be able to take her with us to Rio the difference would be still greater. But we will see to all that and it will be easier now than in summer where all the schools were closed. If we will have to take Eva away and for some reason or other must again place her with others, I'll try to find a continental background. Huebsch[1] and Einsteins I shall consult again, but I don't think that either one could take her — it is not only the question of wanting to take a child but more than anything else the problem of space — flats in Newyork and elsewhere are usually just big enough for the family without any room for guest or even servants. That may be also part of the trouble with Berners and Carmel's boys.[2] They lived in a tiny flat with Rose, — two rooms and sittingroom all rather small — and the flat they have now moved into is hardly bigger. I do not want to defend their behaviour, and I certainly was disappointed that they never even sent a postcard about seeing Eva, but as far as I can remember it was Carmel who cabled that she wanted to send the boys, not they who offered to take them and Berner's were not completely delighted that Rose was taking them. That would explain not their behaviour but their attitude to a certain degree. — We were glad to learn that you were spending more than a week in Bath, and Beheim[3] certainly was an agreeable visitor although I cannot quite imagine where you had him sleep. Have Jungmans[4] left already, and do you take someone else in their place? Give Raumans my thanks for their letter. I believe I wrote them some time ago, but I am not quite sure about it myself, the heat makes one stupid as well as lazy.

[Unsigned letter from Lotte — page missing]

1   Benjamin W. Huebsch, Zweig's American publisher, see p. 198.
2   Carmel was the wife of one of Manfred Altmann's cousins (who lived in London). They had two sons, John and Robin, who were evacuated to the United States together with Eva Altmann.
3   Martin Beheim-Schwarzbach (see p. 194).
4   Friends of Manfred and Hannah Altmann.

Dear Hanna and Manfred,   Rio, 12.I.41

I wrote you yesterday but on re-reading your letter I felt that I have
not quite answered it. First of all I want to reassure you that we will do
everything to see that Eva gets to live in the right surroundings and that
we would like nothing better than to have her with us as soon as there
is some chance of continuity in one place on our part. In any case we
will see Eva immediately after one arrival– and we will report at once.–
secondly: We are very pleased that you like to receive our letters and that
you feel as well as we do that the distance and the complete contrast of
our lives has not really separated us. But please watch out that you don't
acquire your brother's habit of not writing without thanking. There is
really nothing to thank for, you take care of our house and even of our
friends and it is a good feeling for us that in return you get some pleasure
and rest out of it. Furthermore I must remind you of the many years I
spent with you accepting as a matter of course (I did not then realize
that you might have acted otherwise) all you had and sharing your life.
They were happy years for me and I have begun to feel quite sentimental
about your leaving Woodstock Road[1] and so it is nothing more than a just
reciprocity if you now accept just as naturally whatever occurs between
us. — What you write, Hanna, that you wonder whether I could keep
pace with my husband in Argentine, was quite right. As a matter of fact
I could not. I don't know whether it was the rush or the climate which
I did not stand, the constant change of hot and cold, damp and dry,
windy and close, in any case I got a cold and felt so dreadfully tired that
I went to a doctor who made all possible tests without finding anything
wrong, With a number of tonics and vitamins I kept myself awake until
we got back to Rio where after one day I was perfectly allright, although
the Brasilian climate, too, is anything else but invigorating. An interesting fact is that although the law in Argentine — and nearly all South
American States — does not allow foreign doctors, and requires that
they do their studies all over again including the matric[2] and on top of
that must be naturalized, — anybody may give a prescription which
is accepted without name or question by the Chemist. — By the way,
a nose and throat specialist whom we met in Buenos Aires made me
an interesting proposition for an asthma treatment which he said had
success in about 80 percent of the cases in Argentine (and in France
where he has studied and learned the process — introduced I believe
by Ahlfeldt — about 50 percent of success). The treatment consists
in touching a Sanglien[3] in the upper part of the nose with a needle
with some kind of liquid which reduces the oversensitivity and after
repeating this about a dozen times in an interval of 2–3 days each, the

asthma should be cured. It sounds phantastic to us, but this Dr. Bompet is university professor with a high reputation and he would not have accepted payment, so he did not want to do it for the money. Have you ever heard about it? Had I been long enough in Buenos Aires, I might have tried it as I had great confidence in him as he guaranteed that it could have no bad affects whatsoever. But please don't misunderstand and in the sense that I need treatment — I am quite allright and stand the heat just as well as any European summer. Nevertheless we are looking forward to a bit of winter. One gets tired of the heat and through the heat and one is slowly invaded by the Brasilian indolence which is in sharp contrast with the European conscience which still asks for activity, reliability, punctuality. I am also sorry to say that nothing has come of my good intention to go down to swim every morning at 7. I have not the energy to get up just in order to bathe.

Well, enough for to-day. The next letter will probably be written somewhere on the way north. Your letter which arrived after our departure will be immediately forwarded to us. We could not let you know before, we were ourselves undecided when to leave and how to travel. Although we have in reality about enough of traveling for a while, I am looking forward to a week of sightseeing in the North. We are told that the heat will not be worse than here and Bahia promises to be the most interesting. We will have all facilities and conveniences — to be paid by attending receptions and banquets and giving interviews.

With very best love,
Lotte

12 January 1941 Dear Manfred and Hannah, we got today your letter from the 18 Dez. and soon you will have news about Eva. We are flying the 15th to Bahia, Recife, Belem in the North of Brazil and this part (nearly the half way) is paid to us, so that we have only the other half on our own account; you see we manage things all right and as I have nearly finished the book on Brazil, I can always rely upon the people here and I hope, that if for Friedental the Argentine visa should not work — the consul had not only one cable to deliver a tourist visa to him but <u>two</u> — (I hope so at least) I can try to get it here for him as a special favor. Now to Eva. We will stay about three to four months in the States and of course our first idea was to take her there with us, but I am afraid that is not possible as we will be often in town till late at night and had to leave her meanwhile a lone. But I think we will find someone, if she would like a change — all this has to be investigated "sur place".

Should we go back to Rio the question would arise to take her with us. Here all is much easier and we could take a flat or little house, the only difficulty is school. There are good English or American colleges here, but it exists the obligation that all schools here teach (mostly) in Portuguese and she had to learn a new language still and a language which is not so important as French or Spanish. But it is still much to early to make plans as we ourselves have not yet decided — who can make decisions beforehand in such times? In any case, please rely upon us, that we will do our best and not only for yours sake but because we love both Eva and know how important these years of development are. [. . .] remember always that she is safe and you have not to be excited about every alarm while she could be in school or out of the home in England. I am more concerned about you, that you have too much to do and not enough time for rent, let us hope that the worst is over, here everybody is convinced of the British-American final success and then all our pains and losses would be no more without sense- it would be again a world to live within, when this beast Hitler could be definitively overthrown, no price would be too high.

We are somewhat tired and glad to come out of the heat. The weather is splendid, the town beautiful, but we have both the feeling, that a little winter will do us good. Myself I feel, that I have to retire somewhere to do quietly my work and not to see more people — I believe we have been on this voyage six hundred to six thousand and I do not know more, what language I am speaking and this is a heavy strain. We hope to be the 23 or 24 at the Wyndham Hotel 42 West 58 Street but only for a week and you will have our address by cable (please cable always with reply) In any case letter or communication will reach us c/o Viking Press 18 East 48 Street.

Love to Martha[4] and all others and ever yours
Stefan Zweig

1 The Altmanns' home in Golders Green, north London.
2 Matric: an abbreviation for matricula in Latin and Portuguese, or matriculation in English, referring to the formal process of registering to enter a university, or of becoming eligible to enter by acquiring the prerequisites.
3 Sanglien: French for blood vessel. This was a new treatment that involved touching blood vessels in the nose.
4 Martha Kahn, see p. 198.

[Rio de Janeiro, undated]

Dear Hannah, we have frightfully to do before leaving — like in Newyork all things rush together in the last moment. As to our friends, I hope Eisemann[1] will get his visas as my friend the minister Cata has garantied for him, I did not dare to promise it to him but I believe it is quite sure. For Friedental[2] I will do my best and have already arranged something with my publisher. For [–?] I can do nothing as it is my American publisher who has the only right to act and I am only his guest. I am very glad that I shall not be here when Frischauer[3] arrives here, he will spoil the good situation we all enjoy here by his feverish activity. In any case I avoid to introduce him; he will do this himself (for sometimes) with his stories. I understand however that he wanted to find another position and as far as I can I help everybody in this regard. We are thinking continually where you may be and what you are doing — please do not worry about Eva, my sister in law wrote that she feels extremely happy, has a lot of friends and will start skating next month, a pleasure which we could not afford to her in Bath. We are very glad that Heiner[4] can finally go to America, I would like him to take for me my tails (I have taken only the smoking with me) and if he hears from some new music (here you get nothing at all of this kind) I would be grateful. I hope he will not leave too soon, the ideas of traveling in winter-time has something frightening. — I would not like it myself. We do not know more what winter really is, every day sunshine — sometimes a little too much — and blue sky; how you would like the view from our windows!

I see that in your kindness you make the servant and cook for all people in Bath — what are the other women doing? Please advise Manfred to take as much rest as possible in Bath. Could he not work there in a hospital? I am afraid he overdoes his duty.

Kindest regards to all; also to Eisemann, who will I hope, find interesting things and you give him certainly all help he wants. And yourself please don't worry about money and dispose freely as I can by my lectures come through without any difficulty — it is true, it means a great strain, the lecturing in three different languages (or four even) but I have no right to complain. Love to all from yours

Stefan Zweig

1 Heinrich Eisemann, see p. 195.
2 Richard Friedenthal, see p. 196.
3 Paul Frischauer, see p. 196.

4 Heiner Mayer, see p. 200.

Address: New York c/o Viking Press, 18 East Street
Palace Hotel   *Bahia*, 16. I 1941

Dear Hannah and Manfred, we are now here for three days and all what
we have seen is most wonderful; it is the most colourful town I ever have
met and today we assisted[1] the great popular festivity, the Lavagem of Bom
Fim[2] — that means that a good part of the town, most negros, come to
wash the church in honour of their saint and this washing which starts as
a religious ceremony and finishes in orgie of thousand people who danse,
cry, wash and become completely mad. I have never seen any thing of
religious man-hysteria and all this in the brightest colours and without
any artificial tricks — there come never stranger to see this and it would
be in a theatrical production or a film the greatest "hit". Tomorrow we
are driving into the country, we are guests of the Government here and
Lotte is again photografed all day long, we send you only one little photo
of our arrival as the most are more grotesk — myself with a little negro-boy
or with the "intellectuals" of Bahia. You cannot imagine what it means
to see this country which is not yet spoiled by tourists and so enormously
interesting — today I was in the huts of the poor people which live here
practically from nothing (the bananas and mandiocas are growing round)
and the children go like in the paradise — the whole house with ground
did cost them six dollars and so they are proprietors for ever. It is a good
lesson to see how simply one can live and comparatively happy — a lesson
to us all, who will loose every thing and are not enough happy now by
the thought how to live then. In two days — we go tomorrow over land
to the fazendas and tobacco-factories — we will be at Pernambuco, in
five days in Belem, then after a day in English territory (Trinidad) on the
way to your daughter and then it will be to Lotte to write the long letter
you expect so eagerly. I hope you feel alright and will perhaps change
over to Bath, Lotte stands the heat and all the excursions extremely well,
only when we have to go up in the morning at 5 or 5.30 to catch the
plane, she is hard to awaken. Frischauer is in Rio and told me, who did
not believe it, he were our compatriot — in any case he seems to have
never enough money and I am like always his admirer, how he knows to
manage all with his lying technique. Kindest regards yours Stefan Zweig
       5.30 in the morning, waiting for the breakfast, there is not much time
to write. So only kindest regards.   Lotte.

1　Here Lotte borrows from the Portuguese "assistir" or the French assister, meaning to attend.

2　In the *Lavagem do Bonfim* festival, believers wash the steps of the Salvador's Nosso Senhor do Bonfim church in honour of either Jesus or the African god Oxalá — or a combination of the two.

<u>in the 'plane to Miami</u>   22nd Jan 41

Dear Hanna u Manfred,

We sent you a cable yesterday to thank you for the tickets which were given to us in Belem, and we hope to have a cable from you in Newyork as your last letters will have to be forwarded to us from Rio. We could not let you know earlier because we decided rather suddenly. It was very hot in Rio, we had only one room in the hotel and one was losing all energy for work. And as Stefan had to go to Bahia anyhow, we decided to fly. Now we have been on the plane — with interruptions — for a week and we shall be glad to get to Newyork tomorrow morning. Stefan has written you from Bahia; that was our first stop from Rio — 6½ hours by plane. We were delighted with Bahia, and we were spared official banquets etc. through the energy of our companion — a young journalist who accompanied us from Rio to Belem, a very nice and medium-brown Brazilian.[1] Not so easy it was to escape the constant company of the director of the propaganda department in Bahia who was delegated to show us round and who was a great talker — in Portuguese, and we regretted that we ever admitted to understand it, for we have still to listen carefully in order to follow it in conversation, and it was a mental strain. With our companion we could at least speak in Spanish which is a little easier for us; it had been our intention to see the sights with him alone, but this was not possible. The governments of the states of Bahía, Pernambuco and Pará wanted us to be their guest and their representatives wanted not to lose a moment of our stay and to be photographed, of course, on all places except the W.C. That and the fact that we covered enormous distances by plane, was rather tiring and we will be glad to settle down quietly, but the journey itself was extremely interesting that I leave it to Stefan to describe it, I'll keep to the more personal and practical part. I suppose you will have a look on the map to follow our journey and see what phantastic distances we covered, about 2500 miles to Belem and at least that much to Newyork. As to the time we spent in the air, it is quite impressive too: Rio-Bahia 6½ hours, Bahia-Recife 5 hours,

Recife-Belem 10 (!) hours, Belem-Trinidad 6½, Trinidad-Miami 9½, Miami- New York 9 hours. The plane Belem-Miami is a big clipper, with huge armchairs, hot food and comfort, tables, games and room between the seats. The journey along the coast Rio-Belem was by sea-plane, with many landings in obscure little places with beautiful names, interesting but rather uncomfortable journey as the planes were small, narrow and badly ventilated, whereas the clipper flight is extremely comfortable but uninteresting as it goes either above cloud banks or over the ocean. This night we will fly on to New York — no sleeper — after spending the afternoon in Miami. By now we have become early risers as most trips start at 6 in the morning, which means that you have to rise at 4.30 in order to arrive at the airport at 5.30.– Now we will stay about a week in Newyork, seeing Eva, looking for a place to go, seeing people about business affairs and a few friends. I suppose we will take a furnished flat for about 3 months and keep a household as we are tired of hotel food and Stefan wants to retain his slimmer looks which he has acquired through perspiring in the heat and through the uninteresting food in the Rio Hotel. We will try to see as much as possible of Eva and as soon as we have come to a conclusion decide what is best for her. Had we definite plans for more than the next 3 months we would have liked nothing better than to have her with us. But we have to see clearer about our own position in the States and the general situation before we can decide when, for how long and if at all we return to Rio. But in any case we will be near Eva in the next months and as often as possible with her, so you need not worry any more. She will not be lonely and you will get reports. We shall of course write as soon as we have seen her, investigate closely and decide carefully and choose still more carefully should it be preferable to transfer her. — Although your letters to us will be somewhat delayed for the next weeks by having to be forwarded from Rio, we hope to have direct news through Eva. Address until further notice:

Viking Press, 18 East 48th Street
New York.
Love and kisses
Lotte

Dear Hannah & Manfred, I write from the plane, which has become since days our normal way of living. For the first time I must confess that I become a little tired and no wonder; rising every day at 5.30 or even 4.30 and always surrounded by people when you arrive and photographer and interviewer while you are looking for your luggage. You cannot imagine what travelling means today and one pays all the beautiful things one sees with a constant nervousness if all is in order for the different frontier examinations. We carry with us a whole bag of different papers, our passports, our Brazilian permanence identity cards[2], which facilitates visas, our English or Brazilian health certificate, our luggage ticket, our luggage insurance, our air tickets, our American entry-papers, our fingerprints, a dozen photografs, our lecture invitation-letters and I do not know what more and you have continually to fill out papers how old you are and with what ship you arrived 32 years ago and at what date. And to know that if a single of these papers goes lost while you show them continually, you are ticketed and cannot go forward or backward. We change now the countries more than the shirts, yesterday we had to tip in the morning in Milreis[3], evening with English coins and Trinidad Dollars (I never knew that they had other than English money) and now I am perplexed by the problem where to change my tropical clothing against warm one, as all our luggage is in the plane and we have no time to change) believe they will take me in Newyork for a clown if I arrive at 15 below zero in a tropical white and thin suit. By this you can imagine, what distances we hurry through — tonight we arrive after 8 hours plane in Florida, have to fight for the refund of our tickets and to go without sleeper sitting all night to Newyork where we shall arrive at 6 in the morning — the exact time we generally leave. I hope to avoid that any newspaper will know of our arrival, as we want badly a few days of rest and not even days — we are longing to have a few <u>weeks</u> or <u>month</u> without hotel life and publicity. But on the other hand it was a marvel that we could do all this, as the greater part (Brazil) of the voyage ws paid to us and the other procured by the kindness of our dear relatives; and it is not to describe what we have seen all the way long. Lotte is very courageous, she looked very well in Rio and got even complements; the last days we are a little down, because we had no sleep, constant talking and seeing and seen <u>sighted</u> (not only sightseeing.) But I am sure, a few days of rest will give her "pep", as one says here; unfortunantely we will have to be busy a whole week in Newyork before we can settle down for a while. What after these weeks of rest? I cannot tell any thing. We live in a time where it is impossible to make arrangements before hand, but we are nearer now and you will always hear from us.

We follow all the news with keenest interest and it seems that all the terrible sufferings we all go through (and especially you) will not be senseless. If this devil Hitler is finally overthrown no loss, no price, no suffering was too high and too long. I am now very interested to see how the United States feel — you know how depressed we have been in July about her indifference. But all this is now definitely over.

I hope that I shall hear about Friedental[4] and the few other friends. I suppose that Manfred when he has finished his Xray course will have a complete rest and retire to Bath to rest. I do not yet know if we can cable you from Newyork as often as before and will try to arrange it; I know that you are impatient to hear about your daughter and it will be to Lotte to give you as many particulars as possible. I myself will have much to do in Newyork and she has to go alone to La Rochelle[5] the first time.

Now while I write we are going over Portorico[6] and in a few moments we will land there and enjoy a rest of 20 minutes on the earth — this stupid earth, which one loves without to know why. Love to you all

Stefan Zweig

1   Edigar D'Almeida Vitor, a reporter with the Brazilian newspaper *A Noite*. In 1937 Vitor wrote a short book about Zweig entitled *Stefan Zweig, reportagens sobre sua personalidade intellectual, sua vida e sua obra* (São Paulo: Cultura Moderna, 1937).

2   These were essentially permanent resident cards that the Zweigs secured when they returned from their trip to Argentina. While in Argentina (26 October to 15 November), they were issued with visas for permanent residency in Brazil.

3   The Brazilian currency of the time.

4   Richard Friedenthal, see p. 196.

5   New Rochelle.

6   Puerto Rico.

PART II

New York Interlude
24 January to 15 August 1941

Following the Zweigs' hectic five-month tour of Brazil and Argentina, the couple returned to New York City, arriving on 24 January 1941. Apart from a few weeks in New Haven, Connecticut, they would spend the next seven months in New York, immersing themselves in writing projects, including completing both the German edition of *Brazil: Land of the Future* (and revising its English and French translations) and *Amerigo: A Comedy of Errors in History*, producing the first draft of *The World of Yesterday* and returning to the interrupted Balzac biography. As before, the Zweigs continued to write frequently to Hannah and Manfred, their letters now focusing on practical and financial issues. The house in Bath continued to be a preoccupation, as was organizing practical help (visa applications, affidavits, work, food parcels and money) for friends and family in England. But most letters centred on the care of Hannah's and Manfred's twelve-year-old daughter Eva, who had been evacuated from England to New York.

* * *

Following what was to the Zweigs the oppresive heat of a Brazilian summer, the novelty of cold and snow of a harsh New York winter soon wore off. Encamped in the discreetly elegant Hotel Wyndham, at West 58th Street, less than a block from Central Park, the Zweigs initially did their best to remain as anonymous as possible, wanting time to themselves after months of having been the centre of attention. In New York, apart from seeing Alfred Zweig (Stefan's brother), Benjamin W. Huebsch (Stefan's editor at Viking Press) and a few friends such as Thomas Mann, Jules Romains and Stefan's first wife, Friderike, the Zweigs made a point of avoiding company, choosing instead to relax and recover.[1] 'We are glad to have done with flying and sight seeing for a while', wrote Lotte to Hannah and Manfred, 'and that this time our rooms look out on a big stone wall, is almost a welcome contrast after all the beautiful things and views we have seen. We have acclimatised ourselves very easily to the cold, but find it more difficult to get used to the central heating!!'[2] Stefan, though, considered that the weather was 'as bad as possible',[3] a complete contrast with that of Brazil. By March their complaints concerning the constant cold and wind were becoming stronger,[4] with Lotte saying that 'we get already thoroughly tired of the winter'[5] and, at the end of the month, Stefan commenting with frustration on how 'the winter was hard and endless, in more of six weeks we had not a single walk'.[6]

* * *

When not assisting Stefan with his work, Lotte's major preoccupation was ensuring that her niece was being well educated and cared for. 'I have met the proprietress here in Newyork to-day', reported Lotte early on in her searches for a suitable school and home for Eva, 'a little the Galician Jewish type but quite civilized and clever.'[7] Though less involved with Eva's day-to-day welfare than Lotte, Stefan also held strong views on the environment that would be appropriate for their niece, bearing similar central European stereotypes to those of his wife and displaying his tendency towards intellectual arrogance. Commenting on Amity Hall, the small children's home in Croton-on-Hudson run by Olga Schaeffer with her husband, the poet Albrecht Schaeffer, where Eva was placed, Stefan was impressed by the 'philosophic and abstract' atmosphere that was nurtured there. Stefan rather reluctantly felt it was necessary for Eva to attend an American school ('I am sceptical about the manner of pure American education which is superficial and creates but an arrogant halfbilding'), but at least the Schaeffers would offer a counterbalance of a sound moral foundation, the evidence for this being that, as Protestants rather than Jews, they had chosen to leave Germany out of 'disgust and sentiment of freedom without racial or political reasons.' 'They are upright people', wrote Stefan, 'without the resentment [. . .] of the Newyork-refugees.'[8] Being in such an environment would be all the more important given Stefan's negative views on American society ('You cannot imagine how we are disgusted of the impoliteness, the rudeness, the arrogant way of the American children'[9]) and his general distrust of refugees.

✳ ✳ ✳

In contrast to his love of Rio de Janeiro, Stefan Zweig was hardly able to find a good word to say regarding New York. Tired of hotel rooms, restaurants, packing and unpacking and lack of space to work, in February Stefan accepted an invitation to spend two months as a guest of Yale University in New Haven, an hour and a half by train from New York City.[10] Although the Zweigs were unable to find an apartment there, instead taking two hotel rooms[11] (like other American hotels, in Stefan's view, one that offered 'a kind of resemblance with a railway-station, no personal touch and interest'[12]), for a short time they were at least content.

'I enjoy this small quiet life as a rest', wrote Stefan, 'you cannot imagine how I hate Newyork now with its luxury-shops, its "glamour" and splendour — we Europeans remember our country and all the misery of all the world too much. Here we live like in Bath immidst provincial peoples and I enjoy the facilities given by the Yale University to take as many books at home as I like — I have a real hunger to read and study again.'[13] But as they were only a short distance away from New York City, the Zweigs could still see friends and acquaintances when they wanted, yet be able to concentrate on work and consider their future:

> Newhaven is a little place, not nice and one is lost in an American little town without a car. If we are invited one has to bring us back as there are not many buses — it is understood, that even a poor man has his car in America (except in New York where it is paradoxically impracticable.) The advantages are 1) the library of the University. I can take as many books at home as I want and go to the shelfs myself. And that is for me a delight as I have been without books for nearly a year. 2) I am not bothered by all this people which is now crowded in New York — the whole Vienna, Berlin, Paris, Frankfurt and all possible towns. So I have time to work and even think. 3) We have opportunities to see those who are real good friends quickly. There was Sholem Asch[14] here, Joachin Maass,[15] Jules Romains,[16] Bertold Viertel,[17] Friday comes van Loon,[18] you see a very good choice. 4) it is altogether cheaper: not the Hotel which I do not like very much but all the daily expenses and the schnorrers.[19] I do here some little work and prepare for the greater one which I will write in Rio if we should return there.[20]

After two months, and having completed his short book on the explorer Amerigo Vespucci, the Zweigs were again ready to move on. 'We are glad to be back in Newyork', wrote Lotte after their return to the city in April, 'Newhaven had at least this good effect that I like Newyork again.'[21]

✳　　✳　　✳

In New York, the Zweigs again tried to keep to themselves, Stefan regretting that most of his German-speaking friends in the United States were in California. That said, they formed links with a small 'but interesting' circle of British writers such as Somerset Maugham, A. J. Cronin, Bertrand Russell and W. H. Auden, who were all either permanently or temporarily living in or near New York.[22] Presumably persuaded by his friend Jules Romains, the president of the international secretariat of the PEN Club, Stefan rather reluctantly agreed to speak at a fund raising event — 'one of this enormous dinners with 1000 persons which I have avoided all my life long'[23] — to mark the opening of a European branch of PEN in New York. The PEN Club was one of the few organizations that Stefan was prepared to publicly endorse and he felt that he could not refuse this invitation, as 'everyone has to do his duty', despite the fact that he had been very critical of what he felt was the egocentric nature of the 1936 PEN conference in Buenos Aires.[24] Even so, he would be cautious and 'try at least to avoid all phraseology of democracy which will be poured over this evening by a half dozen other speakers'.[25] Given the event's distinguished list of speakers, the absence of Stefan Zweig from the event's programme would certainly have looked odd to anyone aware that he was living in New York: 'Somerset Maugham[26] will speak — everyone ten minutes sharp — for the English, Sigrid Undset[27] for the Scandinavians, Jules Romains[28] for the French and I for the German-speaking writers, the other get 1 minute every one; I have to speak one half in German, the other in English. All this will be relayed by short-wave all over the world'.[29] For Stefan the gathering brought out the 'pettiness authors develop on such occasions', adding that '[s]ometimes one wonders that these are the same people who really wrote beautiful verses and show in their books wisdom and psychology'.[30]

According to Lotte, the event went well — indeed she even appeared to have enjoyed the evening, perhaps recalling similar grand occasions that she attended in Argentina and Brazil:

> For me it was quite interesting and entertaining because it was my first big public dinner, sitting at the celebrities' table between Somerset Maugham (who was very nice and not at all stiff as I imagined him to be) and Count Sforza.[31] Most of the European writers whom we ever read were present and I hope it was not disappointing for the thousand people who paid 3 dollars each for this privilege to see that writers really do not look different from other people. There were lots of speeches, and fortunately, on account of the radio, the speakers were strictly rationed in time — Stefan — Jules Romains, Maugham, Dorothy Thompson,[32] Sigrid Undset, between 6 and 10 minutes, the others who spoke in their native language to two minutes each. Then there was the inevitable auction to raise money for refugee funds and we were surprised that really a number of people publicly donated three or four hundred dollars each. They raised about 5000 dollars and that will be just sufficient to pay the travelling expenses of 10 persons from Europe as they can only get out by the most phantastic routes — via Russia and Japan or via Africa and Martinique and only a few lucky people via Lisbon direct to USA.[33]

✳ ✳ ✳

From the outset, Stefan could barely abide New York. 'I get depressed', he wrote shortly after he returned from Brazil, 'in seeing the luxury-shops, the thoughtlessness of all this people, the stupidity of the refugees and the lack of real compassion.'[34] By April, following the relative isolation of

New Haven, Stefan was lapsing into something resembling narcissistic self-pity:

> We do not see many people, I am tired of the monotony of the war — the Jewish — the affidavit talk; with his thousand variations it remains sterile. I even go not to theatres. I feel not the right mood for everything which is amusement while Europe breaks down under the heals of the beast and while you and all our friends in England are in daily danger.[35]

In marked contrast to the advice and financial and other practical help that he provided to exiled friends of his and Lotte's in England and elsewhere, Stefan could also be extremely intolerant. As a group, Stefan viewed refugees with a mix of suspicion and annoyance, resenting the demands placed on his time of people requesting favours due to his perceived wealth and influence. One person whom he singled out for ridicule was the Viennese writer Paul Frischauer,[36] an acquaintance who Stefan expected would soon arrive in New York 'to meet all the other Frischauers'[37] — a reference to refugees already settled in the city. 'There is a kind of genius in him', Stefan remarked of Frischauer, 'to overcome all difficulties and the dirtier the waters the better he swims. I wish I had his tenacity and courage. We are not fit enough for such times with our "alergic" moral concience.'[38]

Within days of arriving in New York, Stefan visited the British consulate to discuss the possibility of returning to England but he was told that this idea was for all intents and purposes impossible, with flights fully booked for months.[39] Instead, his thoughts increasingly turned to Brazil. 'But', he mused, 'who can make plans! Who can say "I will" "I intend" — one must be satisfied to live and I want all my will-power to continue working in the midst of this turmoil.'[40] For Stefan, life was on hold: 'We live and wait and wait and live.'[41] He obsessively weighed up the pros and cons of possible courses of action, but felt that he was powerless to act on any decisions that he might reach:

> Nothing is sure and we make no plans. America has its advantages — libraries, possibilities of income etc — But Brasil — beauty, quiet life, cheap. Our decision depends from so many things, especially the developments in the world. Everyone's life is but a microbe in this monsters body which we call: The War. Shall we ever see a more sensible mankind?[42]

Stefan continued to be consumed by feelings of being trapped by war and bureaucracy:

the great difficulty is how to assure in advance how to come back [to New York] when the [Brazilian] summer begins as visitors visa will not be available (especially in case of declaration of open war) on the other hand if we would take an immigrants visa it could easily be misunderstood as if I would change my citizenship. You cannot imagine how many of such questions asked every day and in the same time the daily letters and cables for affidavits and visas. But I continue working, my book on Brazil (which will be perhaps useful to tighten the cultural relations between the English-speaking and Latin world) will appear here in English in autumn (the translator[43] is frightfully slow) and I have some new work on hand; so we have no material worries, but moral ones are big enough. The United States will give England all possible help, the whole country is transformed in an enormous factory. What we are afraid of personally is to become cut off during the duration of war and also for Eva we would not like that, as nobody can foresee how long this will take . . .[44]

Frustration dominated his thoughts as well: 'We lose here much time by thinking what to do next.'[45] He accepted that many of his European friends appeared content with the new lives that they were building in California but this option — one that was surely open to the Zweigs — was not one that Stefan, at least, was interested in pursuing:

The others have established themselves in little houses and started a new life, while we are not sure, how long we shall stay and how to decide — will it be possible to go to Brazil? Will there still be ships and planes? . . . So we wait and waiting is not very appropriate for concentrated work, but I have been idle and have different offers and choices at hand.[46]

Expressing views mirroring those of her husband, Lotte also agonized about whether she and Stefan should remain in the United States, go to Brazil or, despite the practical difficulties involved, return to England:

Both countries have their great advantages — here are some really good friends of real intellectual niveau, and the libraries, down in Brasil life in itself is pleasant and interesting and the country stimulating for Stefan. The people are extremely nice and cultured, but cultured somehow in an old-fashioned way, and intellectually there is a difference of niveau, so to say. — It is difficult to decide and lots of things are to be considered — not the least the enormous distance and the fact that travelling with all the necessary permits, visa and the journey itself will probably become more and more difficult. Sometimes we wish we were back in 'Rosemount' in spite of everything which made us leave it, and we wonder sometimes whether this would not be the best solution. Rationally it probably is not and probably Stefan would again feel useless or be given an unimportant job which others might do just as well, and besides this it is nearly impossible to get home without special official priorities. It is just a dream and only to be hoped that one day circumstances will allow its realisation.[47]

Increasingly, however, Stefan became certain that it was Brazil where he wanted to be:

Brazil has the advantage that I could stay as long as I wished and have all possible opportunities; what here will become in case of war is in any case not agreeable, we cannot take a flat and I hate the packing and unpacking, this life which is contrary to all concentration with its daily decisions and deliberations. And I see no end of all this for years and years.[48]

✳   ✳   ✳

At the beginning of March, soon after taking up residence in New Haven, Lotte suffered a series of acute asthma attacks, her first in two years.[49] The return of Lotte's asthma would complicate matters for the Zweigs, further delaying travel plans as she sought medical help to manage her condition. 'Lotte has behaved very badly last week', reported Stefan after her first difficult episode, 'she had her asthmatic episodes in best Vienna style', and he explained that the attack was a consequence of the extreme change of climate and that their New York and New Haven hotel rooms resembled Turkish baths.[50] A few days later Stefan reported further attacks:

Lotte has behaved very badly against me. She knows that I have retired to Newhaven for work and instead of helping me she gets asthma-attacks and now a thick influenza so that I, poor chap, have to care for her. I hope she will be able to leave the bed tomorrow. In any case she must be careful as the weather is disgusting, sharp winds blowing with ice and rain, the streets so muddy that I who hates this since childhood has to buy rubbers.[51]

Repeating this tongue-in-cheek tone — presumably to reassure Lotte's brother and sister-in-law — Stefan reported on the consequences for him of his wife's condition:

Lotte has behaved badly against me, as I wrote you, and is now behaving costly. As her attacks of asthma did not stop we were obliged to let examine her thoughlly for I want for my work and travelling a wife and secretary who keeps fit.[52]

Investigations, Stefan reported, would be needed to find 'allergic points' and, though 'not a serious state', he explained that he wanted Lotte to be thoroughly examined before they next travelled, taking advantage of the asthma specialists in New York.[53]

From previous experience, Lotte believed that following severe asthma attacks, flu and fever, her condition would 'settle' for months.[54] After six weeks and frequent calcium injections, episodes eased to the point that she could sleep through the night.[55] Lotte praised 'poor Stefan' for being 'very patient and helpful' and she expressed concern that because she was unable to fulfil her secretarial duties he was even more anxious to work than usual.[56] Medical tests continued, with Lotte sometimes showing violent reactions to allergic injections aimed at showing the cause of her asthma.[57] With Lotte's doctors claiming to have identified the allergens, an immunization regime was put in place with daily and then weekly injections, the idea being that these would be reduced to fortnightly intervals, then monthly and, eventually every six months. In a year, Lotte had been told, she would be immune from asthma.[58]

✻   ✻   ✻

As summer approached, the Zweigs had still not made a decision as to whether to return to Brazil. Stefan, however, was at least able to consider the months ahead. 'NY is terrible in the summer and an air conditioned apartment would be the only possibility but the prices are fantastic', complained Stefan of the months ahead.[59] Above all what he was again seeking was a period of peace: 'I hate to go to the country here as in the hotels [. . .] I would find no place to work quietly.'[60] Finding an appropriate retreat was not easy as country houses were considered too expensive and, in any case, Stefan felt that places near railway stations (a requirement without a car) were overcrowded.[61] After some effort, they rented for July and August a house (with a maid) that Lotte felt was suitable for 'houseworkers' and the 'car-less', such as themselves.[62] Located at 7 Ramapo Road in Ossining, a small town on the Hudson River that was best known as the location of the maximum security prison Sing-Sing ('one rather tries to forget this fact', commented Lotte[63]). For Lotte, there was nothing in particular to do or see in Ossining but, apart from the town's weather and its peace and quiet, the attraction was being just ten minutes from Croton where her niece Eva was living with Olga and Albrecht Schaeffer.[64] However, in addition to the Schaeffers, whose company both Stefan and Lotte enjoyed, Croton was also home to the writer René Fülöp-Miller and his wife Erika, friends of Stefan's from

Vienna.[65] Stefan's former wife, Friderike, who had recently arrived in the United States from Portugal, was also living in Croton; she would claim later that the Zweigs' decision to take a house in Ossining was made because Stefan needed to consult with her frequently on his autobiography.[66] According to Lotte, however, the proximity to 'wife No. 1',[67] as she light-heartedly referred to Friderike, was purely coincidental. On relations with Friderike, Lotte remarked that,

> the strange thing is that we are almost on better and certainly more normal terms with her than with Stefan's brother who is absolutely egocentric. I remember a conversation I had with you once with regard to the relationship of first and second wifes and husbands, but it all sees perfectly natural and normal and maybe the great difference in age makes it easier.[68]

Initially Stefan was relieved to be moving to Ossining, exchanging New York City's stifling summer heat and humidity for slightly cooler temperatures and more refreshing nights.[69] He was pleased to be in an environment that would allow him to concentrate on his work, in particular the autobiography that he had wanted to write. This would be, Stefan envisaged, 'a long and I hope very substantial book', the main problem being 'the great difficulty that I have only to rely upon my memory as I have no letters, no diarys from all those bygone times.'[70] Apart from this, his worry was 'that the end of it will not be too sad and depressed.'[71]

Stefan immediately immersed himself in his writing, with Lotte reasoning that this was probably 'partly because he wanted to work, partly because he is depressed by the facts of war in their humanity-destroying consequences, partly because there is nothing else to be done here.'[72] Following Germany's invasion of the Soviet Union on 22 June, Stefan was certainly justified to feel pessimistic:

> This new war which is in any case a relief for Britain means again destruction of numberless individual lives and happiness, it will result in starvation of millions and especially the Jews in the border countries will be suffering as never before. In Spain, in occupied France the lack of food is terrific and Europe is but in the beginning — never has a single man brought so much misery over the world than this beast Hitler. One is ashamed to see here the abundance of food and every thing, — only that what is wasted every day and thrown away in the restaurants could feed a population. It makes not so happy to be on this side if one has an instinct of solidarity! And to think that all this will become worse and worse for our mankind — you are much younger and will see after the victory a better world but I with my "three

lives"[73] feel that my generation has become superfluous. We have been a failure and have no more right to give advise to the new one.[74]

Stefan was falling into one of his depressive cycles, dwelling on the state of the world while being ever conscious of the 'terrifying 60th' — his birthday, approaching on 28 November, that would mark, in his view, the final stage of his life — and the consequent need to 'hurry to do what I have to do.'[75] But of his dark mood, Stefan acknowledged certain benefits. 'My deep depression let[s] me work like seven devils',[76] Stefan remarked, as he returned to his 'world of yesterday' in which he had been content or, at least, understood. Eager to complete his life story before reaching the age of sixty, Stefan could at least be satisfied how, 'here in this little house I have done more in three weeks on my autobiography as otherwise in three months, not leaving it from morning to night without to see anybody; in three days I hope (in the autobiography) to be through the first war — I wish I would be through the second in three months!'[77]

As far as the future might hold, Stefan did not want to speculate: 'who can tell what the next months will bring: any curiousity is satisfied for great events and I would like to oversleep the next years.'[78] Although immersing himself in work was a distraction, Stefan was unable to expel from his mind either 'the idea [of] wonder[ing] around for years always packing and unpacking, without my books, without space and service', nor his feelings of guilt for being such 'a very bad companion for poor Lotte'.[79] Feeling guilty at the life that Lotte was leading, Stefan expressed to Manfred and Hannah his sorrow for not 'giv[ing] her brighter hours and only manuscripts to copy and copy', and being unable to 'give her a quiet life as modest as it may be' of the kind that many of his European friends and colleagues were carving out for themselves in America.[80]

Lotte, as ever, was entirely understanding and supportive of the anguish that her husband was experiencing. In a letter written to Hannah without Stefan's knowledge, Lotte tried to explain her husband's torments and his thoughts of what they should do next:

> I am a little worried about him at present, he is depressed, not only because it is really no pleasure to lead such an unsettled life, always waiting what will happen next day before making another short-term decision, but also because of the facts of the war which is now becoming a real mass murder, and its seeming endlessness weigh upon his mind. I hope this mood will pass soon and I wish I had something of those people who can talk others into cheerfulness and somehow inspire courage and hope. My qualities are that I can stand any kind of life without complaining and feeling sorry for myself, but I cannot talk him out of his present mood and can only wait until

he gets over it himself — as he usually did in previous cases. Fortunately this does not prevent him from working but in the contrary induces him to more and more work.[81]

*   *   *

At the end of July — barely a month after arriving in Ossining and starting work on his memoirs, Stefan was able to report, 'I have finished in this month my autobiography, written it with my own hand so quickly that Lotte could not yet follow.'[82] He would now set aside the manuscript, which he explained stopped on the first day of World War II, for two months before deciding whether to make changes. 'I have no hurry to publish it', he wrote, 'I wanted only to have it ready.'[83]

The rapid progress on the autobiography allowed Stefan to finally make real plans to travel to Brazil. Two weeks after moving to Ossining, Stefan reserved passages to Rio, overcoming some of his annoyance at having to deal with wartime bureaucracy ('a lot of new regulations, exit permits, questions and questions, [meaning] our situation is frightfully complicated in every respect!'[84]), dealings that were anathema to the personal freedom that he yearned for. With the completion of his memoirs, exhausted from 'this wandering, this eternal indecision',[85] Stefan felt emotionally and physically drained but firmer in his mind that he was ready for Brazil: 'What I want, badly want, is some rest and Newyork is not the right place for it. I have worked hard and want a little dolce far niente.'[86]

On 5 August the Zweigs left Ossining for New York City, 'our mind is nearly made up',[87] wrote Lotte, over plans to return to Brazil. Even at this stage Stefan was uncertain that they would be able to leave New York, but he yearned to be able to 'sit somewhere quietly for a few months [as] I am extremely tired and a bore for Lotte and myself.'[88] A period of escape was needed, he continued, as 'the war was too long for my nerves with all this travelling around and I feel my age.'[89] But just a few days later, tickets in hand, Lotte was able to sound a more positive note: 'we feel better and more ready and willing to go.'[90] Relieved that a firm decision had been made about where their immediate future would lie, the couple tied up their affairs in New York, began saying their goodbyes and went shopping:

> . . . it is typically American that it is already [in August] difficult for me to find summer dresses. The sales started while we were away and the shops are practically sold out and at this very moment busy with selling furs and winter things. For Stefan it is easier because the mens' sales began much

later and are still on. About the sudden crisis in silk stockings you may have read in the papers. It was quite a panic when the silk import from Japan was stopped, the women rushed out to buy and hoard and it is with a kind of horror that they foresee the necessity of wearing cotton stockings. I cannot get very excited about it and actually bought less than I would otherwise have done as the prices already nearly doubled. I suppose if you get along without silk stockings, the Western Hemisphere will also be able to do so.[91]

While now resigned to be moving on, there was no excitement, let alone pleasure, at prospects ahead, as Stefan expressed in his final letter from New York to Hannah and Manfred:

Our hearts are not light at all, we do not know when we shall return as we have been here only on visitors visas and all depends if America enters the war. Alltogether it has been a very strenous time and especially in the last times we did not feel happy at all. Perhaps Brasil will help with his beauty — but I doubt more and more if ever I shall see Bath again. Sometimes we thought to leave everything and go back, but I feel I shall never in my life have more a real home — had we emigrated here like the others we could have said, here we begin a new life, but I was bound by my nationality which has and will give us still many problems. [. . .] My dear Hannah and Manfred, sometimes I feel very depressed, and doubt if we ever shall be together again, I wish only that you should see your child grown up and more sympathetic as ever — I always am frightened to read that this war will take still more than a year, this war, which has destroyed so much of our lives — I know that there are millions and millions like us, but everyone feels his own life. [. . .] I also have worked hard which means always that I am not in a good mood. Lotte is pysically much better now and perhaps we will have in Brazil a better time: only if this nomadic life would come to an end, I would like to live in a Negro hut in Brazil if I should know if I could stay there. Let us hope at least that you, the young generation, will still have the reward for these enormous efforts — for me it is too late and I could no more enjoy the victory. But you and your child will see a better world![92]

A few hours later Stefan and Lotte would board the SS *Uruguay*, heading for an uncertain future in Brazil.

Notes

1 LZ to HA&MA, New York City, 25 January 1941. Friderike claimed to have met Stefan Zweig at the British consulate, just a few hours after he had arrived in New York, an encounter that she put down to 'destiny' (Friderike Zweig, *Stefan Zweig*, London: W.H. Allen, 1946, p. 249).

2 LZ to HA&MA, New York City, 27 January 1941.

3 SZ to HA&MA, New York City, 27 January 1941.

4 LZ to HA&MA, New Haven, c. March 1941.

5 LZ to HA&MA, New Haven, 19 March 1941.

6 SZ to HA&MA, New York City, 31 March 1941.

7 LZ to HA&MA, New York City, 29 January 1941.

8 SZ to HA&MA, New York City, c. February 1941.

9 SZ to HA&MA, New York City, 31 March 1941.

10 LZ to HA&MA, New York City, 27 January 1941.

11 LZ to HA, New Haven, 15 February 1941.

12 SZ to HA&MA, New Haven, 13 March 1941.

13 SZ to HA&MA, New Haven, 13 February 1941.

14 See p. 194.

15 See p. 200.

16 See p. 201.

17 See p. 199.

18 Hendrik van Loon, see p. 199.

19 Yiddish for 'beggars' or 'spongers'. In German the word has come to mean 'freeloaders'.

20 SZ to HA&MA, New Haven, 12 March 1941.

21 LZ to HA&MA, New York City, 18 April 1941.

22 SZ to HA&MA, New York City, 12 May 1941.

23 SZ to HA&MA, New York City, c. April 1941.

24 SZ to HA&MA, New York City, early May 1941.

25 SZ to HA&MA, New York City, early May 1941.

26 See p. 200.

27 See p. 203.

28 See p. 201.

29 SZ to HA&MA, New York City, c. April 1941.

30 SZ to HA&MA, New York City, 12 May 1941.

31 See p. 202.

32 See p. 203.

33 LZ to HA&MA, New York City, 1 June 1941.

34 SZ to HA&MA, New York City, c. February 1941.

35 SZ to HA&MA, New York City, c. April 1941.

36 See p. 196.

37 SZ to HA&MA, New York City, c. May 1941.

38 SZ to HA&MA, New York City, c. May 1941.

39 SZ to HA&MA, New York City, c. February 1941.

40 SZ to IIA, New York City, 10 February 1941.

41 SZ to HA&MA, New Haven, 15 February 1941.
42 SZ to HA&MA, New Haven, 12 March 1941.
43 James Stern (b. County Meath, Ireland, 1904; d. Tisbury, Wiltshire, England, 1993), whose translations appeared under the name 'Andrew St. James'; he would also translate *Amerigo: A Comedy of Errors in History*.
44 SZ to HA&MA, New York City, 31 March 1941.
45 SZ to HA&MA, New York City, c. April 1941.
46 SZ to HA&MA, New York City, c. April 1941.
47 LZ to HA, Ossining, 21 July 1941.
48 SZ to HA&MA, Ossining, c. 19 July 1941.
49 LZ to HA&MA, New Haven, c. March or April 1941.
50 SZ to HA&MA, New Haven, 7 March 1941.
51 SZ to HA&MA, New Haven, 12 March 1941.
52 SZ to HA&MA, New York City, 5 April 1941.
53 SZ to HA&MA, New York City, 5 April 1941.
54 LZ to HA&MA, New Haven, c. March or April 1941.
55 LZ to HA&MA, New York City, 18 April 1941.
56 LZ to HA&MA, New Haven, c. March or April 1941.
57 LZ to HA&MA, New York City, 18 April 1941; LZ to HA&MA, New York City, 29 April 1941; SZ to HA&MA, New York City, 12 May 1941; HA&MA, New York City, 17 June 1941.
58 LZ to HA&MA, Ossining, 25 July 1941.
59 SZ to HA&MA, New York City, or May 1941.
60 SZ to HA&MA, New York City, or May 1941.
61 SZ to HA&MA, New York City, 17 June 1941.
62 LZ to HA, New York City, 25 June 1941.
63 LZ to HA&MA, Ossining, 4 July 1941.
64 LZ to HA&MA, Ossining, 4 July 1941.
65 LZ to HA, Ossining, 21 July 1941.
66 Friderike Zweig, *Stefan Zweig*, op. cit., p. 252.
67 LZ to HA&MA, New York City, 15 August 1941.
68 LZ to HA, Ossining, 21 July 1941. It is impossible to know whether meetings between the three were as relaxed as Lotte suggests. Certainly Friderike maintained an intense — in her view spiritual — attachment to her former husband. But in her biography of Stefan Zweig, Friderike could barely conceal that she did not consider Lotte as an equal: while claiming to be 'without a trace of bitterness' towards Stefan's young wife, she was also dismissive of what she regarded as 'her quiet, persistent simplicity' (Friderike Zweig, *Stefan Zweig*, op. cit., p. 250).
69 SZ to HA&MA, New York City, 1 July 1941.
70 SZ to HA&MA, New York City, 1 July 1941.
71 SZ to HA&MA, Ossining, 4 July 1941.
72 LZ to HA&MA, Ossining, 12 July 1941.
73 'Meine drei Leben' (My Three Lives) was Stefan Zweig's working title for his autobiography. The three lives that Zweig referred to were the period before World War I, the turbulent 15 years that followed the war, and the Hitler era.
74 SZ to HA&MA, New York City, c. late June 1941.

75 SZ to HA&MA, New York City, c. May 1941.
76 SZ to HA&MA, Ossining, 31 July 1941.
77 SZ to HA&MA, Ossining, c. 19 July 1941.
78 SZ to HA&MA, Ossining, c. 19 July 1941.
79 SZ to HA&MA, Ossining, c. 19 July 1941.
80 SZ to HA&MA, Ossining, c. 19 July 1941.
81 LZ to HA, Ossining, 21 July 1941.
82 SZ to HA&MA, Ossining, 31 July 1941.
83 SZ to HA&MA, Ossining, 31 July 1941.
84 SZ to HA&MA, Ossining, c. 19 July 1941.
85 SZ to HA&MA, Ossining, 31 July 1941.
86 SZ to HA&MA, Ossining, 31 July 1941.
87 LZ to HA&MA, New York City, 6 August 1941.
88 SZ to MA, New York City, 6 August 1941.
89 SZ to MA, New York City, 6 August 1941.
90 LZ to HA, New York City, 11 August 1941.
91 LZ to HA, New York City, 11 August 1941.
92 SZ to HA&MA, New York City, 15 August 1941.

PART III

Letters from Brazil
24 August 1941 to 22 February 1942

VIA AIR MAIL
Aug 24th, 41
ON-BOARD
S.S. Uruguay

Dear Hanna & Manfred,

We will soon be in Rio and I am glad that we took the boat which was very restful while the 'plane journey would have been most tiring. Eva will have written to you that Mrs. Sch. brought her down to the boat to see us off which was a thrilling way to begin her birthday — taking the train for NY long after bedtime and returning about 2 in the morning. [. . .] — We had an agreable trip and a good rest, I refused to work and also Stefan did not do too much. In Rio I shall immediately look for an apartment or small house so that we settle down at least for a few months.

I hope it will not take too long before we hear from you there and that it will be only good news. Has Marta already been in Bath and how did she feel as a guest? And has Mr. Honig who went back to England a month ago already been with you? We told him to come and see you, if necessary in Bath. We were with him quite frequently and liked him well.[1] — I am afraid my letter is not very coherent, but I am writing in the lounge, have heard the BBC News and American news while I read, not to speak of the people who pass etc. Anyhow, you know that my thoughts are with you most frequently. Now it is nearly two years since the beginning of the war and I remember those days most vividly. In these days on the boat, lying in the deck chairs all day long, I often indulged in day-dreaming and wishful thinking and I imagined how I would have enjoyed it could you have been next to me in one of the deck chairs. As this cannot be just now, we must keep contact by letter, and so please write frequently.

Best love and kisses
Lotte

Dear H. & M., Now we have to economise paper as the airmail takes from Rio only 5 grams. We had an extremely quiet voyage and are both again restored after the heavy strain of New York — I have never been so down as in the last weeks and Lotte too has not been too fresh. What we want both is some months in a quiet place and not Hotel life; we hope to find this near Rio. In America you feel already the war in the atmosphere, the preparations are tremendous our life became still more expensive than it was — I believe we have seen for the last time the splendour and the luxury there as this war will unfortunately be a very long one and the expenses are simply fantastic. We have here with the sister of Morgentau, who has the whole financial preparation in hand, her husband is from Vienna and architect since many years in New York; I start already learning Portuguese as I shall stay at least six months here — we do not know when it will be possible to go to the States and if it will be the right thing for us who are longing to have rest from travelling; it was hard for us to leave Eva behind but we feel that she is better there with her "auntie" than with us who do not know where to we go; perhaps I have to lecture again in Argentine. I believe I was right to go to Brazil where I have a right for permanent stay while in America I was only a visitor and in case of war I would have had all these little annoyances as a foreigner (a friendly one in this case). I hope you have got my letter about the house, it is important for me that you dispose in such a way that you can take it over completely — Don't think about me, I have written all in the chimney[2] what I had (as one said in school) and I feel happy with everything you can use of what I have — my clothes, shoes, furniture and so on; I hear that in England clothing, suits, etc are difficult to get and so you could let change some of mine for Manfred, and some of Lottes things for you. We want here nothing of all that and I feel, I shall never use it any more. Please make me the pleasure to use everything but everything as if it were yours. As soon as we have a definitive address we shall wire immediately to you. Kindest regards to you all. Yours   Stefan Zweig

We write this still on the ship and you shall soon have news from us. My book will be sent directly to you by the publisher and I hope to come through soon with the other, which I wrote in Ossining.

1 Camille Honig, see p. 198. Lotte Zweig had been impressed that Honig had 'worked his way up and knows a lot about art and literature'. LZ to HA&MA, Ossining, 27 July 1941.

2 From the idiom 'etwas in den Rauchfang schreiben', meaning 'I have detached myself from everything'. ('Rauchfang' is an Austrian word for 'chimney'.)

HOTEL CENTRAL c/o EDITORA GUANABARA
RIO DE JANEIRO 132 RUA OUVIDOR
BRASIL

31.8.41

Dear Hanna u. Manfred,

We have well arrived on Wednesday and are glad to be here in a somewhat quieter atmosphere. Nothing has changed while we were away,
we have the same room in the same hotel, the same big terrace with
the splendid view on the bay on which Stefan spends most of his time
working, and even the food is still the same. Two days after our arrival we
went to Petropolis by car — a little more than 1½ hours on a beautiful
and well-kept road — and looked for a little house. It is altogether more
difficult than we thought because all the old or wealthy families have
houses of their own and very few houses are to be let. Tuesday we will go
there again and there is hope that we may find something. In that case we
would move up to Petropolis in about a fortnight and come down to Rio
once or twice a week. There are plenty of buses between the two places
and also a railroad of an already venerable age. Going immediately to
Petrop. and settling down there has the great advantage that we need not
move again when summer begins in December. Petrop. is the summer
resort for all who want to remain near Rio, more so than Brighton and
Eastbourne were for London. While still in Rio we gradually see our
friends again and shall also take Portuguese lessons. We read fluently
and understand already fairly well, but now we also must begin to speak
it. — Through the long boat trip of 12 days New York seems already very
far away and besides missing Eva (and Amity Hall also a little) I do not
regret having left the States again. It is strange: nearly all the Europeans
down here in South Amer. dream of going to the States while many of
those who are there find it very difficult to adapt themselves and wish
they could leave and live in South Am. — Arriving in Rio we found
your letter of Aug. 8th, forwarded from Newyk and I hope we will soon
hear from you again and hear more about yourself and Manfred's work.

Best love and kisses
Lotte

We are now four days here and feel allright — happy would be too much because I cannot adapt myself to this nomadic life without a house and without books, we remain Europeans for ever and will feel everywhere strangers. I have no "pep" like the Americans say and also writing will be difficult after the autobiography — all I have to tell is so far away what America likes to read and to hear. Lotte is somewhat better but we dream always to be fresh and enterprising and cannot more find the right "elan" — the war is too long for me and still far from his end. Our life in Petropolis (or here) will be a solitary one because we do not like more society and I have refused to make public appearance for the next time — we will study Portuguese to feel more sure and I hope to continue to work. In New York we had too many people and here not enough of

[Incomplete letter from Stefan Zweig]

Friday, Sept 4th, 41

HOTEL CENTRAL
RIO DE JANEIRO
BRASIL

Dearest Hanna,

Please stop worrying about us, we will be alright, and even if things do not always go for us as we would like it and if we complain once in a while, don't take it too seriously. Those last weeks in USA with all the indecision were difficult, but now that we are here we are going to settle down again. We have already found a house in Petropolis which suits our purpose very well. It is small — bungalow style — has a large terrace with a beautiful view over the mountains, you climb to it from the street on a number of steps, it has a small garden and is tolerably furnished. We are satisfied to have found it, as it is not at all easy and most houses are either dreadfully ugly or dreadfully expensive. The servant question which I am told is also difficult, also promises to be solved for us for the time being as the couple who looks after the house at present will probably remain until I find what I need. Being without servants is in so far very disagreeable here in Petropolis the kitchen stoves are exactly of the type of children's toy stoves and have to be looked after all the time. We hope to be able to go up to Petoprolis next weekend and intend to come to Rio fairly frequently. It is still very quiet in Petr. and the air reminds one even of a European spring. We shall cable you the address as soon as we definately go up there and I repeat it here

34 Rua GONCALVEZ DIAS
Petropolis, Brasil

but please note that it is only for cables. Letters please continue to address to Editora GUANABARA, they will be forwarded immediately from there by a professional messenger which is safer than trust them to the change of the little railroad and delivery in Petropolis. [. . .] — I must close now, first of all our Portuguese teacher just arrived and secondly the mail for to-morrow's clipper closes in a few minutes. — We have received today your letter of Aug, 20th and Mama's of Aug 22nd, not so bad really, just a fortnight.

Love to all, best wishes for the solutions of the serving question[1] in Bath, Lotte

Dear Hannah & Manfred, we have your letter of August 20th today Sept 4th. I am sorry that the house in Bath gives you so much trouble — especially as I doubt more and more that we shall ever see it again. Please to spare yourself and do not do not too much work, the coming times will ask from us all our strength. As to Wilmots[2] boss I wrote you already that you shall not worry too much; I am convinced that I shall have with him serious discussions and I do not wish that you shall be mixed in my personal troubles. Thanks so much to have given the manuscript of my Balzac[3] to Cassells[4]; it would be wonderful if I could get it one day and continue my work quickly. Lotte will write you about our intention in to go to Petropolis; I want absolutely a few months rest and in any case I shall not give any lectures before spring. We cannot see any more trunks, suitcases, we are tired of Hotels, of changes. — I wish I could report to you that Lotte is quite right. Unfortunately she has seldom a quiet night and I hope only that the treatment will finaly give her complete recovery. It is perhaps also the nomadic life whith its danger of climate and surroundings which was not favorable to us both — I have finished the autobiography in the greatest strain only to finish it before leaving New York and will now work on it quietly. At least six months we hope to stay in Petropolis — you know how I like to travel but now we feel we have overdone it. It will be an absolute retired life without society, theatres and (the only thing I miss) without books and we even do not start to think what we shall do afterwards. Here in Rio the first news we received was that the poor Count Huyn[5] died on the consequence of an angina (streptococic poisoning) — Frischauers have phoned but we have not yet seen him, has made a book on the president and will get much money out of the funds: you know how I admire his ability. I have seen so many of the best in New York unable to earn a cent that I find it mesterly how he always invents new possibilities to live largely. Give Eisemann my kindest regards. My indifference against books etc. comes from the condition that I shall never see them and I wish you would keep them or the best of them for you. We are all very confident in final victory, more much more than before but there is no doubt that it will take some time — some years perhaps — as the enormous preparations of the United States will be in full swing from now on. Here everybody is for Britain but you in England will have still much burdens to bear. Kindest regards,

Stefan

1 Servant question.
2 Stefan Zweig's London solicitor.
3 Stefan Zweig's biography on Honoré de Balzac (1799–1850), the French writer and intellectual.
4 Stefan Zweig's British publisher.
5 Until the *Anschluss*, Count Huyn served as press attaché at the Austrian Embassy in London. In 1939 he became a newsreader with BBC radio's German Service.

EDITORA GUANABARA   Rio, Sept. 13th, 41.
~~*WAISEMAN KOOGAN LTDA.*~~
~~*LIVREIROS E EDITORES*~~
~~*RUA DO OUVIDOR, 132*~~
~~*TELEPH. 22-7231*~~
RIO DE JANEIRO
END. TELEG.: EDIGUA — BRASIL

Dear Hanna & Manfred,

No news from you yet this week, but so far two letters from Eva, they are already in the new house and she writes very cheerfully. [. . .] — From us there is not much to report. I had a cold and did not go out much last week, and Stefan spends four to six hours daily at the dentist's. Our only regular "work" were the Portuguese lessons every day, a rather boring business, as we both have no love for this language and rather resent it — Spanish would have been so much more convenient and easy while we are quite sure that we will never master the pronunciation of Portuguese. Anyhow, it has to be done, the Brazilians naturally prefer their language to French in the long run, and keeping a house absolutely requires Portuguese. About the house in Petropolis I have written in detail in the enclosed letter to Mama, and you will hear more about my experiences when we will be up there. — I have thought over what you wrote about mother coming to Bath for a visit, and there is for my opinion not the slightest reason why she should visit there while you have a household and service troubles. I can understand that she would like to return to London and that she prefers being near Manfred, you and her friends to just personal safety which, I have come to think, is not worth too much trouble and isolation. On the other hand I would have acted like you did, declining all responsibility and advising rather that she stays on where she is. But I do not see any reason why she should go to Bath now, and I am sure she does not even want it. She has had country life enough for a while, she does not need a rest, and what else does Bath and Rosemount offer now that neither we nor Eva are there? So do not worry about this now. If mother[1] really returns to London — she did not mention this intention to me and I did not write to her about it — and again has spent a winter there, this problem might arise, but how much will have happened until then?! — I hope that you are both well and that Manfred will soon find the job he wants. Do not bother too much about us and our problems, every European is bound to have his worries in one way or the other nowadays, and if only the war goes well, everything will have been worth while. So do not worry if Rosemount has to be neglected for a while, and don't let other affairs of ours take too much time and thought. We know you manage everything as well or better than we could do it, and we only hate the thought to burden you with our affairs, you must have enough of your own.

Warmest greetings to all and love to you.
Lotte

1 Therese Altmann, see p. 194.

Rio, Sept. 13th, 41

EDITORA GUANABARA
~~*WAISEMAN KOOGAN LTDA.*~~
~~*LIVREIROS E EDITORES*~~
RUA DO OUVIDOR, 132
~~*TELEPH. 22–7231*~~
RIO DE JANEIRO
END. TELEG.: EDIGUA — BRASIL

Dearest mother,

I have received your two letters of Aug 19th (addressed to NY) and of
Aug 22nd and hope to have good news from you again soon and hear
that you can stay on in the same house which you seem to like. We
have taken a house in Petropolis and will move up there some time
next week. It is quite small, really only a bungalow and separate servants quarters as all the houses are arranged up there — I suppose still
a remnant from the days of slavery — but we like it. It is built halfway
up in a hill and has a beautiful view on mountains from a big covered
terrace where I suppose Stefan will spend his days working. You walk up
to it a number of steps through a nice little garden which the landlady
promised will be full of hortensias in the summer. Behind the house
immediately is the hill, but a few steps further up the gardens is just
preparing a plateau and he promised to build a little summer house as
well — so I shall take this as my residence during the day, and maybe
later on, when the season begins, I shall change place with Stefan so as
to hide him from unexpected visitors. I have been very lucky in so far
as the landlady has solved the servants' question for me. The gardener
and his wife will continue to live in the servants' quarters and he will
look after the garden, act as handy-man and do errands if necessary. He
works in a factory and does all for us after his work, and besides their
living in my place I shall have nothing to do with them — they do their
own cooking etc. During the day a cook-general will come and do all
the housework, preparing and cooking. All our friends, meaning well
without doubt, have been warning me how difficult it is with servants in
Petropolis. Those from Rio do not go up there because it is too primitive — the cooking is done on old-fashioned stoves which have to be
heated with wood, the servants quarters are very primitive etc — and the
servants in Petr. itself are supposed to be lazy and inefficient. But I am
not frightened. I know that the gardener lives in the house I shall not be
left quite alone with all the work, and I believe that after England and

U.S.A. I do not expect too much from servants. In any case we are very keen to get settled for a few months at least and to live a quiet retired life. We both have at the moment no desire at all to see people or to go out a lot. Even here in Rio which we both love so much, we go out very little and are satisfied with the view from our terrace which makes for all the defects of the hotel which is clean and has good service but which run too much on the principles of the Haushaltungschule,[1] especially with regard to the food and all possible economies. — So far we have both still been rather tired and I was at home with a disagreable cold for some days. So we declined all invitations for receptions, cocktails etc. and just saw privately a few friends. We have Portuguese lessons every day and can speak although with many mistakes almost all that is necessary and even carry on a conversation in Portugese if there is no other way out. But it is rather an ugly language and a great pity that just this country does not belong to the Spanish group. Spanish is so much easier for us and so much more beautiful as language. The above address remains valid even when we are in Petr.[2]

Love and kisses   Lotte

HOTEL CENTRAL
RIO DE JANEIRO
BRASIL

Dear H & M. We are going to Petropolis in two days and hope to live there quietly for some time. Before I have thought much what you had to suffer at your dentist as I had no less than two protheses to get — now I am a real Englishman having my artificial teeth to take out every evening. It was an excellent Viennese dentist who really worked wonder in making with his craftsman those two big protheses in six days instead of six weeks and without any pain for me. Now this is done and if Lotte would get rid of her asthma we could live and work quietly after the long months of troubles and strain.

I have met here Manfred's brother in law.[3] He arrived here a year ago, was between in the United States and has the intention to stay here for the next months, at least half a year. Last year he had still all his obligations against his former boss, and he hopes as he stabilises here and has his "permanent stay" granted since November 1940 that he will be free of his former obligations for the coming year. You cannot imagine how it complicates his situation to be at once bound to the new firm, the American one and the old one and he hopes that one day he can clear his situation against the former one. He would like to rent an appartment for good — we ourselves have taken the tiny house in Petropolis for seven months only but if it pleases us we can take it for longer so that we have also a permanent address and residence. It is possible that I shall give some lectures in Argentine in spring, but we will keep meanwhile the residence; it contains alltogether 3—4 tiny rooms with a large terrace which will be my real working room and we shall have a black servant girl who lives near the house and if they prove as good as they are cheap we will rejoice. Most important for me is now to finish the autobiography which is practically ready but wants revising and enlarging and then to try to write again some short stories or a novel, something substantial and if the Balzac manuscript arrives I shall be safe. Thanks for all dear Hannah and please use everything in Bath as if it were yours; I hope this winter will be better than the last one and in the great decision the odds are now on our side and whatever happens, a world without Hitler will be a better world. Yours

Stefan

1   A school where one learns how to manage a household.
2   Petrópolis.
3   As Manfred did not have a brother-in-law in either Brazil or the United States, it is not clear who is being referred to here.

---

c/o EDITORA GUANABARA   *PETROPOLIS (BRASIL)*
132, RUA OUVIDOR   *(34, RUA GONÇALVES DIAS)*
RIO DE JANEIRO   3.10.41

My dear Hanna,

We have just received your, Manfred's and Victor's[1] letter of Sept 7th, and nobody can understand your feelings about Eva and things in general better than we do, who on the other side of the question have just the same alternating periods of being depressed, reasonable, and sometimes optimistic, sometimes resigned. And we know from our experience that in such moments of depression the only reasonable answer — that we should be glad that our fears were exaggerated and our precautions perhaps superfluous — does not help one feel better. But I hope that in the meantime you have already got out of that mood, that now you have fewer things on your mind and no urgent question to settle. I can imagine how long it took you to come to the decision to send Ursula back to her parents although on the other hand it seems natural that they should have her at their home again instead of living separately.[2] I hope, especially for your sake, and also because Miller[3] seems a part of Rosemount that he is better again and fully appreciate that you continue with his salary so that he can afford to be cured effectively instead of trying to rush back to work. But I am sorry that in this moment the garden gives you an enormous amount of work and little pleasure, and I do wish I could be with you and do my own share. Instead I am sitting here in our little bungalow, learning again how to cook by showing the maid how to do it, and in spite of the language difficulties am having an easy time of it, being busy mostly re-writing parts of the autobiography for Stefan, and when the weather — in rare moments so far — is good, we go out for walks. We are already quite settled here, Stefan has his barber, his coffee-houses, his writing-table, and I know my shops and already most of the household and shopping expressions. No need to say that sometimes it is a phantastic thought to live in a little mountain town in Brazil, but we are quite happy here and certainly did well to come here instead of remaining in the States. [. . .] — In the meantime you may already have got the Brazil book and will learn more about the reasons of our love for this country. Strangely enough we have now for the first time again a number of books in our own language, there are two lending libraries in Rio and here we met a Mr. Stormberg from Berlin who has all the usual modern books which one had to have. And as the chess takes also some time every day, we are quite busy even without all the people who promised to visit us here. To-morrow I believe Paul[4] will come up. The last time I saw him and Maritza[5] in Rio they looked unbelievably modest, bourgeois and normal. Maritza was cleanly and well dressed with carefully groomed hair, doing needle-work, play-ing chess with Stefan, and Paul too seemed quite harmless and just friendly.

Kindest regards, fondest love,
Lotte

Tell Friedenthal that we found here in the lending library his volume "Marie Rebscheider"[6] and have read and re-read it with great pleasure and regretted more than before that his new novel is not yet finished. Can you find out — perhaps via Hirschfeld, Fairhazel Gdns[7] — what happened to Lotte Schiff.[8] I have not heard from her since June in spite of various letters addressed to the Raebaun address in the country and am worried.

Dear H. & M. I can really confirm that we have here in our little bungalow absolutely the life I wanted after the strenoous times in New York etc. I have as my real workroom a large covered terrace in front of the beautiful mountains, the neighbourhood is very primitive and therefore pitroresque, the poor people are so nice here as you cannot imagine; our black housemaid is silent (she begins to sing now), diligent, clean and grateful to us as she learns to see things she never has seen in her life — for them potatoes are already a luxury and fish is an unknown animal. She takes our empty tins at home as a treasure and uses them there as glasses But nevertheless she is clean and it is the inborn civilisation and humanity I admire so much here in this country. Lotte is busy; you would not believe it as we make very few walks and see no people that the day passes so quickly away, that we are quite suprised to be here already three weeks. I am happy that Lotte likes this kind of life as much as I do; I am only not quite satisfied with her health. She has cheeted me first in having no dowry, now in loosing weight by her damned asthma, which is somewhat better but every night there are one or two dialogues between her and a dog in a house far away. Whenever she begins to cough the dog begins to bark as the air is quite still and transmits every sound in a great distance. I insist that she now makes a cure to get some embonpoint, because here life is so quiet and easy that I wish she should take provisions for her bad times which are expecting us in the future. Alltogether I cannot tell you how happy we are to have left New York where our life did not belong to us and we had all kind of problems, while here we live forgotten and forgetting the time, the world (but not you). Frischauer is as always the object of my most fervent admiration, he earns here with his Vargas book at least twenty times what I with my book having all subventions, connexions and that was not easy coming here without to know anybody or a word of Portuguese.[9] How I regret that I did not move to Brasil five years ago, you have no idea of the fantastic prosperity — a house which was worth 100 £ five years ago cost now 500 or even a thousand, but life still is cheap, all the native things in excellent quality as people have not yet learned to use substitutes. And we told you already what we pay, overpaying the usual rates — 5 dollars a month to our maid while in America one had to pay 60 or 80 and she takes there two holidays a week. I do not generally be mean, but you understand what a relief it is to know that one can still live cheaply somewhere and will not be dependent from newspapers and agents. How you would like this country, so colourfull and peaceful in such a time. — Let me tell you that your letters are expected with the greatest interest — I hope this winter will not be too hard. Give Eisemann my love, I should really write to him, but it is not the higher postage but the feeling that every letter takes much longer than one does not write so easily as in the U.S.A.

Love and greetings to all! Stefan

1 Victor Fleischer, see p. 196.
2 Hannah's niece, Ursula Mayer (see p. 200) had been living at the Zweigs' house in Bath.
3 Mr Miller, the Zweigs' gardener in Bath.
4 Paul Frischauer, see p. 196.
5 Paul Frischauer's wife.
6 Richard Friedenthal's 1927 novel, *Marie Rebscheider*.
7 Fairhazel Gardens, near Swiss Cottage in north London, where many Central European Jews settled.
8 Lotte Schiff, a close friend of Lotte Zweig from Frankfurt.
9 Getúlio Vargas: Brazilian president, 1930–44; 1950–54. Paul Frischauer's book, *Presidente Vargas*, was published in New York by Random House in 1942 and in São Paulo by the Companhia Editora Nacional in 1944; see p. 196.

---

c/o EDITORA GUANABARA   *PETROPOLIS (BRASIL)*
132, RUA OUVIDOR   *(34, RUA GONÇALVES DIAS)*
RIO DE JANEIRO   11.10.41

> You can use the Petropolis address
> but for heaven's sake don't omit
> to mark it very clearly "Brasil".
> My nightmare is that the letter
> might go to Greece instead.

Dear Hanna and Manfred,

Waiting for Stefan to begin his dictation I start to answer your letter of Sept. 18th which only confirms receipt of our letter from the boat. How much time has already passed since our journey, and Mr and Mrs Wiener with whom we travelled down will already return to New York in a fortnight. We wrote you about them — she is the daughter of the old Mr. Morgenthau,[1] he is a Viennese architect living in NY since many years. [. . .] — We are now completely settled, the house is just what we need in its size and position, the maid is improving visibly in cooking and al-right in all other respects, and only the weather is miserable so far. Stefan has been working hard, and in consequence I too and we are

145

very satisfied. We had one or two visitors from Rio in spite of the weather, the first were Paul and Maritza,[2] and — as I wrote before — they appear quite different from what I know them to be — nice, normal, modest and friendly, Maritza well-groomed, even with red finger nails and I do not know if it is their immense ability of adapting themselves to their surroundings or a policy of becoming respectable or anything else. He seems to be writing the book on Vargas, she talks of buying land, starting production of tomato juice, and as I know the man she wants to do it with, there may even be some truth in it. And as she speaks already fluent Portuguese and does really beautiful needlework, I envied her with all my house-wifely instincts which develop in an alarming way — if I see a woman, I am anxious to talk about household, prices and recipees, and one my favourite books is the Portuguese cookery book where I am discovering the most fascinating recipees. — Here in Petr. we have so far seen few people. A very nice woman lives here, Gabriela Mistral,[3] a Chilean writer, and we went to see her the other day. The trouble is that she speaks Spanish, and so my Esperanto mixture became worse than ever. Then we know a well-known doctor next door whom we see on weekends, also very nice, an estate dealer, builder or speculator as you like to call him, of German origin who lives here many years, wants to invite us and is recommended as pro-allied, and that is all so far and quite enough so far. — I was glad to know that Honig[4] had safely arrived and that you were going to see him. I wonder how you liked him, it took me in the beginning some time to find out that he is really a very nice man. — I hope Miller is better and will soon be able to work again. If not, don't bother about anything which is not really essential for your own food. — Is anything decided about Peter going away? And where are they going?

Love and kisses
Lotte.

I asked you about Lotte[5] the other day, but I had a letter last week. She works at Lyons[6] now and lives with her mother.

c/o EDITORA GUANABARA　　　　　*PETROPOLIS (BRASIL)*
132, RUA OUVIDOR　　　　　　　*(34, RUA GONÇALVES DIAS)*
RIO DE JANEIRO

Dear Hannah and Manfred, we came down for one day to Rio to bid farewell to our friends Wiener Morgenthau[7] who leave in two days for New York. It is for us already a very strange feeling to be again in a big town because we live in Petropolis such a peasant life. All is primitive — Lotte will have given you details about the cooking — but this has a great charm; isolation in these moments is a kind of happiness and I have there my natural life, reading, working and I feel myself much more useful than in New York. We really wanted some rest after these long months and I am unfortunately convinced that our nerves in the next months and years have to be prepared for strenuous times; I am glad that Lotte likes this retired life as much as I do. For the moment I cannot imagine that I ever would like to live otherwise than in this retired way but who can tell was if expecting still us all? In this country you feel that one can live with very few money and one does not really want much from life, while in New York you are much more occupied with material things. A foreigner who does not know us would call our life here monotonous and tedious, but you know how we like quiet walks, quiet reading — alltogether we went one single time to the cinema, we have no wish to hear much except from you. I have really resigned to see anything I owned before and I feel much better not more to be troubled by hopes and fears; in my age one has to learn the "vita contemplativa" and to leave all fame and wealth to the others. We are not quite sure if we should not have a dog — only we fear to get attached if one day we should have to move or to leave again. — I hope that you have followed my advice and do not worry about the house in Bath, I see no reason why you should loose your time with lost things and I am sure that also Mrs Raumann will keep it in good order. My dear, I know how full your life is and how many things Manfred and you have to do and it is for me a disagreable feeling that you should care for our things, which are as all others subject to all chances and will be after more a burden than a pleasure. Please go only there if you like it for yourself and not out of a sentiment of duty against us. We are expecting your news about Manfred and if he will find the right position. From our little life without any events there is no more to report — so only our kindest regards to all and love to you both. Stefan

1 Alma Wiener, who was married to the architect and urban planner Paul Wiener, see p. 204.
2 Paul and Maritza Frischauer, see p. 196.

3 See p. 201.
4 Camille Honig, see p. 198.
5 Lotte Schiff.
6 A chain of tearooms and restaurants in London.
7 Paul Wiener (see p. 204) and his wife Alma Wiener, née Morgenthau.

[Petrópolis, undated, possibly the end of October or the beginning of November 1941]

Dear H. &. M. I would not have believed that in my sixtieth year I would sit in a little Brazilian village, served by a barefoot black girl and miles and miles away from all that was formerly my life, books, concerts, friends, conversation. But we feel extremely happy here, the little bungalow with its large covered terrace (our real living room) has a splendid view over the mountains and just in front a tiny cafehaus, called "Café Elegante" where I can have a delicious café for a halfpenny and enjoy the company of black mule-drivers. Life is here very cheap and you have no opportunity to spend. I am working and in my idle hours I play the master-games of a big chess book — one feels far away from all and even the war. It was really necessary for us to stabilise for longer time, we were both frightfully tired, Lotte more by her asthma and myself by psychic depressions; here in the solitude we hope to get new strength also alas, we will want much strength. The news from Europe are so depressing, thank God not the military ones but those from the occupied territories — I am afraid, millions will starve while here all is in peace and full prosperity. There is here now a quite new nationalism starting, Brasil feels that it will become important in war and peace, but the people themselves are very nice. We try to speak Portuguese but it is difficult for me because of my Spanish which interferes continuously. — From Wilmot[1] I have a letter and I see that he tries to clear my position for next year. Altogether I regard everything as lost and would be glad if you could enjoy of all as long as it is possible — nobody has an idea what enormous economic changes this war will produce, also America will be another country after the war. For you, the younger generation all this has practical interest, not more for me — in four years or even three I will not be able and willing to adapt myself to the new world, it belongs to your daughter, who will, I hope, see and enjoy better times. I wish we could send you some chocolate or coffee and sugar, which is ridicusly cheap here but we have not yet found out any possibility. I repeat my wish, my urgent wish, that you may use all clothes, underwear, linnen, overcoats and also whatever we have there — it has not sense to reuse it for years and I am sure I will never use all this. You do me only a favour and you will see that I feel much better with this idea. I have then less to regret of what I shall never see more.

Yours Stefan

1 Stefan Zweig's London solicitor.

Petropolis, 28.10.41

Dear Hanna & Manfred,

Thanks for your letter from Bath (Oct 6th) with Victor's[1] letter and your report about all the changes in Bath. It really is a shame that Rosemount gives you continually so much trouble and that Marta who likes Bath and would make everything so much easier for you there, is not allowed to go there.[2] Looking back over the last year it seems to me that every few weeks you had a different and never very simple problem there, and that makes me feel that perhaps after all it is not worth so much thought, time and work which you seem to give it. I felt alright about it as long as long as I thought that you got more out of it in terms of rest, pleasure and fruit and vegetables than it cost you, but now it seems that you allow Rosemount to absorb too much of your time and thought and I sincerely wish you would not do it. If it can't be helped, let it be closed or even billeted; what does it matter in times like ours if a few books are lost or the furniture spoilt a little! It is more important and quite in accordance with our wishes that you don't allow yourself to be dominated by its problems and certainly you must not spend more time there than you really want. So please — if it makes you stay away from Manfred, close the house, neglect it or leave it to its fate. — As to the changes themselves: I am sorry that Miller is still ill and hope he recovers once more. In the meantime I hope the other gardner does all the essential work so that you need'nt bother about that. — That Rauman's are gone is perhaps — if you have a good help in Hilda[3] — for the best for all concerned, and if they chose to look after Lorle[4] and help her to get on without spoiling her completely also Marta ought to be satisfied. For you, I believe Hilda will be much more useful if she is able to keep house alone without your doing and worrying about every little detail. I suppose that Lore after all had to be told everything and did not do more than that. About the new people I can only hope that you get on well together and that for both parties the different milieu of the other is a matter of interest and not of conflict. How good that you used to read the court circular in former times, so you are not quite so ignorant as you might have been. Did they already suggest some other people you could take in as well? By the way what has become of Lizzie,[5] she has disappeared from your letters completely? Is she still in London? — You ask whether we get all your letters. I hope we do and there seems to be no visible gap between them, they arrive usually in intervals from ten to 14 days. — I am glad for you that Smolletts can stay on, I fully understand that you don't want more changes than you can help. We, too, have enough of that and are content to lead here a solitary quiet life without even being eager to meet one or two really nice people whom we know here. We have been and are working hard to finish the autobiography and now I must go back to work. Somehow it seems to take longer to copy, change and type than it takes Stefan to make the changes.

Love and kisses
Lotte

Tell Manfred he need not bother to read the letter, it really only concerns and interests you, Hanna.

1   Victor Fleischer, see p. 196.
2   Martha Kahn, see p. 198. For the duration of the war many sections of the Admiralty were relocated to Bath where, due to security, 'enemy aliens' were prohibited from residing.
3   Hilda Miller, the daughter of the Zweigs' gardener in Bath.
4   Lorle was a niece and adopted daughter of Martha Kahn.
5   Litzi Philby, see p. 201.

[Undated — between 28 October and 1 November 1941]

PETROPOLIS (BRASIL)
(34, RUA GONÇALVES DIAS)

Dear Hannah & Manfred, before all my thanks I just got a letter from the Viking press that the Balzac manuscript has safely arrived and I have asked to forward it; of course I cannot finish it here having no books and material in this virgin country, but I can revise and — if I may say so — "play" with the book and prepare in some parts the definitive form. Our life is here seen from outward very monotonous, we work and read and go out for a walk without to meet people and so nothing is to tell; in our inner heart we feel as you that the war takes out of lives much of the best — I can understand how you miss your daughter and often we talk if we should not have taken her with us. But how can we offer to her such an isolated life in the years where a child wants society friends and "anregung"[1] and then — we see not all what shall become of us, where we have to go and when we can decide any thing. The proportions of this war are over our human possibility of foresight and I try (in vain) not to think of the far future; I write my books in a kind of tour de force only to suggest to myself that I am still existing, but I know very well, that my real public is gone and will never come back and that I am like this man at Grillparzers[2] goes living behind his own funeral. It is good to read Montaigne[3] in these days and all those who give good lessons in resignation. Would you be so kind to forward the inclosed letter to Maria Budberg,[4] I have lost her adress and would let her know that I have immediately written some lines for H. G. Wells[5] birthday. Yours ever

Stefan

1 German for 'stimulation'.
2 Franz Grillparzers (1791–1872): Austrian dramatist especially known for his tragedies.
3 Michel de Montaigne (1533–92): French courtier, essayist and biographer during the reign of France's Charles IX.
4 See p. 194.
5 See p. 204.

Petropolis, 7. XI. 41

My dear Hanna,

I haven't heard from you for quite a while and I really miss your letter. I hope it is just a postal delay and that there was no special reason to keep you from writing. Today the Balzac-Manuscript arrived from New York which it had reached it seems, in the beginning of last month. Stefan and I can't quite agree; he thinks it is complete as far as he wrote it while I seem to remember that it ended with his death. But no doubt you sent all there was, and I hope that bringing it to Sir Newman Flower[1] it did not take you much time and maybe gave you some conversation material with the new inhabitants in Rosemount. I am anxious to know whether you get on well with them and whether they are the right people for you to have in the house. I would be so hapy to know that at last in Bath you have a settled household without a new problem every few weeks, and especially that it is no more a "must" but only a pleasure for you to go there. How are you satisfied with Hilda Miller? Does she really prove to be a housekeeper or does she bother you with every little matter of shopping and menu. Mr Miller, I hope, has recovered in the meantime, give him our kindest regards in any case. Do you remember how you and I were more in favour of taking another gardner? And now you depend mostly on him and his family. — From us there is little to tell. Petropolis is still quiet and will not become crowded before Christmas. We know a few people here, but do not see very much of them, and it is quite an odd assortment — a Chilean poetess (who is at the same time Consul for Chile up here), a very nice and intelligent woman, a German refugee whose main pride is the family reputation they once had in Spandau, a German emigree of post-war and ardent anti-Nazi, and a French-Brazilian intellectual who now lives here with his old mother.[2] And to-morrow we are invited in a house of people who once stopped us in the street on the ground that the woman had written an article on Stefan's book. They seem nice and speak French, so it may be a pleasant evening. But we are not eager to see people and not even to go out for walks as the weather lately has again been bad, although fortunately no more cold. — As I gave you such long information about my household troubles in the beginning I just want to mention that now I have got over the first difficulties and also over the household complex which possessed me for a few week's during which my only desire when I met people was to discuss prices and cooking. My maid is not a genius, but has learned (and so have I) to make Palatschinken,[3] Schmarren[4] and Erdapfelnudeln[5] and other "European" dishes. When I have time and feel well I even have pleasure in showing her new things, if not, I carefully make the menu so that I need not talk to her. My memory in what regards household is going back further and further and Marta[6] would be able to give me good advice from what she remembers from early times in Ettlingen. We have a plain wooden floor, and lately the gardner came to wax it. For their purpose they took out all the furniture, placed the poor little carpets somewhere outside and beat them with a stick; my laundry is carefully treated with Waschblau,[7] the Mayonnaise is again made by hand instead coming out of a bottle, and the chicken you buy alive on the market and kill them at home — but so far I have not had the courage to go and buy one and carry it home in a piece of paper, tucked under my arm, and my maid is too modest to buy well. Soon, I suppose, I shall take to making my own cream cheese (it is not known here) and pickling my meat. Also the memory of our old lemon cream is sometimes trying to come back, and I wish I could buy custard powder or know how to produce it from natural ingredients. But please believe me — I am not an ardent and possessed housewife and would not have the time for it if I wanted it for I have been working hard as secretary again and suppose that it will continue. Besides this I am playing chess and reading a few classics, while the study of Portuguese has come somehow to be neglected, although of course the newspapers are only in Portuguese now and our radio does not pick up other than Brazilian stations. If you see Frederick Kuh[8] you may tell him that for a while there were daily articles from him in the *Correio da Manhã*[9] which I read with great interest. Lately there have been very few what I regret. — A fortnight ago we sent a sample package of chocolate and I am curious if and when and in what condition you receive it. It is only allowed to send one pound including wrapping. Would you be interested — if the regulations allow it — in getting similar little parcels of rice or coffee or sugar? Cigarettes, I am afraid, are forbidden. I know you are not badly off with food, yet it seems such a shame to have so much of everything here and one feels like sending parcel after parcel to share it. Is the central heating still working this year? And in your flat?

Our friends Wiener[10] must be home in New York now and I hope they will go and see Eva soon and bring her our love as well as a small parcel. And they even promised to write me how they find her. — In these days we expect a man from New York who was with us on the boat going over and whom we since met in every country. He has even been in Amity Hall because he knows the Schaeffers,[11] but I am not sure whether he has seen Eva as he is a business man and only was there at night. But he will probably have something to tell us about her.

Do write again soon, and please try to enjoy Bath more and work as little as possible for it.

Love and kisses
Lotte.

Stefan is busy working, and as the boy just goes to the Post Office — we never trust our letters to an ordinary letter box — I send the letter for once without his greetings. Sorry to have bothered you about the second copy of the Balzac. I thought the first was lost and anxious to have it.

1 Sir Walter Newman Flower, see p. 196.
2 The 'poetess' was Gabriela Mistral (see p. 201); the 'French-Brazilian intellectual' was Domenico Braga whom Stefan Zweig had first met in Paris when Braga was

with the League of Nations' International Committee on Intellectual Cooperation; it has not been possible to identify the other acquaintances of the Zweigs.

3   Thin pancakes, comparable to the French crêpe.
4   A pancake that is served cut up into small pieces.
5   Potato dumplings.
6   Martha Kahn, see p. 198.
7   A homemade bleach, bright blue in appearance.
8   Frederick Kuh (1895–1978), an American-born journalist, was the respected London correspondent of the *Chicago Sun* newspaper and the UPI (United Press International) agency.
9   The *Correio da Manhã* was an important daily newspaper published in Rio de Janeiro from 1901 to 1974.
10   Paul and Alma Wiener, see p. 204.
11   Olga Schaeffer (see p. 202) ran the children's home in Croton-on-Hudson, New York, where Lotte Zweig's niece, Eva Altmann, stayed.

Petropolis, 7. XI. 41

Dear Marta,

I have not yet thanked you for your letter, yet I often think of you. Especially when Hannah wrote me that Lorle[1] is back in London, working at R.'s office. I imagine that you feel half pleased about it because Raumans takes an interest in her (perhaps they will even try to provide her with a husband in good old-fashioned manner) and half displeased with their educational methods. Where does Lorle live now? And Kate? You never wrote what she is doing and whether you have any news of the girl's brother at all. Hanna wrote that you were not allowed to be more than a visitor to Bath and I am sorry although I do not know whether you don't prefer being in London now again. I wish I could have you here, not that I need your help, but I got so used to having you in the house with me, and I miss our domestic and other talks. I wrote Hanna — you would feel here like in your grandmother's household; everything is done by hand and at home and I have had some trouble at first trying to remember the old recipees as on my primitive stove (heated with wood and, if I am luxurious, a bit of charcoal) there is no way of grilling and au gratin as I was used to. One funny thing is that here in Petropolis you can buy everywhere good Streuselkuchen[2] and Bolus[3] and our old-fashioned biscuits, home-made in every bakery-shop. This comes from the fact that a hundred years ago there was a German immigration to Petrop, and they have not forgotten their tradition.[4] — Do you still do a lot of needle-work? Maritza is making beautiful crochet milieus and table mats and showed it to me, but this little bungalow, pleasant as it is, is not worth such fine needle-work. So maybe I shall begin a jumper for cool summer evenings — we are told that in summer it rains nearly every afternoon (while now it rains the whole day) — but who will finish it if I don't get along? I left Eva, too, with a pair of socks for British soldiers, the one was nearly finished when we left, but I have my doubts about the second. But she has an excuse, she wrote that she had painted decorations on the nursery furniture, and now they are making mats and things like that. Needle-work is old-fashioned, it seems.

With kindest regards and best wishes for your birthday which must be in these days,

Yours,
Lotte

1 Lorle was a niece and adopted daughter of Martha Kahn, see p. 198.
2 Crumb cake.
3 A 'bola' in England was a Jewish brioche-like yeast cake. 'Bolos' is Portuguese for 'cakes'.
4 German immigrants first settled in the Petrópolis area in 1837, joined in the following decade by several hundred more settlers. These labourers, artisans and peasant farmers had a significant impact on the development of the small town and its hinterland.
5 Maritza Fischauer, see p. 198.

10.XI.41

PETROPOLIS (BRASIL)
(34, RUA GONÇALVES DIAS)

Dear Hannah & Manfred, So many thanks for your kind wishes — you are quite right that they find me in a melancholic mood. All hopes of a short end of this war would be foolish and you will understand that my special situation is not favorable. We have no more a publisher for the original version of the books, France, Italy and most other countries are lost, the United States are not in my line of writing and it has not much sense to contribute for magazines with a deduction of 27% at the source 10% for the agent and a part for the translator. My Balzac can not be finished here without a large documentation; thanks God the autobiography is at last ready but when will she be translated and how — all the flavour, the tempo the colour is gone. But I have started already new work and life is at least here so easy. Let us describe our day; morning a delicious Brazilian coffee, then on the verandah work and reading, a primitive lunch, a game of chess, a walk and work again — we spend nearly nothing, I have not been in a theatre since a year, in a concert since half a year, I see strictly nobody for weeks, but the surroundings are marvellous, the climate agreable, it is a monkish life but a very healthy one and this was necessary. I must confess that I had a break down with black thoughts what all may happen (and some of it may happen / Lotte was only bones and cough for weeks; now I feel more indifferent against all possible annoyances and worries and Lotte looks much better, we live together like turtle-doves and try to forget the world and I wish the whole world would forget us. All my efforts to learn Portuguese are in vain and I cannot adapt to America — much better to Brazil and the Spanish countries. — [. . .] — I am so sorry for Eisemann[1] and much more because I have gone through the same desperate mood myself. And I know how his brother expects him and would do everything for him! Please do not worry about the house, do not loose your time with my damned things, I hate the idea that you feel the responsibility for the upkeeping and I am afraid that you will be paid only with worries and difficulties. Let things go easy, you have to do enough to make dear Manfreds life as happy as possible — "ich hab mein Sach' auf nichts gestellt"[2] how the old song says and I am sure I shall be right in the long term. I hope you dont forget your own expenses for voyages to Bath and I know that I nevertheless will be in moral and material debt to you.

Kindest regards to all and love from
Stefan

Petropolis, 10.XI.41

My dear Hanna,

We just received your letter of Oct. 22nd which we had been awaiting impatiently as your last letter was from Oct. 6th. — [. . .] — About us Stefan has written. He somewhat exaggerates, I was not so very bad although there was a kind of relapse again when I came here, but this seems to be over and I am ready to climb all the mountains. There are hardly any excursions as we know them from summer resorts, but if you follow a smaller road you usually come into very beautiful country with a great variety of views and nature. We have worked hard lately and the autobiography is finished. I am still busy transcribing corrections into the carbon copies but Stefan already works on something else and there is no time to get bored. On the household I don't spend much time, my maid has learned quite a number of — in her opinion — exotic dishes and the house itself gives little to do. We have had a few fine days and on those I really got up between 6 and 7 because it was so beautiful outside. On rainy days — and we had plenty — ½9 seems early enough. — I hope to hear in the next letter that Manfred got the job he was looking for and that the Miller family really does all the work for you in Bath so that you need not worry.

Love and kisses
Lotte.

1 Heinrich Eisemann, see p. 195.
2 'My trust in nothing now is placed': the first line of Johann Wolfgang von Goethe's poem 'Vanitas! Vanitatum Vanitas!'

15.XI.41

PETROPOLIS (BRASIL)
(34, RUA GONÇALVES DIAS)

Dear Hannah & Manfred, we just coming back from a beautiful walk through the virgin forests and under myriads of stars. You cannot imagine how beautiful it is in the tropical countries now the rains are over. We live our primitive life working all day on our cool terrace and looking on palms and the donkeys which bring fruits and big loads of bananas to the markets — the oranges are brought in automobiles because they are so cheap (50 for 5 pence). In the evening we start our walks and find us often after half an hour in midst of the most perfect. Often we think how beautiful it would be to have here a own house unfortunately the enormous prosperity of this country has raised the price of terrains enormously — when I was first here six years ago I could have got houses at the tenth of what they cost today but life is still very cheap. We live here at a third or fifth what we had to spend in New York and much more quiet and health because we are from morning to night in the open air. Naturally — if I had not my work I would not know what to do for except the nature there is noting except a few cinemas which have all American pictures. From war nothing is to be observed except that what we see in the newspapers no restrictions, no great change in the prices like in U.S. where life becomes very expensive and where — much to my disadvantage — the taxes on the source for literary work have been raised to 27% (six years ago they were 4% and before zero) Fortunately I have for the first time since nearly two years leasure to work and to read; if I had not the fear that I should be disturbed by annoyances from outside and if our health continues to be good we could not have chosen better. How often do we wish you could have some of our peaceful days and enjoy this mild and sunny climate while you have hundred worries and over you the clouds of the winter and the war! I am so grateful to you that you have arranged all about my book with my publisher; he is such a nice man and I always was at best terms with him as with the American; the only one I am expecting disagreable things is Wilmots[1] [–?] but it may be also my fault. The new book the autobiography will be probably translated in America because I do not know if the Blewitts[2] (which have been much better) could accept the work and the difficulty in sending the manuscript is great. We will have in any case a Spanish and Portuguese edition and the Swedish if Hitler spares their country — all other translations are gone as long as this beast still in a position to terrorise France and Italy. But let us try to forget those bad things. I have still to thank you for your good wishes and we try to fulfil them. Lotte is much better, her asthma is not more so painful and I hope the good and perfumed air will stop it soon completely — I myself feel quite well except some gray on the temples and a nice set of false teeth which I take out every night to remember that I am not the bright boy of yore. [. . .] Now Lotte will tell you more about our monkish life but do not commiserate us, I remember that Tolstoi said, that a man of sixty should retire into the wilderness and our solitude is a very beautiful one — I never have been in a more beautiful scenery than here in Brazil and people are so nice; last year they have spoiled us with invitations and festivities and this year as we told every body that we would like to work they leave us completely in peace. If I had my books here and my notes I would miss with pleasure all I ever possessed, collections, pictures — fortunately we have here found a little library, of course not like the American and English ones but enough that the mind does not get completely dry. Please give our love to all the friends. Is Kormendi's[3] novel finished? And what about Friedenthal?[4] Does he finally complete a book? Oh my dears, sometimes it seems ages to us, that we had a house and believed to have a home; now we know that all this will never come back again and I cannot imagine the new life I have to start and how and where. But for the moment we are perfectly happy to have still for four month this little bungalow for work and rest and we forbid ourselves to think on new plans. Do not forget that for us letters are more precious than ever — we get very few as we have no more the international connexions with publishers and the friends in America and England have her own worries and do not like to write letters which take weeks to arrive. We are so frightfully sorry that we cannot send from this "canaan"[5] coffee, sugar, etc which are so cheap and so abundant here to you, but there is no organisation like in the U.S.A. and we are ashamed to see these things here and not to be able to lay somewhat of it on your Christmas table. Love to you all!

Stefan

Dear Hanna, The enclosed letter for mother is just as much meant for you even though it does not show yours and Manfred's name. I really began to get worried about mother, her last letter was from the end of September. But you would have let me know if she were ill.

Love to you all,
Lotte

1 Stefan Zweig's London solicitor.
2 In England, Phyllis and Trevor Blewitt had translated into English Stefan Zweig's *Beware of Pity*, published in 1939. *The World of Yesterday* was translated in England by Cedar and Eden Paul, where it was published in 1943.
3 Ferenc Körmendi, see p. 199.
4 Richard Friedenthal, see p. 196.
5 Canaan, the Biblical promised land of the Israelites. Despite the difficulties that Jewish refugees had in securing visas for Brazil, there is no sense of irony in Zweig's use of the term here.

PETROPOLIS (BRASIL)
(34, RUA GONÇALVES DIAS)

16th Nov. 1941

Dear mother,

It is quite a long time now that I did not hear from you and I hope just as much that no illness prevented you from writing as that no letter has been lost on the way. I am always afraid of this on account of the rather unusual sounding address and wish to emphasize again that if you write to the Petropolis address (where mail seems to arrive always punctually) you must mark "Brazil" very clearly to avoid that the letter goes to some other country or even to another continent. It happened to a friend of ours that his letter addressed to Charlotteville, United States, on account of the way the address was written, went to Africa, passed various censorships, kept erring about for two months until he finally got it back. Our life continues here in the same quiet way. Stefan has finished revising his autobiography and I am still busy transcribing alterations into other copies etc. In the meantime he is already working on other things, so that I need not fear being suddenly without work. Nevertheless I am planning to begin some kind of needlework, probably a jumper as nothing better or more useful has occurred to me. And as I am told that also in summer the evenings are always fresh, I might have use for it — if I finish it in time, for summer is beginning soon and I have no one like you, Hanna or Marta to finish it for me if I don't get on with it. What are you working on now? Only soldiers' socks or something for yourself? Is it cold already and will you be able to remain in the house after December? You wrote once that this was doubtful. Is Mr. Eisemann still in Harrogate[1] and how is he? Do you see them or only his mother-in-law? We have had, after an unusual amount of rain, some very fine days, and those days of sunshine are really delightful, and I always regret that you cannot go with us on all those summer resorts, as Brazilians do not walk and already tell us that the fifty steps which lead up to our house from the street, are almost too much for their hearts! But if you leave the main streets and follow a lane or smaller older looking path, you almost always get after a very few minutes into the most pittoresque tropical wilderness, jungle, primitive huts, wild flowers, little streams, and in between surprising views on the mountains. For Petropolis is not situated in a large valley but in many different valleys so that from everywhere you get a different view on different mountains and in entirely different valleys. Fortunately most of these more distant valleys are inhabited by more modest people so that these districts are served by busses and we need never be afraid of losing our way completely or having to walk back the whole way. We have now a few acquaintances here, Brazilians, Chileans, French and refugees, all very nice and tactful — that is to say that we were invited everywhere and so far did not invite them back because we were very busy, and they are all understanding and leave us alone as much as we want to. In any case I cannot give real "invitations", because my maid is not perfect and never will be, although she is very nice and does all I tell her. But contrary to what I was told about dark maids she is not especially gifted for cooking and I have to show her again and again so that she does things right. In a way this is excellent practise for me, for I get used to doing and showing things, also to experimenting new dishes, but it does not induce me to invite people because every new or a little unusual dish means that I keep my thoughts during the morning more on the kitchen and table than on my work. But I am quite satisfied that I have something to do besides my typing, and on the whole things do turn out right and the household does not give me much trouble. Sometimes we go to Rio for the day, but with two hours journey each way and lots of things to do in Rio it is a tiring job and not the pleasure trip which we originally imagined that it would be. For pleasure purposes we would have to stay in Rio overnight and we have not yet got over our dislike of hotels and luggage and prefer our own hard beds.

Hoping to hear from you soon, with best love,
Lotte

1 The family of Heinrich Eisemann (see p. 195) were good friends of Lotte's mother, Therese Altmann (see p. 194), who was also in Harrogate to escape the wartime bombing of London.

24.XI.41

Dear Hanna, and Manfred,

We had no letter from you last week and hope for one this week. Now it is almost time, dearest Hanna, to send our best wishes — I am sorry I cannot send anything else and wish you would buy yourself something nice from us — for your birthday and hope that you spend the day pleasantly and in good spirits. Let us wish that the next one Eva is already back at home! [. . .] — Your birthday letter for Stefan travelled very quickly and reached us some time ago. This week he will have to pass this hard day and we plan to spend it with the publisher in Friburgo, another little mountain town, 3 or 4 hours from here. — Otherwise nothing is to be told about us. We had a visitor or two, were invited once or twice, continue to play chess (although Stefan is not satisfied with my progress), and the only new thing is that I have begun to knit a jumper and taught my maid to make Semmelknoedel[1]. Do not laugh at me if I ask you to send me a recipee of Linzertorte and Lemon cream. I cannot give great invitations, but I feel the need to specialise as the things you can buy here are always the same — Streusselkuchen[2] or a kind of Petit Four and I prefer home-made things. And whereas Sachertorte is rather heavy and I believe impossible to make in my stove, I think Linzertorte does not require much or regular heat. Do not think I develop into a model housewife — even though I did go to the market last Saturday. Yet I vaguely dream of making salt meat and would welcome a ladies tea with stupid household talk. But I believe after December this will be easy as many Brasilian friends send their families up here.

Fondest love and heartiest birthday wishes
Lotte.

I have been long without news from mother. But Eisen[3] wrote a few days ago that he sees her almost daily (and he seems to be recovering), so I hope that she is alright.

24. Nov. 1941 Dear Hannah & Manfred, now the black day[4] is very near and we will pass it not at home but on a excursion to a little place in the country; I have asked all my friends not to mention it in the newspapers (where even the birthdays children are printed with an overflow of pathetic phrases) but it is better to be away. We feel here already somewhat at home, Lotte is much better and we wait for the summer which will be delicious here as one escapes the hot nights and has all the day open door life (we live since months with open windows also the doors are not locked when we go away, — patriarchic times.) — About Eva we have news from New York. It was a misfortune that Mrs Schaeffer[5] broke her arm just now, where she was necessary for the new installation but we all live somewhat in the provisory, why not Eva and it is perhaps good, that she learns in time how to overcome little difficulties. She was over weekend at my sister-in-law, who has the best intentions; unfortunately they are both, my brother and she,

somewhat pathological with her continuous fear. He — in comparison with whom I was even in my best times a poor man — has fear to die as a beggar (and they have no children!) she cooks and washes, while all others find servants — I am so sorry that they are as they are and much would have been easier also for me if they would be otherwise, but she is at least willing to do something while on the others one cannot rely. (all people have their worries there and everyone is gifted with at least ten refugee-relatives) I am glad that Mrs. Wiener[6] invited her and she had lunch at her father, the great Morgenthau[7] (on golden & silver plates.) Of course we wish she had somebody who is her real friend in New York and I would be glad, if my sister in law would get attached to her with all her awkwardness — my dear, how easy life would be if people were quite normal, but I am not sure to be it myself. If one would leave her longer with my sister in law she would wrap her in flannels and give her medizine all day (they have killed three dogs by giving them constant medizine) and at the smallest cold they would go to the doctors and specialists — her neurotic fear exaggerates everything and it would not be a good [–?] for Eva; on the other hand I am glad that there is somebody who cares for her as unfortunately we are away. So do not worry about her, she is in best health and good spirits, likes her house, her aunt Olga[8] and her school; thats the most important except that she is perhaps longing for you secretly as you are doing quite openly. Yours Stefan

1 Bread dumplings.
2 Crumb cake.
3 Heinrich Eisemann, see p. 195.
4 Stefan Zweig had long been fearing the arrival of his sixtieth birthday on 28 November 1941.
5 Olga Schaeffer, see p. 202.
6 Alma Wiener, see p. 204.
7 Henry Morgenthau.
8 Olga Schaeffer, see p. 202.

[Undated — October/November 1941; pages 1 and 2 missing]

About the business and financial arrangements you had to make for us with Wilmot etc. I suppose Stein[1] will write you himself. I feel sure that you have done everything at least as well as we could have done it ourselves, and I am afraid you spent as much time and thought on it than Stefan would have done. Many, many thanks! Tabori[2] wrote us a letter some time ago, that he is not allowed to have any relations with people in Hungary and that the money the Hungarian publisher has or had in England is blocked, so that no payment may be expected.[3] — Now I have written more than my share and must leave the rest of the page to Stefan. Please send the two first sheets of this letter on to mother so that I need not repeat myself.

[Lotte Zweig – not signed]

Dear H. & M. We like our stay here very much. It is life like our parents and grandparents had and the people are so extremely nice and even clean in their great poverty. Food is still not artificial, the baker bakes his bread and his (excellent) cakes himself and our life expenses are one third as those in America. Others would call Petropolis out of season a frightfully dull place but for somebody like me who wants no other thing than to work and to read quietly, to enjoy walks in the beautiful surroundings it is the perfect thing. You cant imagine the variety of types and characteristic topics in the Brazilian life, I enjoy it enormously after the monotony of American streets. Dear Hannah, you will understand that one gets more and more sceptic against "civilisation" seeing the glorious results of it and that this peaceful, more primitive, more natural life has a quite new attraction; the only weak point are books but I have bought a Shakspeare, a Goethe, a Homer and with this and some others which I can lend from others one can live for a certain time especially if one writes his own ones. What I miss are reference-books when I need some details and in urgent cases I have to wait 4–6 weeks to get information from New York. As to the material things I feel much more free and care less than there; I had certain things and fears which worried me very much and which I cannot explain to you as they are too complicated but I repeat that from here all looks much more indifferent and we become more and more able to forget the bad possibilities of the future. This war takes such proportions that all provisions and all fears are futile, every thought of a post war living or of consequences of former mistakes is wasted. I do quietly my work and hope to be through my autobiography in a few weeks having completed still in Ossining the second draft — Lotte's health is somewhat improved and so we have not to complain; I wish you could see our little bungalow in the mountains. Lotte with her black cook, myself in the Cafe "Elegante" (in reality a tiny poor but pittoresk open café, in which I am nearly the only white man and Lotte the sensation as never another white lady would enter such a popular place) Perhaps we shall even get a dog! Yours Stefan

From Wilmot[4] I had direct information. As far as all is in order, let us hope the same for the future.

1 A British solicitor whom the Zweigs consulted.
2 Paul Tabori, see p. 203.
3 On 20 November 1940 Hungary joined the Tripartite Pact, drawing close to Germany, Italy and Japan. By mid-1941 German pressure on Hungary was mounting, leading to further isolation, including financial, from Britain. On 7 December 1941 Hungary and Britain declared war on each other.
4 Stefan Zweig's London solicitor.

Rio, 2. XII. 41.

My dear Hanna,

Coming to Rio for the day we found your letter of Nov 8th and that of the Mayer family.[1] I was very happy to hear from you again after a pause of 3 weeks (your last letter was of Oct. 22nd and we were waiting for another one since a fortnight) and while Stefan is busy seeing people, being shaved and then photographed I remain in our publisher's private office in the bookshop in order to write to you. Stefan begs to be excused if he does not write to you to-day, I shall meet him only in Petrop. and want to post this letter in Rio. — I am very happy that Stefan is feeling better and got over the period when he thought everything useless on account of the war and postwar and even lost the pleasure of his work. Thank God, this seems to be definitely overcome, his work interests him once and he even went to see some people to-day who might give him information and lend him some books he needs. It was fortunate that in Ossining, being a lot with Fuelops[2] and also Schaeffer[3], I had learnt that Stefan's depression was not an isolated case but was attacking — and leaving — the different European authors one after the other. This knowledge did not cheer Stefan but it helped me in a way, having understood why writers, owing to their imagination and on account of the fact that they are free to indulge in pessimism instead of their work, are more liable to be affected by these depressions than others, and — as Viertel[4] said to Stefan — these spiritual crisis in such times are even necessary for a writer who is bound to feel and suffer even what does not directly regard himself and his life. — But you can imagine how happy and thankful I am that he feels more cheerful now and works with pleasure again. The autobiography is finished and Stefan occupies himself with various projects without quite knowing yet which one he will really undertake. I managed to find a complete French Balzac here and gave it to his birthday and I am very glad that the first copy of the manuscript arrived safely. A few pages are missing — my fault still — and next time I will give you the exact numbers of the pages and chapters so that you may send them occasionally. You need not bother Cassell[5] with it, just mark it "pages from a manuscript on Balzac" and send it by ordinary or air-mail. Another request for your next stay in Bath which I did not want to make without Stefan's consent so that now, after having spoken to Stefan about it, it comes just too late and after Fried's[6] visit. — Stefan left all his notes on the Balzac in Bath, part of it in one or two black quarto ringbooks. I believe I even typed part of it and in that case a copy probably exists in a cardboard folder. My idea was — and Stefan agrees — that Friedenthal (in whose intelligence, discretion and understanding he has full confidence) should take the notes and copy them on the typewriter, partly to facilitate the work of the censor[7], partly to diminish the risk of postal loss, and then send them to Stefan. This will take some time, I suppose, and I leave it to you, first of all when you are in Bath to find the notes, secondly how you transmit them to Friedenthal and thirdly whether to send them through Cassell[8] or yourself. Whichever gives less trouble to you. — Maybe at the same time you can send me the bibliography, the printed and typewritten part (which Heiner[9] wrote).

[. . .] Of course, if the war and our stay here are much prolonged — and I am afraid they will be — the question of taking Eva here will become acute. It is too early to discuss it and we would have to think everything over with you by means of writing, so don't worry about this yet. Eva is in good hands and it was certainly better for her, much as we would have liked to take her with us, not to be torn out of her surroundings and to undertake a complete change of language, education and milieu without knowing that she will have time to stabilise again. If we remain and settle down either in Rio or Petrop then only can I write you in detail about everything, and make a proposition, for of course the decision on such a decisive change will be with you. Then the advantage of having her with us would have to be weighed against a change of language and educational system, but as I say it is too early yet, and in any case don't worry about it. We try to do the best we can for Eva and I give the matter careful thoughts in all directions, and take all possible informations on schooling possibilities (public, private, convent, mixed schools etc etc).

It is good that by you are interested in my reports about the household. I am afraid that in the beginning when it was really not quite easy for me, poor Stefan had to listen to all my problems as I had to communicate them to someone and so far have not found a woman friend to talk things over. I know a few women in Petrop. but they are either enraged housewives or too little interested, and I have to wait for January when the men from Rio send their families up to Petropolis. In any case the worst of my household troubles are over, and after the hard beginning of teaching a maid who did not know anything in a language which I could hardly understand and had never spoken before, things which I did not know well myself, I am not afraid of anything any longer. My maid is adequate now although she will never become perfect, and I have little to do with the household. One important change has occurred, and that is a 10 months old wirehair fox terrier which Stefan got from the publisher on his birthday (spaniels seem not to be had in Brazil).[10] About this in the next letter Stefan will certainly write you in a day or two, and I have to catch the bus home — that is to say to the beautiful but rather rainy Petropolis. Fondest love to you and Manfred and once more best birthday wishes,

Lotte.

What is the matter with mother? Her last letter was written before the holidays. I have not heard from her for many weeks.

1 Most likely the family of Heiner Mayer, see p. 200.
2 René and Erica Fülöp-Miller, see p. 197.
3 Albrecht and Olga Schaeffer, see p. 202.
4 Berthold Viertel, see p. 203.
5 Cassell, Stefan Zweig's British publisher.
6 Richard Friedenthal, see p. 196.
7 All post being sent to and from Great Britain was subject to official censorship. Lotte obviously recognized the difficulty that censors would have had in reading Stefan Zweig's handwritten notes relating to Balzac, suggesting that Richard Friedenthal type them and keep a copy. Apart from the value of having the notes, Lotte's idea is likely to have appealed to Stefan as way of providing financial support to Friedenthal without offending him.
8 Cassell, Stefan Zweig's British publisher.
9 Heiner Mayer, see p. 200.
10 The dog — Pluckee (or Plucky) — was a gift from Abrahão Koogan, Stefan Zweig's Brazilian publisher. Zweig had owned a spaniel in Salzburg.

[Undated — Petrópolis — December? 1941[1]]

Dear Hannah and Manfred, To your letter I want to tell you my fear, that Hannah has an exaggerated feeling of responsibility concerning the house in Bath. I am of course happy if she takes a few days there, but I do not wish that she has the worries of a house-mother. It is quite indifferent to me if the house is kept some what better or worse and the Raumanns will look themselves to it — you cannot imagine how indifferent I have become to all material things and how far the house is from my thoughts, how I have resigned ever to see the books any more; concluding my autobiography I have said fare well to all the past. For me one thing is important — to concentrate after many month of travelling and the depression through the war. I have lost all pleasure on entertainment, we have even not been a single time in a cinema and I am so thankful to Lotte that she does not protest against this rather monkish form of life. The idea to stay now for half a year without to move is for me a relief; may be that I shall be disturbed from outside, but all is here much easier, much indifferent and I would not mind to live such a retired life, forgetting the world and forgotten by her. For you this war is what the other was for me — an intervall — and fast his terrors and difficulties will let you love life more afterwards, especially if you have back your daughter more happy than ever and full of experiense. I myself can no more live in promisory forms, I must know, that I have not to change and will not have worries . Here is for the moment the maximum of such possibility of complete retirement and that's why we do not want to change. Believe me that I think quite clear and if I do not fulfil your wish which would give you Lotte back before Eva, it is because I see the possibilities of some complications which may arise; we all must have patiense now and I for my part would not complain even if our small life here would continue for many months. I am glad to have left Newyork. I can work here better, life is easier and certain primitiveness have her great charm. As to the material matters I insist that your expenses for travelling etc should be paid back to you regularly; if there should be no more cash don't worry, one will then sell some of the investments; it is important that you and your family have all you want. I wish we could send you parcels from here but till now we could not find an opportunity. I know that the food situation has improved a good deal, but if you would know how cheap sugar caffé is in Brazil you would understand our desire to send over some specimens. Give Victor[2] my kindest regards, he may excuse me that I do not write him — but not-writing letters means always that I am writing books. Let us hope that this winter (here begins the summer now) will not be too hard and if some good signs do not deceive me I hope it will be the last winter of the war and all our expectations fulfilled. So cheer up — it is to us, the old ones, to resign and not to you. Yours Stefan

1 As Stefan Zweig writes, 'here begins summer', the letter was likely written in early to mid-December.
2 Victor Fleischer, see p. 196

---

10. XII 1941

PETROPOLIS (BRASIL)
(34, RUA GONÇALVES DIAS)

Dear Hannah and Manfred, We write to you under the impression of the Japanese war declaration which isolates us perhaps somewhat more from home and you; there is not yet clear if Brazil will declare war to Japan as well but in any case the life here is not so influenced by the war as the country is self-sufficient.[1] We are so happy not to be in the U.S. inmidst of the terrible excitement and I am so glad that Lotte too likes so much this country and the peaceful small life of our beautiful solitude. The new member of our family, the little dog "Plucky" proves to be a very affectionate companion; he is happy with us except in the evening when we cruel persons force him into the bathroom; he would like to stay also the whole night with us and weeps that we do not allow him to sleep with us. So when you think about us be sure that we have without to have merited it the better part and even the best compared with the others; we often have deliberated if we should have taken Eva with us, but our life would be too dull for her and I am sure for her education is much better provided at Mrs Schaeffer.[2] The photos will have shown you that she is in splendid health and development. We are anxious to have good news from Manfred — please be so kind as to forward the inclosed letters to Warburg[3] and Eisemann; stamps and postage cost us more than our daily life and so we send letters always to three persons at once. Now I leave the word to Lotte! Love to you all

Stefan

Dear Hanna u Manfred,

There is little to tell about us at the moment. Only I am beginning to get very worried because I am without news from mother for such a long time and also you did not mention her for a long time. I hope that nothing serious is the matter with her. — In the meantime you will have received Eva's photos they will give you a good idea what she looks like now. And Erica Fueloep's[4] amateur photos which she promised to sent soon, will, I hope, show you something more of the house and its inhabitants. It was a nice idea of Mrs. Sch.'s to have these pictures made without my asking and it proves you anew that she takes a personal interest in Eva. Also Mrs. Wiener[5] wrote to tell me she had Eva with her and that she is "a darling". Hoping you are well and cheerful,

Yours
Lotte

1   The United States declared war on Japan on 8 December 1941, two days after the Japanese air attack on Pearl Harbour. On 12 December the United States declared war on Germany and Italy. Brazil did not declare war against Japan until 6 July 1945, though on 22 August 1942 it declared war on both Germany and Italy.
2   Olga Schaeffer, see p. 202.
3   Stefan Zweig's stock broker in London, as well as a friend.
4   Erica Fülöp-Miller, the wife of René Fülöp-Miller, see p. 197.
5   Alma Wiener, see p. 204.

[Postmarked 21 December 1941]

Dear Hannah & Manfred, there is nothing to relate as we have no news from you; mail has been rather irregular during the last weeks after the declaration of war in U. S. and due to the Christmas postage. My book has appeared since in Sweden, both Swedish and in the original language, but I have no copies — I hope you have received from Newyork the lecture of Romains[1] on my humble person in English; there is also a French version, but we get no copies; we are nearly cut off with books from the whole world, that this shall continue for two or three years is nearly as hard for me than for you to be so far from Eva. Please transmit this letter to Neumann[2]. Here is no change in our life, all quiet, but the perspective to live for years in such a Brasilien solitude not just that what I expected formerly for my old age.

Love to you all!
Stefan

Kindest regards from our little dog!

1 Jules Romain, see p. 201.
2 Robert Neumann, see p. 201.

PETROPOLIS (BRASIL)
(34, RUA GONÇALVES DIAS)

31. XII 1941

Dear H. & M. we got today your letters of 21. Nov and 7th Dezemb. at once; mail is now more irregular owing to the extension of war and there is for me no possibility to see my own books abroad. We have not much news. Lotte is somewhat better but her nights are not absolutely quiet and I am not satisfied with her weight. I had hoped that the fact that we are day and night summer and winter with open windows or on the terrace would cure her asthma because there is no dust at all but we have still to wait. She is not at all hindered and in good spirits — as much as this is possible in such a time and world as ours. Our dog behaves nicely only he imitates too much his master; yesterday night he escaped from the garden and whereto did he go quite alone? To the Café Elegante! Now Petropolis starts its season, all streets are full of children and even the great Panamerican-union of ambassadors in Rio on the 15. January will not stop this flow or flight to the mountains. We had already the first visits after our long lonliness. About the indenture Lotte has already called to you our consent for six years — but how does one in reality know what will happen in six months? I am as you know very sceptical if after this war anybody will have any thing to live as what he works for, the time of out fathers and grandfathers has gone where on[e] was sure to have a little security for his old days. I continue my work slowly but steadily, but I do not see my own books when they are published in Sweden and Portugal and still less what I should get for them. Every thing becomes more and more complicated; now I have to send my manuscripts by air-mail and I am afraid the postage will cost more than they bring. But how happy have I to be that I can continue at least any hope that with the victorious end of the war I shall have my publishers again. All is now provisory what we do, what we prepare to do — we must not forget that we live in the greatest catastrofe of history and that it is a miracle life continues in midst of this ordeal — a poor, a shabby, a undignified individual life as we are everyone fixed like with nails on one place and cut of from the great stream of life, but we live, we hope, we wail and are here in this little place have at least the favour of a splendid nature. We will have everyone still great worries, difficulties, before we can look again quietly and happily into our eyes, I am prepared for every thing and you too and all countries; the question for me remains if after the war I will have still strength and sense enough to enjoy life. You with your daughter will have it and this idea makes me happy for you. — I enclose a few words for Friedental[1] and Victor.[2] I hope to be able to write one day more and longer to them but there is in reality not much to tell as our private life is of no importance now and the public events have enough publicity. I am glad Manfred is with you and not only your husband but also your child: spoil him, in his age it does no more harm! Yours affectionately

Stefan

1 Richard Friedenthal, see p. 196.
2 Victor Fleischer, see p. 196.

Petropolis, 10. I. 42

My dear Hanna,

[. . .] I hope you have spent pleasant Christmas days, or better weeks, at Rosemount, and that on the whole everything is going as you want it to go. — About our life I must so far repeat the same story again and again: It is raining almost constantly and that is why the season is very bad and hardly any of our own friends are up here yet. So we continue our quiet life, having company by our dog and going for walks whenever the rain stops for a few hours. The description of our walks I leave to Stefan. It is clearly his job, being a writer, to give you an idea how, 10 minutes from the town, one can be inmidst almost complete wilderness and primitive life, in some lonely valley with beautiful and varied views and lots of children around poor little huts. Needless to say that where we go, none of our friends has ever set foot.– Next week there is the great Pan-American Conference in Rio,[1] but the Brazilians have been so spoilt with attention and visitors this last year that they don't get very excited about it. — The communications with the USA continue as before, only letters take longer, and so I hope that the cardigan I knitted for Eva and which I dispatch Monday, will arrive in due time (and that it will fit). Working at it I thought of all the knitting we have done together and wished I could have you here. Also the fog which frequently surrounds us and all the English woolens I am wearing on account of it, bring back memories. Well one day we will talk about all this again. Fortunately time really flies and soon we will have to think again what to do when our contract expires in May. I suppose we shall try to remain in this little place which for our needs has many advantages. — Don't forget to write us a lot!

Fondest love,
Lotte.

10.I.42

Dear Marta,

I must profit of this extra space to write you a few lines and to assure you that I think of you not only while knitting or making genuine Shinkenknödel and trying to prepare Powidl[2] but that I miss you just as Hanna on many other occasions. I suppose you have a lot of work shopping and inventing new recipes, but I nevertheless would like to hear from you about Lore and Kate and how you are satisfied with their development. They must be almost grown up and may soon present you their boyfriends, and I wonder how you feel about it. Won't you go to Bath again soon to have a rest? And what kind of needlework are you doing now? I might even do an a-jour tablecloth now that we have decided to keep the house for a longer period and now that the maid's cooking is fair enough to invite occasional informal guests. We have had marvelous summer weather lately and in this remote mountain place war seems still far away in spite of newspaper, radio and the fact that our mind is almost constantly occupied with the latest and coming events.

With kindest regards,
Lotte

1 The Pan-American Conference was held in Rio de Janeiro on 15 to 28 January 1942. Attended by representatives of twenty Latin American countries and the

United States, the main purpose of the gathering was to persuade Latin American countries to break relations with Germany, Italy and Japan.

2 Plum jam.

Petropolis, Jan. 16th, 42

Dear Hanna & Manfred,

I am sorry you were ever made to believe that on account of the new theatres of war mail connection between us would be cut off. On the contrary, we received your letter of Dec. 29th already on the 14th — a record after the long delays of the last months. I also believe that you need not worry that Amity Hall will be directly affected by the war; I had been a little anxious too in the first days, but all letters from USA show that life is going back to almost normal after the first great shock, and nobody of all those who reported that they wanted to invite Eva over Christmas even mentioned such a possibility. — You seem to have had a hundred percent English Christmas this time and I hope you enjoyed it. I am glad in any case that you could spend it at Bath. — In the meantime, Hanna, you probably have already started work of one kind or the other, and I can imagine that the work for the children with Anna Freud[1] is just the right thing for you. I fully understand that committee work did not satisfy you. You must write us in detail just what you are doing. I believe Miss Laquer, my former teacher in the domestic school, is also working there, although certainly in quite another department. In spite of your temporary mood of dissatisfaction with your life I am very content that Rosemount finally runs smoothly without occupying your mind and your time constantly and I wish the Miller family all the very best, for their and mainly for your sake. — [. . .] The aspect of the centre of Petropolis where everybody meets everybody has changed completely with the arrival of the summer guests and you can wear trousers or cotton dresses just as well as carefully tailored silk dresses. So far we have seen few people yet, the weather was too bad, the Inter-American Conference may had had an influence too, for the diplomats on account of the work to be done, for the others from the social point of view, receptions, dinners etc. but at least the very bad weather and the constant rain seems to be over now and we had a few really perfect summer days and thoroughly enjoyed a little sunshine and dry, warm weather. — You will have been to visit mother in the meantime, I suppose, and she wrote that she was greatly looking forward to it. — Please tell Koermendy[2] that

Stefan never got his letter; in this first period of the Japanese war quite a number of letters which we sent or which others wrote us have been lost or unduly delayed, and I was doubly glad that yours arrived so quickly. "There is nothing more to tell", as Eva would write, so only warmest love and kindest regards to all,

Lotte

Today only kindest regards and love to you all. Lotte plays half the day with the little dog and we admire all your "pep" as one calls in U.S. youthfull activity. Stefan

Dear Mother,

Since a fortnight I have the intention of writing you a really long and informative letter, but I have been very lazy mentally these last weeks, we had to invite a few people from Petropolis in the evenings which are my personal correspondence times, and in daytime the constant rain had finally made us quite restless and unable to concentrate on anything. Now the summer seems to arrive definitely, and with it the last summer guests. Petro is getting more lively, and although we have not yet had many visitors it is sufficient that Stefan does not want to dress and sits on the terrace in his pyjamas to make people come and catch him in this negligee. This week we have been in Rio for a day and found it again perfectly beautiful, being lucky to catch a clear, sunny and not too hot day. — I hope you have had all the expected visitors meanwhile and enjoyed seeing them again. We did not know about the engagement of Eisemann's[3] daughter. Which one is it? Forgive the damaged paper, the typewriter catches these very thin sheets in spite of all precautions.

Love and kisses   Lotte

1 Hannah had trained as a doctor in Germany and was beginning to specialize in psychiatry. For a time in London she collaborated with Anna Freud in her work with children.
2 Ferenc Körmendi, see p. 199.
3 Heinrich Eisermann, see p. 195.

[Petrópolis, undated, c. mid-January 1942]

Dear Hannah & Manfred, in our monotonous and quiet existence was today a little excitement; our gardeners wife (he is all day in a factory) who lives in the little hut behind our bungalow got a child today and Manfred would have had something to learn — how primitive the thing happens here which is quite complicated in our world. In a little room, half of my study in Bath, were during the great moment the husband, the midwife, a sister, her child, a dog so that was no room at all; every even the smallest comfort like running water is missing in this small space which has still the kitchen-stove in it and nevertheless a brown boy was brought to the world, a very quiet child, which makes no noise till now. Lotte was very excited about, not so the husband who immediately after went quietly to the café. One is always astonished by the poverty of the people here and one learns how many things of our life are superfluous — if I remember René Fulops[1] child with all kind of sterilizations and protektions; here a black midwife does (and not very cleanly) all the work and the children grow nevertheless here like strawberries — our black maid has no less than five. Living here means to get knowledge of life, all is here (except in the Frischauer luxurious quarters[2]) like two hundred years ago and this gives life here a great charm; people live the old family life and are happy to have a dozen children without to worry how to feed them and God helps. It would be strange for us to return to European and Northamerican ideas after all this experiences — the one big advantage is that one is not more so afraid to become poor. In such countries one could live with very few if one would forget his former standard. We had not very good weather here; since 40 years it did not rain so much in Brazil but we make every good moment our long walks (mostly with our dog) and discover always here pittoresk sceneries; at night there are views of the whole forest glittering like a christmas-tree. Alltogether we are very happy to be here instead of Northamerica and Lotte feels somewhat better — I am not yet satisfied completely, but I hope that she will stop soon her night-music[3] especially as summer is now beginning. I have not worked too much — depressed by the eternity of war, the daily rain, but I hope now to start as it is senseless to wait for better times one two three years. From Eva we have very good news and our confidence in Mrs. Schaeffer is like before very great — I believe it was a thousand times better that Eva has grown up with children of all ages, kinds, religions, languages and was obliged to do many things herself as to remain always at home as the only child — I envy you the moment when you will have her again. I hope you have a fairly good time and my matters give not too much annoyance to you — I myself have written everything I had in the "Rauchfang"[4] and cannot understand September 1939[5]. We hope to get soon good news from you. Give regards and love to all. Stefan

1 René Fülöp-Miller, see p. 197.
2 An apparent reference to the special treatment that Zweig believed Paul Frischauer (see p. 196) expected for himself in Brazil.
3 Lotte Zweig's asthma attacks.
4 An Austrian word for 'chimney'; see note 2, p. 134.
5 Germany invaded Poland.

---

21. I 1942   *Petropolis (Brazil) 34 rua Goncalves Dias*

Dear Hannah & Manfred, [. . .] The weather has finally cleared up and we take long walks, Lotte feels much better, her attacks have nearly ceased, only at night to wakes up (and wakes me up) once or twice for a little coughing and her weight is far from satisfying me, but I have to take her as I took her and the law does not allow to send her back only because she has two or three kilogrammes less weight than before. From the conference at Rio[1] we see not more than you read in the papers, our little dog is sweet but behaves badly, strolling away in the neighbourhood, especially in cafés or houses with children and for the third time negros brought him back. Perhaps he finds life a little too tedious with a single couple and I find it tedious myself sometimes; we have books but one feels somewhat isolated — on the other hand, there is no place in this mad world where you feel less interference from the war. Our solitude has the bad effect that my Portuguese does not make no progress at all — there is also some interior repression in me; when I studied French, English and Italian at fifteen, I knew that I made an effort for forty or fifty years and that was worth-wile. But for how many or better for how few years shall I study Portuguese. Lotte learns much better as the house-hold obliges her to conversation. I believe we told you that the workman who lives in a hut connected with our bungalow got a baby, a tiny creature; so Lotte could have some "Ersatz"[2] by it and the dog, but she is not so interested in it as I supposed. — We follow every line in the papers about England and the war. We are glad that there was no more bombing since months, but all seems to indicate that the war will be still a very long one as the real preparations in the U.S. which are enormous have not yet full activity in the battle but nobody can realise how enormous they are. I continue to work, in the U.S.A. we find not yet the right translator for the autobiography but next month will appear the little booklet about Amerigo Vespucci and I am working here on another book. We will soon know if we can have this bungalow longer than April — the house is somewhat damp and shoes and all leather things, even books, gets moisture (mouldy) after one day of rain, but we hate changing, packing, new addresses and would like to remain. Now I have only written about us and nothing about you but you know that with all our wishes we are with you. Love to all

Stefan

Petropolis, 21.I.42

Dear Hanna & Manfred,

[. . .] Also about me Stefan has reported almost everything and leaves me little to tell. At first he laughed about me when the baby was just about to come and I got somewhat excited and then told him in detail that I had seen it the moment it had come out of the doctor's tongues — and things must be very bad here when you get a doctor for a birth — before it had even had its bath the whole family inclusive their dog was already back in the room. Now I just look at it every few days and make some mental comparisons between this baby and Fuelop's³ child for whom even after a year still every spoon and pan is sterilised after or before each meal, and whom the parents for weeks were only allowed to approach with a mask. This one just sleeps in his parent's bed and when it is hungry the mother opens her dress and gives it a drink. — Thanks for the recipee of the Linzertorte. I have not yet been able to make it as the kitchen stove is worse than usual and besides I have days where I avoid my maid because I hate to speak Portuguese with her it is so unnecessary difficult with its complicated grammar and pronunciation and I do not always feel like it. But once in a while I still try your new dishes, only whenever I ask Stefan what he would like, it is something to which Powidl⁴ is essential (tell this to Marta, it will remind her of old times). And one day I probably will give in and make some of dried plums. — The struggle with mouldiness which attacks leather, dark dresses and suits some books and papers, is a continuous one and worse in summer than in winter which is supposed to be cold (5–8 degrees Celsius above zero) and dry. It does not really hurt the tissues, but gives much work, for you have to put everything into the sun, brush it off — and a few days later begin the whole thing again. Our whole district has the reputation of being particularly damp and to get especially frequent mist and fog; on the other hand it is very convenient nearer to the town and in our opinion prettier than most of the pretendedly dryer districts. And we have got used to our bungalow and find many advantages in it. And we also got used to our so-called gardener (he hardly does more in the garden than cutting back the hortensias when they threaten to overgrow everything) and his family and also to our maid whom I only did not send away the first day because I had not the courage to interview another one and face the task of introducing her to our foreign ways and to my strange Portuguese. The Petropolis season this year still has not got into full swing partly on account of the weather and partly on account of the Conference which keeps people in Rio. And so far our fear of getting too many unexpected visitors has been unfounded, and we even welcome those who come. — In every sense of the word your life is more exciting than ours and you certainly are more up to date than we are in everything. That is another reason why you ought to write more and still much longer letters than before, and so please oblige your loving sister, sister-in-law, friend and relative,

Lotte

1 Pan-American Conference.
2 Substitute, or replacement.
3 René and Erica Fülöp-Miller, see p. 201.
4 A plum jam.

Petropolis (Brasil) 34 Goncalves Dias 1.II.1942

Dear Hannah & Manfred,

Mail has been irregular last weeks owing to the Conference and the extension of war, but I am writing without to expect your news. Our life is not at all changed by the season in Petropolis, we see very few people, only the summer time has made our house more vivid. The wife of the workman who has a room next to us, has got a baby, we have got a dog, the dog has got fleas, we are getting them from him mixed with bites of mosquitos, spiders and other little animals and two snakes have appeared in our garden (not dangerous ones as one told us/ so we have a good picture of the tropical summer and it is visible on

our skin especially Lotte's of whom the animals are so fond as she is of
our doggy — all her suppressed mother-instincts are heaped upon him.
Her health is not yet as I would like it and perhaps we will give her liver
injections to regain the lost weight — of all our losses this one affects
me most. I suppose we all feel not very happy in these times especially
as is it to be supposed that they will continue and a real bright peacetime
(also social and personal peace) lies far ahead but on the other hand
we have resigned to so much that at least with our exterior form of life
we get accustomed to war, incertainty and isolation. My little book on
Amerigo Vespucci will be sent to you this month from my American
publisher[1] — I will remind him to do so; it is no big work and I have the
autobiography which shall be published first in the original in Sweden
is more personal.[2] Next week we hope to get the decision if we can have
the bungalow for next term — we do not like to move and are already
accustomed to the neighbourhood; you know how important it is to
have kind reliable people and especially here where doors and windows
are open day and night. It is true we have no precious things but for the
people here everything even an old trousers are a treasure. Excuse if I
have spoken only of us, but you know that all our thoughts are with you
and Lotte will write you more. Love for you all.

Stefan

34 Rua Gonçalves Dias Petropolis, Febr. 1st 1942

Dear Hanna and Manfred,

I have very little to write except a few annotations to Stefan's letter. My
health is not at all bad and I am sorry that what he writes must give you
that impression. I may have lost a kilo or so in weight but he is the only
one to notice it and in a country at war I would still stand out as being
particularly well-fed. Anyhow, to give him pleasure, the doctor will
make me a few liver injections. The asthma, too, has not at all been bad
recently and I even gave Stefan the pleasure of a few quiet nights. Since
we are in Petropolis, I have had but one attack and that one very slight,
just strong enough to get an injection and to allow myself the luxury of a
day in bed. The flea-bites is what annoys me most at present. Since about
a week Plucky's fleas have developed a tendency to change over to Stefan
and me and I seem to have a specially wonderful taste for them because
I get ten bites while Stefan gets one. I hope to dominate that invasion
very soon, however, and fortunately my maid is not one of those refined

ones and I can talk and ask her assistance freely without hesitating. Officially we are now in the middle of the season, but it is not half as bad as we thought. Contrary to European summer resorts the people do not go out much and if they do, they just drive from one place to the other. If we went to the Casino or the one fashionable Café we would probably meet everybody we ever met in Rio. But as we don't we do not see many more people than during the quiet time. We have had a few new visitors lately and met some nice and in Stefan's sense cultured Frenchmen, but on the whole our life continues on as before.

One request for an hour's work, dear Hanna when you are next in Bath. Now and then Stefan gets not offers but enquiries about the film rights of his older books, and as we have no documents at all here, I would be very grateful if you could find the folder of film agreements — it once was in my writing desk in the study and should be either a slim cardboard folder or the folder enclosed with the big box for agreements in general — and just make me a list of the film agreements there are, 1) name of the work, 2) name of the company, 3) whether world or language rights, 4) — this the most important — whether there is a time-limit for the durations of the agreement. I hope this does not give you much work, as those agreements are not very many, I should think about a dozen altogether.

As again a fortnight has passed without bringing a letter from you, we are again expecting it impatiently and are carefully watching the postman's round every day, just as carefully trying to explain each other when he has passed without entering, why your letter may have been delayed. In any case the best method to avoid long gaps between letters from you would be, just as usually do, to write frequently even if there is little to tell.

We have better weather now and greatly enjoy not to watch the change between rain, mist and fog all day long. The Conference has brought many and long newspaper articles, but on the whole no change at all in the usual life. In a fortnight Rio will have its famous carneval, and although we avoid on principle all festivities, we will go to Rio for a day to watch the Carneval of the people in the streets which is supposed to be a unique spectacle.

I, too, have only written about ourselves. But what is the good of writing questions, you know very well that every little detail, however insignificant in itself, greatly interests us, especially me, and all you have to do is to sit down and write.

Fondest love,
Lotte

Unfortunately I never got Komendis[3] letter. Give please Eisemann my kindest regards. Stefan

1 Zweig's *Amerigo: A Comedy of Errors in History* was published in 1942 in the United States by Viking Press.
2 *Die Welt von Gestern*, Zweig's autobiography, would be published in September 1942 in Stockholm by Exilverlag Bermann-Fischer.
3 Ferenc Körmendi, see p. 199.

10. II 1942

PETROPOLIS, (BRASIL)
(34 RUA GONÇALVES DIAS)

Dear Hanna and Manfred, We have no news from you since ages but we know, it is not your fault — also from New York all mail is endlessly delayed, may be because the conference wanted all the avions or because there is now much more mail to forward owing to the fact that all letters to the last neutral countries in Europe go no more directly over to Lisbon but over U.S. So we have the impression to be still more away from you than ever. How we would like to have you here only for one day (rather for more — Lotte) for you cannot imagine how beautiful it is in the summer days, the air sunny and clear, the mountain beautiful, the vegetation gorgeous, — all would be perfect without the cloudy thoughts. We do quietly our work without to be very active, there is something in the atmosphere which makes you lazy and also the idea that a book in these times of inimaginable decisions is but a ridiculous trifle hampers the intensity. We prefer to think that one has to enjoy these quiet, peaceful and beautiful days in a country which has no restrictions as something we will later remember with envy and regret, so we are not as eager as we should be and play more with the little sweet dog than reasonable people would do in a normal time. Now in the season we see some friends and next week we go down to Rio for one day to see the popular carneval (not the fashionable one)[1] which is a unique thing on earth; one has of course some mixed feelings to assist to such fantastic explosion of joy in a time where nearly in the whole world explosions kill people but it would be stupid not to assist such a unique spectacle (as we have been in no theatre, no concert and nearly no cinema since half a year and more.) By your letter only I remember that the house in Bath exists for myself here nearly forgotten that we had once one: to forget bygone things, to resign is not the great art we have to learn for all imagination cannot visualize the coming world. I wish you could see our quiet and peaceful life, Lotte bears wonderfully the monotony of this existence and enjoys the beautiful surroundings; our life would be rather sad in an Northamerican village but here the eye enjoys even if it looks up from a newspaper the glorious nature. Pardon me, if I write only about us but we have nothing to say about you as your letters have not yet reached us. Will you be so kind to forward the inclosed letter to Leni Hermann[2] I like to send her only a few words. I hope you are in best health and Manfred has much to do. Yours ever,

Stefan

Petropolis, Febr. 10th, 1942

Dear Hanna & Manfred,

Nearly a month has passed again without a letter from you or mother and also from USA we have not had mail for almost a fortnight. We spend every morning between 11 and 12, sitting on the steps and watching out for the postman — unfortunately in vain. There are many reasons for post delay and we explain them to each other, but this does not make us less impatient. I hope you have not had the same experience but are in continuous contact with Eva. I am longing to hear how you are, what you are doing, whether there are any changes in your life, that is to say whether Manfred has found a job or whether Hanna is working with Anna Freud or anything else, etc. etc. and hardly less we like to know about all our friends and acquaintances. We have been slightly more busy seeing people these last weeks and rather enjoyed it after four months of almost complete solitude. We have made the acquaintance of a few more European couples, pleasant and cultured people, and my poor maid even had to stand the extra strain and excitement of lunch guests — tea guests do not excite her any more, this has already become routine work. Also the weather has been fine the last weeks, real summer weather, warm during the day and cool at night, but nevertheless we have not yet managed to attain our ambition: to get up at 6 or 7 like most Brazilians do, in order to profit from the fine morning. Also our walks have been reduced lately on account of the more frequent visitors and invitations, and our dog whom I took to Rio the other day to have him trimmed and who now looks perfectly ridiculous, is rather reproachful about this matter of going out only in the evening. But it can't be helped, it is too hot for long walks in daytime, and the dog is not allowed either in trains or busses. I suppose these few details give you an idea of our life which is more quiet even now during the season than we had dared to hope. But I am convinced the steps up to our house detain many potential visitors from just dropping in, and as we carefully avoid the two or three places where you can meet everybody we only meet those people we really want to meet. Stefan was at the reception of the prefeito[3] of Petropolis the other day (by some mistake I was not invited too) but it seems that he kept in a corner with a few friends and only learned by the visitor's list in the newspaper later on, how many acquaintances he has missed. He continues working and so I am occupied too, but on a somewhat reduced scale, in the morning we wait for the mail half of the time, in the afternoon there are often visitors, sometimes also in the evening, and so I am enjoying a half-holiday which I partly use for trying out some more cooking recipes. Linzertorte I could not make yet as the stove is so bad that our landlady even promised me a new one, but I am mentally ready for it, as well as for knitting another jumper for Eva as soon as I have news from her that the cardigan arrived and how it fits. You see I am falling more and more in the mentality of those women who once bored me to death, and I also understand now the writers' wives who do not always want to listen to their respective husbands' intelligent conversation but prefer to discuss women's problems among themselves. I simply have to get rid of the trifling details like the one that my maid when she needed greaseproof paper for a cake used the wrapping paper of a tilsit cheese, or that she uses the dog's special comb for herself (fortunately they both are very clean) and other interesting things, and I badly need someone to talk over dress problems and hairdresser and the many kinds of insects in the house and so on and so on. So far I have not yet found the right woman for all this as most of our European friends have no household of their own, and mostly the acquaintance is so new that they prefer to talk or to listen to Stefan instead of small talk. So I unload part of these problems on Stefan, who listens with great patience and as the conditions here are so totally different, even with some interest. Therefore you need not pity me too much.

Please send this letter on to mother, she will see from this one that I really have nothing special or interesting to tell, and I am waiting to hear from her again to write her at length (as I did about three weeks ago with an enclosure to brother Jan[4]).

Lotte

Stefan wants me to inform you that we will keep this little house for a longer period and that we will spend the so-called winter here.

1 The 'popular' carnival was a street event centred on Praça Onze, a working-class, predominantly Afro-Brazilian area in the centre of Rio de Janeiro that was also known for its long-established Jewish population. The main 'fashionable' event took place in the city's Theatro Municipal.
2 The wife of the German writer Max Herrmann-Neiße, see p. 197.
3 The mayor.
4 Hans (Jan) Altmann, see p. 193.

[21 February 1942 — postmarked 26 February 1942]

PETROPOLIS, (BRASIL)
(34, RUA GONÇALVES DIAS)

Dearest Hanna,

Going away like this my only wish is that you may believe that it is the best thing for Stefan, suffering as he did all these years with all those who suffer from the Nazi domination, and for me, always ill with Asthma. I wish we could have done more for Eva personally, having her with us all the time, but on the other hand it is my sincere conviction that it has been better for Eva to be with Mrs. Schaeffer[1] whose understanding love and way of education is so much similar to your own. Having her with us, she would have felt our moods, been lonely probably and have had without doubt great difficulties adapting herself in such completely different surroundings. On Mrs. Sch. you may count, I am convinced, like on one of the family. My sister-in-law will also look after Eva and maybe even offer to take her herself or send Eva somewhere else. But I who know you and your ideas, would advise you to leave Eva at Schaeffer's. Let us hope it is not too long until you can take her home.

Many thanks for all you have been to me and forgive me for causing pain to you and Manfred. Believe me it is best as we do it now.

Lotte

Dear Hannah and Manfred, you would understand us better had you seen how Lotte suffered in the last months from her astma and I for my part was oppressed by our nomadic life which did not allow me to do my work efficiently. We liked this country enormously but it was always a provisory life far from our home, our friends and for me with sixty years the idea to wait still for years of this terrible time became unbearable.

Had Lotte's health been better and had we could have Eva with us it would have had sense to continue but living in thought always with the others far away and without any hope to love the quiet life I was longing for and to see Lotte's health restored (the long injection-cure did not help at all) we decided, bound in love, not to leave each other. I feel responsibility against you and Lotte's mother, but on the other hand you know how perfect we two have lived together these years and that there was not a moment of disagreement between us. Let us hope that you will see your daughter soon and she can give you all the love you merit; I have written to my brother and I am sure they will do all they can for her. Our devoted friend, my publisher Abrão Koogan will tell you one day about our last hours and that our thoughts have always been with you.

Stefan

1 Olga Schaeffer, see p. 202.

PART IV

Postscript
Letter from Ernst Feder
5 March 1942

Dr. Ernst Feder[1]
Petropolis, March 5, 1942
(Estado do Rio)
Rua Major Ricardo 133

Dear Doctor,

I don't have the honour of knowing you personally. However, I feel a great need to inform you about some details pertaining the last [weeks] in your brother-in-law's and your sister's lives since my wife and I were the only compatriots who had a regular and intensive exchange of ideas with Mr and Mrs Zweig up to the eve of their death. The information I will supply will be a bit unorganized because we are still deeply affected by their loss and can hardly believe that it really happened. Our thoughts of deepest sympathy are with you.

When we moved to our summer home in Petropolis from Rio on December 1, the Zweigs had been here for several months. They lived about five minutes from us. As you know, he did not want to escape the heat as much as he wanted to escape his numerous acquiantances and social life. Even when we first visited the couple, we noticed Mr Zweig's depression. Your sister always displayed the same amiableness although a shadow seemed to weigh upon her, as well. We met once or twice a week for three to four hours. When they came to our house, Mr Zweig called himself a "squatter" because they stayed for such a long time. After we had come to see them on the high verandah of their modest little house, they would accompany us home. The beautiful nights under the Southern star-clad sky would entice them to take an occasional walk. "We are turning you into night owls", your brother-in-law once said jokingly. Supported by your sister, we often tried to lighten up his mood with jokes. He would smile, and it was not until later that we realized that we had never laughed together. Your sister always asked us to come more often because he didn't have much stimulating social exchange and hardly met any kindred spirits; he was sorely missing an exchange of ideas in German.

On my part, a great amount of conversational effort was used to fight his depression and pessimism. He would remain silent, but didn't seem convinced. He felt relatively well in Brazil. He once expressed it in the following manner, "We are in the part of the boat that rolls the least." An accidental circumstance that further added to his low spirits was the persistent rain, which was unusual even in the very wet [climate] of Petropolis. The weather didn't start to clear up until mid-January.

He was deeply affected by the [global] situation. "Atrocious" was a word with which he often described the horrors of war. There was no indication of his extreme decision, however. He often talked to me about whether they would stay in Petropolis or go back to Rio in the winter. "When are you going back?" he would often ask me in a tone that showed that he was considering the same matter. Both of them were repeatedly looking at other houses in case the contract with the landlady would not be renewed. He spoke at length about his literary plans. He wanted to write a novel set in the time of the inflation and asked me whether I could supply him with factual material. He was deeply saddened by having to abandon his Balzac plans because all of his materials had remained in Bath. He dedicated most of his time to a biography on Montaigne. Since he didn't have all volumes of Montaigne's complete edition at hand, I left him mine. The last work he completed is a "Chess Story". He sent it to me, asking for my comments and subsequently expressed his infinite gratitude, as you know he would have. In addition, your sister said that she was very sorry that I hadn't gone through his autobiography with him. He had sorely missed somebody with whom he could talk about literary matters.

On Saturday, February 14, we went to have tea at their house with Mr and Mrs Strowski[2] and a Brazilian, Mr Braga,[3] from Paris. Your brother-in-law held all three of them in very high esteem. The seven of us stayed together until about 7 p.m.

The lively conversations had visibly refreshed him and your sister. They both urged the two of us to stay on and we remained together until midnight. It was the only time that I felt like I had coaxed him out of his melancholy. "Do you really think we will be able to return to Europe?" he asked me that night. "As certain as you sit here at this table, I am strongly convinced that you will one day sit at your table in Bath, maybe together with us."

On Monday, February 16, his publisher, Mr Koogan[4] drove us [all] to the Rio carnival. Not only did he want to get to know the famous festival himself, but he also wanted to make your sister particularly happy. I am sure that he hadn't made his final decision at that point. In the car, he talked to us about a response to a note in "Correio da Manha."[5] While we were driving through decked-out suburbs and first carnival floats, he developed such an elaborate idea for an article for "Readers Digest" that I was taken with awe. In Rio, we parted ways and didn't see each other again.

He already returned to Petropolis Tuesday evening; I came back later. On Wednesday or Thursday, both of them must have made the decision. On Friday, they returned to Rio (he would normally only go [down] on rare occasions. If something had to be done, it was usually your sister who ran the errands). Evidently, [they wanted to] take care of business matters [such as] lawyer, publisher, bank.

In the morning of Sunday, February 21, he phoned us to invite us to their house. When we got there, your sister greeted us on the verandah. She was very serious and didn't feel quite well. She had suffered from asthma during the carnival in Rio. We encountered him at his desk where he was writing. He normally did not work in the evening. Of course, I couldn't fathom that he was busy writing his farewell letters. He was even more depressed than usual. Your sister was more silent than normal; both were their amiable, gracious and empathic selves. We have seldom met anybody like your brother-in-law and sister for whom we felt such a liking and with whom we became close so quickly.

He told us that he had slept little in the past few nights and had read a lot. Bainville's Napoleon was his last book.[6] He gave me the book because he knew that I was working on new documents on the French Revolution. Of course, I couldn't foresee that it was meant as a farewell gift. He returned my Montaigne. When I asked him whether he had [obtained] a complete edition, he gave me a vague answer. I didn't insist any further. Your sister returned an Austrian cookbook to my wife that she had borrowed to cook some of Stefan's favourite dishes occasionally. We played chess, as was our custom. Your brother-in-law read one of my works with the greatest attentiveness. He had asked me to bring it and made some splendid remarks. [There was] no inkling of a last farewell. At our usual time, 11:30 p.m., we set off to go home. His last words were, "Please excuse my mood. My black liver [is to blame today]."

On Sunday, your brother-in-law and your sister didn't see anybody anymore. They used the day to write and go on walks where they must have visited all the places they had grown fond of. When we received the phone call on Monday evening, we were both were completely stunned. When we came [to their house], some acquaintances and many journalists had gathered. Your brother-in-law and your sister were completely unchanged in their last repose; they even seemed almost cheerful. He was lying on his back, she on the right side with her left arm around him. You are well aware that the funeral [had caused] a deeply moving demonstration [of sympathy] in all strata of Petropolis society; that all shops closed spontaneously during the ceremony; that the death of Stefan Zweig and his young wife sent shock waves through all of Brazil; that his unique significance as a writer and human being and the love and courage of his "last heroine" were celebrated in thousands of articles; that [public officials] want to name a street after him and erect a monument in his honour.

If you, dear Doctor and your dear mother and wife, would like to know any more details, I am at your complete disposal. Mr and Mrs Zweig spoke about family matters only on rare occasions. When your sister talked about her mother, brother or sister-in-law, it was only with most loving feelings. In Rio, I was told that your brother went to consult a neurologist twice. However, we didn't notice anything in him that would point to a disease.

May you, dear Doctor, your wife and your mother find the strength to bear this terrible blow that has hit many people so hard. Every day, we find out about how popular both of them were with the population. Once, a stranger left a whole armful of roses at their garden gate. Your sister came down, took the roses, pressed her face into them and thanked the stranger by saying, "grand pays chéri, Brésiliens généreux et hospitaliers". Similar scenes took place on various occasions. Your brother-in-law and your sister never mentioned them.

I greet you and your loved ones very warmly, also on behalf of my wife and send you my most distinguished regards.

Yours sincerely,
Ernst Feder

If you would like to obtain newspapers or magazines, please don't hesitate to contact me. I am adding [the article] I wrote about your brother-in-law and your sister as printed matter.

Translated from German by Karin Hanta

1 See p. 195.
2 Fortunat Strowski, see p. 203.
3 Domenico Braga, who had worked with the League of Nations' International Committee on Intellectual Cooperation in Paris.
4 Abrahão Koogan, see p. 198.
5 A Rio de Janeiro daily newspaper.
6 Jacques Bainville, *Napoléon* (Paris: Fayard, 1931).

Dramatis personae

Altmann, Eva, *b. Berlin, Germany, 1929*
Eva Altmann was the only child of Manfred and Hannah Altmann
and the niece of Lotte Zweig. In 1933 Eva moved to England with her
mother, joining her father who had previously settled in London. In a
private arrangement, Eva was evacuated to the United States in 1940 and
returned to London in 1943. Like her parents, she qualified as a medical
doctor and went on to become a professor of clinical epidemiology.

Altmann (née Mayer), Johanna (Hannah), *b. Ettlingen, Germany,
1898; d. Turtmann, Valais, Switzerland, 1954*
Hannah Altmann was the wife of Manfred Altmann and sister-in-law of
Lotte Zweig. A medical doctor, Hannah met Manfred when both were
working in Berlin. Together with her daughter Eva, Hannah followed
Manfred into exile in London in 1933; unlike her husband, she did not
requalify as a doctor there. In Germany she had started to specialize in
psychiatry and for a short time worked in London with Anna Freud.
Hannah Altmann died in a car accident together with Manfred and
the political scientist Franz Neumann (a close friend from Kattowitz).

Altmann, Hans (Jan), *b. Kattowitz, Germany (now Katowice, Poland),
c. 1895; d. London, England, c. 1980*
Jan Altmann was an older brother of Lotte Zweig. Following the
independence of Poland in 1918 he opted to remain in Katowice to
manage the family's business. Jan arrived in England in 1938 without
his non-Jewish wife but he found it extremely difficult to settle and he
made unsuccessful attempts to emigrate to Brazil and the United States.

Altmann, Manfred, *b. Kattowitz, Germany (now Katowice, Poland),
1900; d. Turtmann, Valais, Switzerland, 1954*
Manfred Altmann was an older brother of Lotte Zweig. He studied
medicine in Germany, working mainly in Berlin. A few months after
the Nazis gained power in 1933, Manfred moved to England, with his
wife, Hannah, and their young daughter, Eva, soon joining him there.

He requalified as a doctor and in 1934 he established himself in general practice in Golders Green, attracting among his patients large numbers of German-speaking refugees who lived in the area. Later he trained in radiology and radiotherapy, giving up his general practice in 1948 to specialize entirely in this field. Manfred and Hannah Altmann were the main heirs to the estate of Stefan Zweig. The inheritance included literary rights and the house in Bath.

Altmann (née Hirsch), Therese, *b. Frankfurt, Germany, 1868; d. London, England, 1949*
Therese Altmann was the mother of Lotte Zweig. Following the death of her husband, Therese Altmann left Germany for London to join Lotte, and her son, Manfred, and his family. Therese Altmann was the grand-daughter of a well-known rabbi, Samson Raphael Hirsch, whose philosophy was that orthodoxy could be practised within a secular context. She was very orthodox in her religious beliefs and practices, unlike her own daughter and three sons. In London, she lived in Golders Green, near to Manfred and Hannah, though she moved to Harrogate, Yorkshire, during the wartime Blitz.

Asch, Sholem, *b. Kutno, Russian Empire (now in Poland), 1880; d. London, England, 1957*
Sholem Asch was a Yiddish-language novelist, dramatist and essayist strongly influenced by the Haskalah (Jewish Englightenment). Asch first moved to the United States in 1910, becoming a naturalized citizen. He later returned to Poland before moving to France and then, in 1938, back to the United States. Stefan Zweig spent time with him in Salzburg, London, Nice and New York.

Beheim-Schwarzbach, Martin, *b. London, England, 1900; d. Hamburg, Germany, 1985*
Martin Beheim grew up in Hamburg, where he became a writer. He fled to England in 1939 and remained there until 1946, working for the BBC. After the war he worked for the British Control Commission in Germany. He published his first literary work in 1927 and was the author of many essays, novellas and biographies, and books about chess.

Budberg (née Zakrevskaya), Maria Ignatievna, *b. St Petersburg, Russia, c. 1892; d. Florence, Italy, 1974*
Born into an aristocratic family, in 1921 Baroness Maria Budberg fled post-revolution Russia for Estonia, to join her children from her first marriage. There, due to a marriage of convenience with a Baltic German

baron, she acquired Estonian citizenship and the title that she used for the remainder of her life. She is best known as a 'Mata Hari', due to her involvement with the British diplomat and secret agent Sir R. H. Bruce Lockhart, Maxim Gorky (for whom she acted as interpreter when Stefan Zweig visited him in Italy in 1930), and H. G. Wells. Budberg was also a translator of Russian literature, a writer and literary agent.

Cahn, Alfredo, *b. Zurich, Switzerland, 1902; d. Córdoba, Argentina, 1975*
Alfredo Cahn was Stefan Zweig's long-time Spanish-language translator and literary agent in Argentina. Of Jewish origin, Cahn settled in Buenos Aires in 1924, following a short period studying in Spain. Cahn was also a literary scholar and became a professor of German literature at the Universidad Nacional de Córdoba.

Eisemann, Heinrich, *b. Frankfurt, Germany, 1890; d. London, England, 1972*
Heinrich Eisemann was an antiquarian book and manuscript seller in Maida Vale, London, and a friend of the Altmann family, in particular of Lotte's mother, Therese. An orthodox Jew, Eisemann was a specialist in Judaica. Stefan Zweig purchased a substantial number of manuscripts from him but he grew increasingly disillusioned with him, believing that his prices were excessive. Zweig was helping Eisemann and his family to secure visas for Cuba although they never went there.

Feder, Ernst, *b. Berlin, Germany, 1881; d. Berlin, Germany, 1964*
Ernst Feder was editor-in-chief of the newspaper the *Berliner Tageblatt* but left Germany in 1933 for France, where he worked on the *Pariser Tageblatt*, a German-exile newspaper. In 1941 he fled to Brazil where, using the pseudonym 'Spectator', he contributed an opinion column in the Rio de Janeiro newspaper *A Noite*. Feder was one of the last people to see Stefan and Lotte Zweig before they committed suicide. He returned to Germany in 1957, where he remained until his death.

Ferro, António, *b. Lisbon, Portugal, 1895; d. Lisbon, Portugal, 1956*
António Ferro was a Portuguese journalist and supporter of 'cosmopolitan fascism', writing several books, including *Viagem à roda das ditaduras* (1927), an apologia to the importance of authoritarianism. In 1933 he was appointed the director of culture and propaganda in the Portuguese government of President António de Oliveira Salazar. Stefan Zweig met him in 1938 while visiting Estoril with Lotte. Ferro was instrumental in helping Zweig to gain visas for his ex-wife Friderike

to Portugal and onward passages to the United States. After the war he pursued a brief career as a diplomat, first as Portugal's ambassador to Switzerland (1950–54) and then to Italy (1954–56).

Fleischer, Victor, *b. Komotau (Bohemia), Austria-Hungary (now Chomutov, Czech Republic), 1882; d. London, England, 1952*
Victor Fleischer was a dramatist, editor of books of art and founder of the German publishing house Frankfurter Verlagsanstalt. One of Stefan Zweig's closest friends, Fleischer moved to England in 1938. His wife (until they divorced) was the theatre producer and film director Leontine Sagan (*Mädchen in Uniform*, 1931 etc.).

Flower, Walter Newman, *b. Fontwell Magna, Dorset, England, 1879; d. Blandford, Dorset, England, 1964*
Sir Walter Newman Flower was an author and influential publisher. In 1927 he purchased Cassell & Company, which was responsible for publishing many important works of biography, including those by Stefan Zweig. Newman Flower's own publications include studies of George Frederic Handel (1923) and Franz Schubert (1928).

Freud, Anna, *b. Vienna, Austria, 1895; d. London, England, 1982*
The youngest child of Sigmund and Martha Freud, Anna Freud left Vienna for London in 1939 with her family. In London she founded the Hampstead War Nurseries. After the war she started the Hampstead Child Therapy Course and Clinic, a non-profit institution for research and training in child psychoanalysis.

Friedenthal, Richard, *b. Munich, Germany, 1896; d. Kiel, Germany, 1979*
Richard Friedenthal was a close friend of Stefan Zweig. In 1938 Friedenthal fled Germany for England, where, despite his anti-Nazi background, he was interned as an 'enemy alien' during the early years of the war. Following Zweig's death, Friedenthal took on the unofficial role of his literary executor. A literary scholar, Friedenthal posthumously edited Zweig's biography of Balzac, as well as volumes of Zweig correspondence. His published work included novels, novellas and other writings, including biographies of Luther, Goethe and Leonardo da Vinci.

Frischauer, Paul, *b. Vienna, Austria, 1898; d. Vienna, Austria, 1977*
Paul Frischauer was an Austrian writer who emigrated to England in 1934 with his wife, Maijan Ivana (Maritza). In 1940 he travelled to Brazil, where he had been commissioned, apparently by the dictatorship's Departamento de Impresa e Propaganda (DIP), to write a

biography of Getúlio Vargas, the Brazilian president. The resulting book, *Presidente Vargas*, was published in New York by Random House in 1942 and in São Paulo by the Companhia Editora Nacional in 1944. In 1945 Frischauer moved to the United States and in 1955 he returned to live in Austria. Apart from his book on Vargas, Frischauer was the author of biographies and historical novels with subjects including Garibaldi (1934) and Beaumarchais (1936).

Fülöp-Miller, René, *b. Karansbesch, Hungary (now Caransebes, Romania), 1891; d. Hanover, New Hampshire, USA, 1963*
René Fülöp-Miller was an Austro-Romanian novelist, historian and sociologist who had been friends with Stefan Zweig in Vienna. Fülöp-Miller and his wife, Erica, fled Austria for France in 1939, moving to the United States in the same year. While the Zweigs were renting a summer house in Ossining, the Fülöp-Millers lived nearby in Croton-on-Hudson.

Grubb, Kenneth, *b. Oxton, Nottinghamshire, England, 1900; d. Downton, Wiltshire, England, 1980*
Kenneth Grubb was an Anglican missionary and author of widely circulated books, pamphlets and other publications relating to evangelism, indigenous people, and travel relating to Central and South America, including *South America: The Land of the Future* (London, 1930), a title that Stefan Zweig adopted for his book on Brazil. With the outbreak of World War II, Grubb became the director of the newly formed Latin American Section of the British Ministry of Information.

Hernández Catá, Alfonso, *b. Aldeadávila, Salamanca, Spain, 1885; d. Rio de Janeiro, Brazil, 1940*
A Cuban diplomat, journalist, essayist and writer of novellas and short stories, in 1938 Alfonso Hernández Catá became his country's minister in Rio de Janeiro. There, the Zweigs formed a close friendship with Hernández Catá and he made considerable efforts to secure Cuban visas for their friends and family members still in Europe; he also supplied Stefan Zweig with Cuban cigars. Hernández Catá died in a plane collision above Rio de Janeiro's Botafogo Bay.

Herrmann-Neiße, Max, *b. Neiße, Germany (now Nysa, Poland), 1886; d. London, England, 1941*
Max Herrmann-Neiße was a dramatist and poet, closely associated with the Expressionist movement in Berlin. A non-Jewish opponent of the Nazis, Herrmann-Neiße fled Germany in 1933, first to Switzerland, then to England, where he died in exile. Stefan Zweig, a close friend,

contributed an obituary on Herrmann-Neiße that was published in *Aufbau*, an influential cultural and political journal published in New York for German-speaking Jews.

Honig, Camille (Rachmil), *b. Tomaszów-Mazowiecki, Russian Empire (now in Poland), 1905; d. London, England, 1977*
The son of orthodox Jewish shopkeepers, Camille Honig moved to Warsaw in the 1920s to establish himself as a journalist. Seeking to expand his horizons, he moved to London in the early 1930s, where, as a struggling writer, Honig was helped by Stefan Zweig. In 1938 Honig married Patricia Hamilton-Moore (a member of an English-establishment family), who would convert to Judaism. With the outbreak of war, the Honigs went to Australia for safety; there, he raised funds for Allied war efforts within the Jewish community. Returning to England for military service, Honig stopped off in New York, where he again met with the Zweigs.

Huebsch, Benjamin W., *b. New York City, USA, 1876; d. London, England, 1964*
The son of a prominent American rabbi originally from Slovakia, Benjamin Huebsch started work as a lithographer with his brother's small print shop, gradually transforming it into the important publishing house of B. W. Huebsch Co. In 1925 the company amalgamated with Viking Press, with Huebsch becoming the new corporation's vice-president and the chief editor. Huebsch was especially attracted to European literature and was the first American publisher of James Joyce and D. H. Lawrence, as well as commissioning the translations of works by important writers such as August Strindberg, Anton Chekhov, Maxim Gorky and Stefan Zweig.

Kahn (née Mayer), Martha, *b. Ettlingen, Germany, 1887; d. London, England, 1983*
An older sister of Hannah Altmann, Martha Kahn joined the Altmanns in London in approximately 1935, following the death of her husband. In London, she first lived with Hannah and Manfred, then with the Zweigs as their housekeeper in Bath, continuing to look after Rosemount in their absence in North and South America. After the Zweigs' deaths, she returned to Hannah and Manfred, remaining with them until they died, when she went to Eva's family as their housekeeper.

Koogan, Abrahão, *b. Bessarabia (now Ukraine/Moldova), Russian Empire, 1911; d. Rio de Janeiro, Brazil, 2000*

In 1920 Abrahão Koogan emigrated to Brazil with his parents. In 1930, at the age of just 19, he and his brother-in-law Nathan Waissman founded a publishing house, and four years later they purchased Editora Guanabara, which had specialized in medical books. Editora Guanabara expanded beyond medicine, publishing translations, including works by Freud and, in 1937, the work of Stefan Zweig.

Körmendi, Ferenc, *b. Budapest, Hungary, 1900; d. Bethesda, Maryland, USA, 1972*
Ferenc Körmendi was a Hungarian novelist and journalist. In Budapest Körmendi worked for the *Pesti Napló* newspaper and in 1939 he moved to London, where he joined the Hungarian Section of the BBC World Service. His *Escape to Life* (1932) won an international novel competition in 1932 organized by leading London publishers. Among his other translated novels are *The Happy Generation* (1934, tr. 1945) and *That One Mistake* (1938, tr. 1947).

Landau, Jacob, *b. Vienna, Austria, 1892; d. New York City, USA, 1952*
Jacob Landau was director and founder of the Jewish Telegraphic Agency, established in New York in 1917 as the Jewish Correspondence Bureau, to collect and circulate news relating to Jews in the Diaspora as well as in Palestine.

Landshoff, Fritz, *b. Berlin, Germany, 1901; d. Haarlem, the Netherlands, 1988*
Fritz Landhoff was an owner of the Potsdam publishing house Gustav Kiepenheuer, whose authors included Bertolt Brecht, Heinrich Mann and Arnold Zweig. In 1933 Landshoff moved to Amsterdam, co-founding a literary magazine and the publishing house Querido for exiled writers. After the Nazi occupation of the Netherlands, Landshoff fled to the United States, where he continued his publishing activities.

Loon, Hendrik van, *b. Rotterdam, the Netherlands, 1882; d. Old Greenwich, Connecticut, USA, 1944*
Hendrik van Loon was a Dutch-American journalist and popular historian. In his 1938 book *Our Battle — Being One Man's Answer to 'My Battle' by Adolf Hitler* (1938), van Loon urged Americans to fight totalitarianism and he went on to campaign on behalf of Franklin Delano Roosevelt in the 1940 presidential campaign. During World War II van Loon broadcast to occupied Holland and assisted European refugees in the United States.

Maass, Joachim, *b. Hamburg, Germany, 1901; d. New York, USA, 1972*
Joachim Maass was a journalist, poet, novelist and essayist, who during the late 1920s and 1930s received considerable encouragement from the likes of Hermann Hesse, Thomas Mann and Stefan Zweig. Maass emigrated to the United States in 1939, where he taught German literature and wrote his best-remembered novels.

Mannheim, Karl, *b. Budapest, Hungary, 1893; d. London, England, 1943*
Karl Mannheim was the founder of classical sociology. After the suppression of the Hungarian Soviet in 1919, Mannheim fled to Germany. With the introduction in 1933 of the Law for the Restoration of the Professional Civil Service that excluded Jews from state employment in Germany, Mannheim lost his university position there and moved to England, where he taught at the London School of Economics. Mannheim was part of the Altmann family's circle of friends in London, probably introduced by Franz Neumann, a childhood friend of Manfred Altmann's who moved to New York in 1936 to work at the Frankfurt Institute of Social Research.

Maugham, Somerset, *b. Paris, France, 1874; d. Nice, France, 1965*
Somerset Maugham was one of the best known (and wealthiest) of English novelists, short story writers and playwrights of his time. Maugham was living in the French Riviera at the outbreak of World War II, from where he moved to the United States for the duration of the conflict. There Maugham continued to write, in particular working on Hollywood film scripts, and he campaigned for the United States to aid Britain in the war.

Mayer, Heiner, *b. Ettlingen, Germany, 1889; d. London, England, 1947*
Heiner Mayer was a brother of Hannah Altmann. Along with his wife Alice (b. Berlin, Germany, 1902; d. London, England) and daughter Ursula (see below), in 1933 Heiner Mayer fled Germany, where he had owned a silver and chrome-plating business. The family first took refuge in northern Italy before managing to reach England in 1939. Following the outbreak of war, Heiner was interned in the Isle of Man by the British authorities as an 'enemy alien'. On his release, he eventually found work as a book-keeper. Although the Zweigs attempted to help him obtain an American visa, he never received one.

Mayer, Ursula (Ursel), *b. Berlin, Germany, 1927*
The daughter of Heiner and Alice Mayer, and a niece of Hannah

Altmann, Ursula accompanied her parents to England in 1939. Soon after the outbreak of the war, Ursula was sent with her cousin, Eva Altmann, to stay with the Zweigs in Bath. As she was not yet a British subject, Ursula was unable to accompany Eva to the United States. Instead she remained in Bath where she attended the City of Bath School for Girls until it was felt safe for her to return to her parents in London.

Mistral, Gabriela, *b. Vicuã, Chile, 1889; d. Hempstead, New York, USA, 1957*
Gabriela Mistral was the pseudonym of Lucila de María del Perpetuo Socorro Godoy Alcayaga, a Chilean poet, educator, diplomat and feminist. Mistral served as Chile's consul in Petrópolis from 1941 and it was there, in 1945, that she received the news that she was to be the first Latin American to win the Nobel Prize for Literature.

Neumann, Robert, *b. Vienna, Austria, 1897; d. Munich, Germany, 1975*
Robert Neumann studied medicine and chemistry and moved to England in 1934. Shortly after the outbreak of the war he was interned by the British as an 'enemy alien'. Neumann became a writer, focusing on Jews and fascism. He was a considered a master of parody and was much admired by writers such as Thomas Mann and Stefan Zweig.

Philby (née Kohlmann), Litzi (Alice), *b. Vienna, Austria, 1910; d. Vienna, Austria, 1991*
Litzi Philby was an Austrian communist of Hungarian-Jewish origins. Following the Austrian government's February 1934 crackdown on leftist activists, she married the British communist (and future Soviet spy) Kim Philby, whom she had met through the Comintern underground. In April 1934 they fled Vienna for England, with the marriage effectively ending soon after, although they did not divorce until 1946. In London she became a good friend of the Altmann and Smollett (see p. 202) families. She formed a relationship with Georg Honigmann (1903–84), a German communist refugee also living in London, and in 1947 the couple moved to East Berlin where he became an editor of the *Berliner Zeitung*; she remained in East Germany until 1984 when she returned to Vienna.

Romains, Jules (né Louis Henri Jean Farigoule), *b. Saint-Julien-Chapteuil, France, 1885; d. Paris, France, 1972*
A French poet and writer, Jules Romains was a founder of the literary movement known as Unanimisme. After the German occupation of

France, Romains went into exile in the United States, where he broadcast to Europe on the Voice of America. In 1941 he moved to Mexico where, along with other French refugees, he established the Institut Français d'Amérique Latine.

Schaeffer (née Kurnik), Olga, *b. Glauchau, Germany, 1899; d. Croton-on-Hudson?, New York, USA, 1949 or 1950*
Olga Schaeffer was the proprietor of Amity Hall, the home in Croton-on-Hudson for refugee children where Eva Altmann (Lotte Zweig's niece) stayed. Olga Schaeffer was married to the writer and poet Albrecht Schaeffer (b. Elbing, Germany, 1885; d. Munich, Germany, 1950), a friend of Stefan Zweig. Albrecht Schaeffer's diverse body of work covered ancient and medieval mythology and he was a translator of Oscar Wilde, Paul Verlaine and Homer among others. Accompanied by their children, the Schaeffers emigrated to the United States in opposition to Nazi rule, arriving in New York in April 1939. In 1950, soon after the death of Olga, Albrecht returned to Germany where he died the same year.

Sforza, Carlo, *b. Montignoso di Lunigiana, Italy, 1873; d. Rome, Italy, 1952*
An antifascist Italian diplomat, Count Carlo Sforza refused to serve under Benito Mussolini. He lived in exile in Belgium, from where he fled to the United States in 1940. After the war Sforza returned to Italy and served as the country's foreign minister from 1947–51.

Smollett (né Hans Peter Smolka), Peter, *b. Vienna, Austria, 1912; d. Vienna, Austria, 1980*
Born into a wealthy Jewish family, Peter Smolka (later Smollett) went to England in 1933 to represent the Viennese newspaper *Neue Freie Press* before working for *London Continental News* and *Prager Presse*. He was invited to the Soviet Union in 1936 and published articles and a book on his travels, which attracted the attention of *The Times* in London and the British Foreign Office. He became involved in the shadowy world of espionage and counter espionage, working for the British as the head of the Soviet section of the Ministry of Information and, apparently, for the Soviets. After the war, he returned to live in Vienna; there he was a vital help for Graham Greene researching his screenplay and novella *The Third Man* (1949). Peter Smollett and his wife, Lotte (b. Slobodzia Banila, Bukovina [now in Ukraine], Austria-Hungary, 1913; d. Vienna, Austria, 2000), were friends of the Altmanns, with Litzi Philby also part of their circle. Both the Smollett and Altmann families have always maintained that Peter Smollett introduced Lotte to Stefan Zweig.

Strowski, Fortunat, *b. Carcassonne, France, 1866; d. Cervières, France, 1952*
Born into a Jewish family from the Austro-Hungarian province of Galicia, Fortunat Strowski was educated in France. A professor of French literature, in 1939 he accepted a position at the recently created Universidade do Brasil in Rio de Janeiro. Strowski is best known for his critical editions of the work of Michel de Montaigne, the sixteenth-century French courtier, essayist and biographer.

Tabori, Paul, *b. Budapest, Hungary, 1908; d. London, England, 1974*
An author and journalist educated in Hungary, Switzerland and Germany, Paul Tabori moved to London in 1937. Initially he worked in journalism, including for the *Daily Mail* and the BBC, and later writing for the theatre and film. His many novels were widely translated. For many years Tabori was active in the International PEN Club.

Thompson, Dorothy, *b. Lancaster, New York, USA, 1893; d. Lisbon, Portugal, 1961*
Dorothy Thompson was an influential American journalist who had been expelled from Germany in 1934 due to her anti-Nazi writings. In the United States, she went on to do much to publicize the cause of Jewish refugees in France and elsewhere in Europe.

Undset, Sigrid, *b. Kalundborg, Denmark, 1882; d. Lillehammer, Norway, 1949*
Sigrid Undset was a Norwegian novelist, essayist, historian and translator who in 1928 was awarded the Nobel Prize in Literature. She fled Norway for Sweden in 1940 following the German invasion and spent the remainder of the war in the United States, pleading the cause of occupied Norway and the plight of European Jews.

Viertel, Berthold, *b. Vienna, Austria, 1885; d. Vienna, Austria, 1953*
After a promising career in the theatre, Berthold Viertel became a screen writer and director, and moved to Los Angeles in 1928 to gain experience in the movie industry. From 1928–47 he worked as a film director, mostly in Great Britain and the United States. In 1947, he returned to Europe and worked in Zurich, Vienna and Berlin. He was a close friend of Stefan Zweig and in 1940 he worked with Stefan and Lotte on his last film script for *Das Gestohlene Jahr*. The film was finally filmed in Vienna in 1950.

Wells, H. G., *b. Bromley, Kent, England, 1866; d. London, England, 1946*
H. G. Wells was an English science fiction writer, known also for his pacifist and socialist stance. Wells visited Zweig several times in Salzburg, continuing their friendship in London, in part because of their mutual support for PEN, the writers' organization of which the latter held the position of international president.

Wiener, Paul Lester, *b. Leipzig, Germany, 1895; d. New York City?, USA, 1967*
Paul Wiener emigrated to the United States in 1913 and returned to Europe soon after he became a citizen in 1919. Wiener studied architecture and worked in Berlin, Vienna and Paris, returning to the United States in 1928. He was commissioned by the Brazilian government to organize and design the interior of the Brazilian pavilion for the 1939–40 New York World's Fair, working together with Oscar Niemeyer and Lúcio Costa. In the 1940s he designed the Cidade dos Motores, a new town in the state of Rio de Janeiro. Wiener was married to Alma Morgenthau Wertheim (1887–1953), a daughter of Henry Morgenthau, Sr., a businessman and senior United States diplomat of German-Jewish origin.

Zweig, Alfred, *b. Vienna, Austria, 1880; d. New York City, USA, 1977*
Alfred Zweig was the older brother of Stefan Zweig. He took care of the family business in the Sudetenland, in western Czechoslovakia. He remained there until the *Anschluss* of Austria and the annexation of Czechoslovakia in 1938–39, after which he fled to the United States with his wife, Stephanie.

Zweig (née Burger), Friderike Maria, *b. Vienna, Austria, 1882; d. Stamford, Connecticut, USA, 1971*
Friderike Zweig was Stefan Zweig's first wife, whom he married in 1920. Raised Catholic, Friderike was the daughter of a Catholic mother and a Jewish father. In 1906, she married Felix von Winternitz, an Austrian public servant, with whom she had two daughters, Alix Elizabeth (1907–86) and Susanne Benedictine (1910–98). Neither daughter developed a close relationship with Stefan Zweig. Friderike and her daughters left Austria for France after the *Anschluss*. With the outbreak of the war, they fled to Portugal, from where they moved to New York. Stefan and Friderike Zweig divorced in 1939.

Index

INDEX

Letter from an Unknown Woman
(1922) 3
Lewin (Mrs) 78
Lisbon 10, 22, 59, 118, 182, 197, 205
Liverpool 41n. 65
London 4–8, 10–16, 20, 21, 41n. 65,
50, 52–62 *passim*, 65–86 *passim*, 72,
76, 79–80, 83, 85, 90, 92, 94, 100,
105, 135, 138, 139, 145, 148–50, 161
Loon, Hendrik van 117, 127n8, 199
Ludwig, Emil 1, 9
Luxembourg 12

Maass, Joachim 117, 200
Machado de Assis, Machado de 23
Magellan, Ferdinand *see Conqueror of
the Seas: The Story of Magellan*
Maio, Marcos Chor 42n. 90
Malamud, Samuel 35
Mann, Heinrich 1, 201
Mann, Thomas 1, 115, 203
Mannheim, Karl 86, 200
Maranhão 98
Mariana (Minas Gerais) 57, 60
Marie Antoinette (1933) 4
Martinique 118
Marxist-Leninism 23
Mary, Queen of Scots (1935) 7
Masereel, Frans 1
Matuschek, Oliver 2, 38n. 5, 45n. 152
Maugham, Somerset 117, 118, 200
Mayer, Alice 50, 51n5, 54, 55n8, 69
Mayer, Heiner 50, 51, 52, 54, 57, 60,
71, 75, 83, 92, 200
Mayer, Ursula, 11, 51, 69, 92, 96, 97,
143, 200–1
Mello Franco, Afonso Arinos de 29, 35
Metsch, Gerhard 34, 36, 43, 44, 45
Mexico 1, 19, 22, 52, 59, 204
Miami 37, 101, 108, 109, 110
Milan 10
Miller, Hilda 149, 152

Miller, (Mr) 64, 65n. 7, 78, 93n. 2,
143, 149, 152, 174
Minas Gerais 57, 60, 62, 65 *see also*
Mariana *and* Ouro Preto
Mistral, Gabriela 29, 146, 152, 154n2,
201
Montaigne, Michel de 26, 151, 190,
191, 205
Montevideo 63, 68, 69, 71, 73, 75, 79,
80 *see also* Uruguay
Morais, Antônio and Dulce 30, 140,
176, 177, 178, 179
Morgenthau, Henry 163 *see also*
Wiener, Alma Morgenthau
Müller, Hartmut 38n. 5
Mussolini, Benito 22, 204

Naples 10
Netherlands 12, 82, 201
Neumann, Robert 58, 67, 70, 170 195,
201
New Haven 37, 116–19, 121
New Rochelle (New York) 64, 86,
111–12
New York City 7, 10, 12, 26, 49, 52,
53, 54, 57, 66, 68, 71, 75, 81, 83, 87,
90, 94, 95, 96, 105, 111, 115–29,
144, 147, 163, 164
Niemetz, Serge 38n. 5, 45n. 152
Nietzsche (1925) 4
Norway 12 *see also* Scandinavia
Nova Friburgo 162

Olinda (Pernambuco) 98
Orchard (Mr) 64, 78
Ossining (New York) 34, 122–6, 134,
164, 165, 176
Ouro Preto (Minas Gerais) 17, 60

Pará *see* Belém
Paraguay 80, 82
Pernambuco *see* Olinda *and* Recife